GET
REAL

GET REAL

49 Challenges Confronting Higher Education

WILLIAM G. TIERNEY

Cover art: Paul Klee, *Composition with the Yellow Half-Moon and the Y*, 1918. The Berggruen Klee Collection, 1984, the Metropolitan Museum of Art.

Published by State University of New York Press, Albany

© 2020 State University of New York

For information, contact State University of New York Press, Albany, NY
www.sunypress.edu

Library of Congress Cataloging-in-Publication Data

Names: Tierney, William G., author.
Title: Get real : 49 challenges confronting higher education / William G.
    Tierney.
Description: Albany : State University of New York Press, 2020. | Includes
    bibliographical references and index.
Identifiers: LCCN 2020009137 | ISBN 9781438481272 (hardcover : alk. paper) |
    ISBN 9781438481289 (pbk. : alk. paper) | ISBN 9781438481296 (ebook)
Subjects: LCSH: Education, Higher—Aims and objectives—United States.
Classification: LCC LB2322.2 .T57 2020 | DDC 378.001—dc23
LC record available at https://lccn.loc.gov/2020009137

10 9 8 7 6 5 4 3 2 1

Contents

Acknowledgments

I have benefited over the years to have worked in the Pullias Center for Higher Education at the University of Southern California. My students, research assistants, postdoctoral students, and colleagues helped me think through what I present here. Monica Raad and Diane Flores, who staff the center for us, are the absolute best at what they do. Although many folks read a part of this book, Michael Lanford provided extraordinary help in his editing and feedback. He's a gem. My editor, Ariel Lewiton, not only line edited the text but argued with me about various points that helped me clarify my thinking. Rebecca Colesworthy at SUNY Press has been thoughtful, positive, fun, and reflective about how to improve the text. I had the good fortune to put the finishing touches on this manuscript first at the Rockefeller Foundation's Bellagio Center in Lake Como, Italy, and then at the European University Institute in Florence, Italy. I could not have had better environments to complete this book. Through it all, Barry Weiss has been my sounding board and best friend. To everyone: Grazie Mille!

Preface

I have taught the introductory class for our PhD students at the University of Southern California for close to twenty-five years. Every fall, we discuss difficult theoretical texts that many of them are reading for the first time. I say from the outset that I don't want people to agree with me if they think that's what I want to hear. I acknowledge that they're going to recognize my biases implicit in the readings and an occasional aside, but my job is to help them think through their own particular stances on the issues. Their answers to issues are less important than their ability to understand the issues and then to build an argument about why they think what they think.

I am fortunate in a doctoral seminar that most everyone will have attempted the reading. I usually ask one student to offer some prefatory comments that summarize the article we're discussing and then that student facilitates the start of the conversation. I explain at the start of the semester that if students don't talk, I may call on them, not to embarrass them, but to solicit their thoughts. We all have opinions on important articles, I say. Inevitably, I ask students, "What do you think?" I ask the question again and again.

Class discussions are robust, and students frequently disagree with one another. At some point, a facilitator of the reading will get a smirk on his or her face, look out to the group and, mimicking me, will ask "What do you think?" People laugh, and we have a good conversation.

Although the topics in what follows are certainly different from an introductory PhD seminar on theory, I have written the text in the same vein as my class. Many readers are likely to have gone to college and will have opinions on some of these issues based on their personal experiences. Or you may have a viewpoint on certain topics because they are "hot button" issues debated on talk shows and social media. Other topics may be entirely new and unfamiliar. You probably will be able to glean my particular stand on an issue, but this book is neither a polemic nor dispassionate argument for one or another position. I am trying to help you think through some of the thorniest issues that higher education faces today, especially now, as we deal with the aftermath of the COVID-19 pandemic and the structural racism exposed by the murder of George Floyd. I also want to caution against the worry that "higher education will never be the same" because of the pandemic. The sky is not falling. I have intended this book to help us think through in as calm a manner as possible the problems that confront us and how we might move forward to create not the same system, but a better one. I have not burdened the text with citations, but I have listed readings that I either have referred to or are supplementary if you want to read more about the topic. With each essay, I am asking, "What do you think?"

CHAPTER 1

A Crisis Is a Terrible Thing to Waste

The Benefits of a Postsecondary Education

From 1837 to 1842, Horace Mann, then-secretary of education for Massachusetts, gave a series of five lectures for common school conventions that were held throughout the state. Three years later, these lectures were published within a single volume, and in his fifth lecture, Mann made two significant points that had a critical impact on the US conscience. First, he argued for the importance of education, making the following claims: "In a land of liberty . . . there must be internal restraints; the reason, conscience, benevolence, and reverence for all that is sacred, must supply the place of force and fear; and, for this purpose, the very instincts of self-preservation admonish us to perfect our system of education, and to carry it on far more generally and vigorously than we have ever yet done."[1] Second, he stressed that, because of education's significance, schools should be public and open to everyone: "For this purpose, we must study the principles of education more profoundly; we must make ourselves acquainted with the art, or processes, by which those principles can be applied in practice; and, by establishing proper agencies and institutions, we must cause a knowledge both of the science and the art to be diffused throughout the entire mass of the people."[2] At that time, education was neither widespread nor public. Most young people developed basic literacy due to efforts by their churches, private tutors, or family members. Approximately 90 percent of the country lived in rural areas, where children were compelled to balance informal education with work in family farms and businesses.[3] Moreover, the United States was an economic backwater that boasted no more than ninety municipalities with more than twenty-five hundred people in 1830.[4] The majority of young people who were privileged to enjoy a formal education were predominantly white and male, hailing from an elite, urban area of New England. Mann reckoned that if the United States was to succeed, then the fledging nation needed to expand educational opportunities to its citizens. Educational reformers like Mann, such as Thaddeus Stevens of Pennsylvania and Henry Barnard of Connecticut, advocated for school taxes and a formalized, public school system along the Eastern seaboard. By 1850, public schools were widespread in New England, even though opportunity for formal education remained limited to students in southeastern and midwestern states and territories. Over the next fifty years, public education in the United States extended into more rural areas, and from 1910 to 1940, a high school movement pushed the expectations of universal education beyond grammar school. When a new state was admitted into the Union, it had to have a provision for schooling. Areas that quickly embraced high school education saw their investment rewarded in the form of greater wealth, less social stratification, and a more diversified economy that was less dependent on manufacturing.[5]

Until the middle of the twentieth century, higher education, however, remained the preserve of a chosen few—largely white, middle- and upper-class men. Well-to-do individuals did not seek a vocation because their life's work was laid out for them. Large universities trained the elite for positions of authority in society. Small religious colleges came and went with rapidity in the nineteenth century, all with the same goal: to inculcate religious doctrine in the local population. By the end of the nineteenth century and into the early twentieth century, however, the utility of a college education became more apparent. Congress created land-grant public colleges during the Civil War where tuition was nonexistent. Teacher-training schools were created. Women became participants in some institutions and attended single-sex institutions, and separate universities were created for African Americans.

By the middle of the twentieth century, the United States recognized the economic importance of a college degree to the individual and society, and its predominance took hold. Indeed, ever since Horace Mann spoke about the critical role of education in United States' progress, the country has agreed about the significance of education and extended it.

California stands as a useful example. In December 1846, Olive M. Isbell opened the first English-language school in California on the Santa

Clara Mission grounds.[6] The first public school followed in 1848. The first private college opened in 1851, and a women's college was founded one year later. Although the state ranked eleventh in population in the early twentieth century, it had the largest enrollment in public education of any state. By the 1930s, 24 percent of California's college-age population matriculated to higher education, a figure well above the national average of 12 percent. California enacted what the rest of the country imagined: a belief in the importance of education and the will to provide it to as many people as possible.[7]

The value of a college degree has historically swung between two purposes: vocational training that leads to employment or a transformative experience that enables individuals to gain an understanding of the social fabric that binds humanity together. Some have argued that a degree must enable both purposes, whereas others lobby for one goal to the exclusion of the other.[8] What is no longer in doubt, however, is the significance of a degree for many careers.

I shall not suggest here that everyone needs to go to college. About two-thirds of California's working-age adults, for example, need to have some training beyond high school if the state wants to meet its workforce needs. A community college, where one earns a certificate or two-year associate's degree in a specific vocational area intended to fill a workforce need, will suffice for many students. By 2030, for example, policymakers and stakeholders of higher education (such as those at the Public Policy Institute of California) estimate approximately 30 percent will do just fine with an associate's degree or simply a postsecondary certificate in a particular field of study. This estimation still leaves around one-third of the state's high school graduates who can find employment with a high school degree, which I shall discuss in a later chapter.[9]

Unfortunately, the United States now lags behind other industrialized countries with regard to college participation and attainment. According to 2016 Organisation for Economic Co-operation and Development data, the United States ranked third worldwide in the percentage of the population aged fifty-five to sixty-four years that had completed higher education, but tenth among adults aged twenty-five to thirty-four years.[10] The nation is falling behind in the global race for human capital development, and it places the country at risk. The Lumina Foundation and Gates Foundations, among others, have called for the United States to regain its competitiveness and to once again be the number one nation in the world in terms of college access and attainment.[11] Why?

For one, wage earners will earn more if they hold a bachelor's degree. Sure, Bill Gates ditched Harvard, and Peter Thiel awarded $100,000 checks to twenty "uniquely talented" teenage dropouts who eschewed college to conceive and develop a "radical innovation that [would] benefit society."[12] Richard Vedder, a conservative economist, likes to point out that there are too many Domino's Pizza delivery drivers with bachelor's degrees in Washington, DC.[13] In Los Angeles, we also have an awful lot of waiters who hold postsecondary degrees in theater arts and want to be actors. These anecdotes have less to do with the need for more college-educated citizens and more to do with the value and real-world application of various degrees. If I'm trained to be a pianist and end up driving for Uber, it does not negate the fact that the country needs more nurses. Learning to be a pianist also provides auxiliary skills and benefits. If I'm a trained historian who currently waits tables, it does not mean that we have enough individuals trained in STEM fields or that I will never land a job in music. All sorts of people make strategic choices so that they might pursue their dreams while they are young. Other individuals make decisions to work in fields that are less financially lucrative but fulfill important societal needs. Interestingly, several of Peter Thiel's fellows raised significant venture capital for budget hotels in India and topical energy sprays, yet none of them produced the radical innovation that an avoidance of college would purportedly inspire, leading one entrepreneur to caustically remark, "Peter Thiel promised flying cars; we got caffeine spray instead."[14]

Bill Gates and Peter Thiel notwithstanding, the Public Policy Institute of California, among many other groups, has pointed out that unemployment rates are much lower among college graduates, and wages are substantially higher.[15] A college graduate earns roughly a million dollars more than a high school graduate over the course of a lifetime.[16] Degree holders also are more likely to vote, volunteer, give to charity, engage in civic activities, and send their children to college.[17] A college education makes good economic and civic sense.

We need more people participating in higher education not only because they will earn higher wages but also because the economy and our democracy need a better-educated workforce. In California, we need about one million more people participating in higher education if we are to have people fill the jobs that will be available in 2025. Indeed, we need them not just to participate but also to complete their degree, and in timely fashion.[18] We also need more individuals participating in the democratic public sphere.

Deficits in higher education participation and college degree attainment are most stark among a state's racial and ethnic minorities. African American and Latinx students remain the most at-risk for dropping out of high school, not transitioning to college, and not completing a postsecondary degree. This deficit has little to do with individuals and more to do with structural inadequacies that our country has yet to fix. The implications of this concern are significant: these populations will be left out of the high wage economy, which in turn will exacerbate inequities, reduce state revenues, and inhibit economic productivity.

Although we frequently focus on the economic benefits of higher education, we cannot dismiss the social benefits of a college degree. Mann saw public schools as the great equalizer that enabled the poor to move into the working and middle class, but he also thought education was a way to civilize the uneducated. Mann's language would likely be attacked today for suggesting that too many students are not civilized, a term that has often been associated with racial and class-based values systems. Still, education should not just be about learning vocational skills. We want students to be participants, not passive bystanders, in this experiment called democracy. To be participants, we want students to learn how to engage with the critical issues of the day. I do not really care if students come to diametrically opposite conclusions to mine, as long as they come to their conclusions based on concrete evidence, and they are able to ask intelligent questions. I'll discuss that in a later essay, but I raise the point here because I do not want us to reduce education to merely a vocational task. The danger to democracy is not that people disagree with one another but that they have no opinion or voice in their own futures. If our colleges and universities are not fostering a sense of engagement in the democratic public sphere, then we are failing at what we are supposed to be doing.

In a celebrated essay entitled "A Talk to Teachers," James Baldwin spoke eloquently about the purpose of education a half century ago:

> The purpose of education, finally, is to create in a person the ability to look at the world for himself, to make his own decisions, to say to himself this is black or this is white, to decide for himself whether there is a God in heaven or not. To ask questions of the universe, and then learn to live with those questions, is the way he achieves his own identity. But no society is really anxious to have that kind of person around.

> What societies really, ideally, want is a citizenry which will simply obey the rules of society. If a society succeeds in this, that society is about to perish. The obligation of anyone who thinks of himself as responsible is to examine society and try to change it and to fight it—at no matter what risk. This is the only hope society has. This is the only way societies change.[19]

Let's recognize, however, that these twin purposes are no easy tasks. As I discuss in chapter 3, simply completing college in a timely manner sometimes seems beyond students' abilities. And what students learn (or do not learn) in college is under enormous scrutiny. Yet, it seems facetious to ignore the individual and societal benefits of a degree. Jobs increasingly call for advanced skills, or the know-how to learn new ones. A mature democracy—paraphrasing and updating Horace Mann—requires an educated electorate.

At the moment, however, we face a crisis on multiple levels. In 2020, we had a pandemic race through society and change higher education in unexpected and immediate ways. All of a sudden, everyone was teaching online. Unexpected costs ranged in the hundreds of millions of dollars for some universities and state systems. Colleges that already were struggling to meet their enrollment goals faced closure. At the same time, state tax revenues for the 2021 fiscal year were estimated to drop by more than 25 percent.[20] A general panic set in where the only certainty was the uncertainty of the future. I tend to think we are in for a rough few years, but doomsayers need a sense of history. Yes, this pandemic is different from other crises we have faced, but I write this book with the understanding that higher education is always in a state of change—sometimes slow, sometimes fast, sometimes planned, and at other times unplanned. What we really need is a collective understanding of where we want to go as an industry, and then we can develop the plans to get us there.

Washington, DC, provides little guidance on how to improve educational outcomes and recently has done little to suggest that postsecondary degrees are important. Academic leaders have become more caretakers than visionaries. Faculty understandably concentrate on their own economic concerns, and they provide little guidance on how to enable universities to flourish again. It's easy to think an optimal strategy is to keep your head down and stay out of trouble. A crisis, however, is a terrible thing to waste. It's precisely because we are in crisis that we have the opportunity to create changes that tie our visionary past to a creative future. My purpose here will be to outline the various issues that confront us and to suggest where I stand, but more importantly, to help readers think through where they stand on these often thorny and confusing issues. I am assuming if we can discuss and come to an agreement as to what we believe, then we can come together about how to put those beliefs into concrete actions and policies. Too often, however, we are not clear on what we believe.

The Worth of Universities to Society

One of the curiosities of US higher education is the value placed on research, even though so few faculty actually do research. Here's how it works. Faculty are first socialized to do research as graduate students. As of the 2016 to 2017 academic year, the United States had 4,360 degree-granting institutions of higher education, yet only 311 offer doctoral degrees that lead to faculty positions.[21] Only a handful of those universities actually send a significant portion of their graduates to tenure-line positions in academia; one research study found that only one-quarter of doctoral degree–granting universities produce more than 75 percent of all tenure-track faculty.[22] The same holds true across disciplines. Everyone who has earned a doctorate degree has gone through the drama of doing research during their coursework and their dissertation. Insofar as mimicry is part of socialization, graduates have learned to love doing research because they learned at the feet of their advisors that research is most rewarded. It's a curious system: the vast majority of faculty positions, tenure track and adjunct, do not require much, if any, research. It's as if we train people to be neurosurgeons when the jobs they will obtain are in nursing.

Nevertheless, some faculty learned to love research when they were graduate students, and they want to continue it even if it is unnecessary at their institution. Others recognize that, all things being equal, faculty who do research reap greater rewards than those who merely teach. The result is a crazy system where teaching is the handmaiden to research even though research is not necessary at most community colleges, public state universities, or for-profit institutions.

To say that research is not necessary everywhere is not to imply that it is unnecessary anywhere. The nation and the state benefit from both applied and theoretical research that have the potential to increase the social and economic well-being of the citizenry. After World War II, the United States made a strategic decision to situate the bulk of research at its universities. We could have followed other models, such as establishing stand-alone institutes as in much of Europe. We could have said that spending federal and state dollars on research is not in the national interest. To the country's credit, we instead invested in a vast research infrastructure for our premier institutions that led to scientific and social breakthroughs. The research infrastructure of the United States, until recently, has been second to none, and it has contributed to the nation's prosperity. We have the bulk of the world's Nobel Prize winners, and a vast majority of innovations have occurred at research universities.

Throughout the rise of the US university, two forms of funded research have emerged. On the one hand, federal, state, and foundation leaders have commissioned work with specific outcomes in mind. Whether it was research funded by NASA to contribute to the space program or the scientific programs of the National Institutes of Health to find cures for disease, a great deal of public funding has been authorized toward very specific outcomes. On the other hand, universities have left faculty to their own devices to develop research projects that are more theoretical or suppositional, where the immediate benefit to society is less clear. Indeed, one might argue that we support research in the humanities because the historian who undertakes a study of a particular moment during the Renaissance, or the theoretical physics professor who undertakes research on quantum mechanics, enlarges our understanding of ourselves and the planet we inhabit.

These are two modes of research done for the public good, but in very different manners: studies conducted to aid us in reaching a solution to a vexing problem and research that has no clear usable outcome but advances our understanding of particular phenomena.

Both kinds of research are expensive. We know, for example, that research universities are costlier to operate than comprehensive universities and community colleges. The faculty teach less and do more research, the faculty are paid more, and many have expensive labs and buildings. The payoff can be esoteric in that it is very difficult to demonstrate the worth of all the research activities taking place. Other sorts of research have very clear outcomes that improve society, such as cancer research or a greater understanding of the causes of bullying in schools.

As a society, we need to come to grips with determining how much research is enough research. Surely, we do not need every individual and every institution engaged in research. If that is the case, then how many research institutions do we need where a sizable number of its faculty are conducting research? When the University of California, for example, added its newest campus in Merced, California, there were arguments about the economic benefits to the region and why the university needed an additional campus for a variety of student-focused reasons, but those arguments had little to do with research. By overemphasizing research, we risk shortchanging the importance of teaching.

One of the ironies of academic life is that we like to claim that the board of trustees, the president, and the faculty are at odds. However, they are actually aligned together more often than not. Whenever institutions have morphed from a teacher's college to a state university or added a new campus, everyone agrees about the change, even if additional research will cost the state more money than a teaching institution. The more prestige an institution garners, the happier everyone is. Does the state benefit by adding another research university? That question is rarely asked.

We also do not differentiate our research universities in a manner that might enable some to focus on research and others to focus on teaching and community engagement. Instead, we have a one-size-fits-all mentality such that all research universities operate in lockstep. One by-product is that our research universities, by virtue of needing costly labs and so forth, cost more to operate. One way to keep costs down is to hire part-time adjunct labor for low wages to teach the classes that faculty would ordinarily teach.

Every advanced, industrialized nation has a coordinated set of research universities that aid in the economic and social development of the country. China recognized a generation ago that part of its economic advancement depended on expanding its research capacity; in turn, it has outspent the United States to catch up. India is slowly coming to the same realization. The social and economic benefits of research universities are vast. We need to affirm the import of research and then develop a plan at the state and federal levels to adequately support our public research universities but also recognize how much research needs to be done.

The Challenges That Exist

In an interview from 2013, Clayton Christensen, originator of the theory of disruptive innovation, predicted that "higher education is just on the edge of the crevasse":

> Generally, universities are doing very well financially, so they
> don't feel from the data that their world is going to collapse.
> But I think even five years from now these enterprises are going
> to be in real trouble. . . . [Online learning] will take root in its
> simplest applications, then just get better and better. You know,
> Harvard Business School doesn't teach accounting anymore,
> because there's a guy out of BYU whose online accounting
> course is so good. He is extraordinary, and our accounting
> faculty, on average, is average.[23]

Obviously, Christensen had no idea that a pandemic would strike the
world in 2020. His predictions had not come true prior to the pandemic,
and there actually is evidence from the pandemic that his predictions are
not entirely correct. Previous institutional investments in technology and
support staff made it easier for faculty to teach online, but many students
wanted interaction with one another and their professors. In fact, colleges
and universities became concerned that a sizeable number of students
would take a "gap year" if in-person classes did not resume in the fall of
2020.[24] As with any evolving medium, the technology will improve, but
that improvement does not necessarily mean that face-to-face classes are
an artifact of the past.

Similar doomsayers who suggest that "the end is near" for colleges
and universities are not unlike their religious brethren who have regularly
predicted the apocalypse for centuries. There is little evidence that higher
education as a system is unsustainable. Institutional transformation has
been relatively common—from teachers' colleges to state colleges, or
perhaps a state college upping its game, in search of institutional prestige, to become a state university. In the nineteenth century, hundreds of
small religious colleges existed throughout the United States; some have
survived, most have not. We will also see market adjustments in the
coming years. We are seeing it already with a handful of mostly small
liberal arts colleges at death's doorstep. Small, tuition-driven campuses
will find it increasingly difficult to attract students unless they are able
to put forward a convincing argument about why they should have their
students fork over several thousand dollars for a product that might be
cheaper at a public institution.

Again, I appreciate the challenges we now face. State budgets have
been decimated; precisely at a time when state postsecondary systems need
more revenue, they will get less. And yet, in the last recession, dramatic

cutbacks occurred. We need to think of revenue and readjustments over a longer time horizon than the next week. We will climb out of the fiscal ditch we are currently in, but it may take a half decade. The question is where we want to be.

Nevertheless, I have been in academe long enough to recognize the slow pace of change and the difficulty involved in wholescale transformation. Not so long ago, conventional wisdom held that online education was going to swamp traditional teaching methods. And then came the rise of for-profit higher education, which purported to offer the secret for getting students through expeditiously, with employment as soon as they graduated.

We know how those predictions worked out. Online education is still a poor second when it comes to teaching and learning, even though we learned a great deal from the rapid transitions we had to make during the pandemic. For-profit higher education has been riddled with corrupt practices leading to enormous debt and crappy jobs for students. Some online classes are great, offering alternative learning environments for nontraditional students. Some for-profits are great insofar as they do what they claim: they train students for a distinct profession, and by the end of their training, the graduates are able to find gainful employment. Like so many other predictions that cautioned that the end is near, what seemed certain to our prophets a decade ago has not come to pass. Their prophecies were warning signs, however, and we should think of what those warnings are about, and who is most at risk.

Cost

The cost of something is the price incurred to produce the product. The price is what the consumer is charged. At one point, both the cost and the price of higher education were not that difficult to understand. Of consequence, more than a half century ago, the cost of college was not much of a conversation. A college-going culture did not exist in the vast majority of high schools in the United States. While higher education was not populated solely by the sons (and some daughters) of the wealthy, by and large, the poor and the working class did not attend college. However, during the 1950s, college enrollment grew by 49 percent, and during the 1960s, it grew by an astounding 120 percent.[25] Today, a significant number of college students come from working-class backgrounds and find it necessary to work while they attend college. From 1989 to 2008, between 70 and 80 percent of all undergraduates were active in the labor market while they were attending college. Today, it is estimated that approximately 40 percent of undergraduates work at least thirty hours a week, and around 25 percent are simultaneously working full time while they attend classes full time. Sixty percent of all working students are women.[26] The point is not simply that we have greater fiscal needs because the consumers are poorer. The cost of higher education has risen precipitously, and of consequence, the price of a college education has risen, even after adjusting for inflation. Within a mere ten years (2005 to 2015), the price of undergraduate tuition, fees, room, and board rose 34 percent at public institutions and 26 percent at private, nonprofit institutions.[27] From 1987 to 2017, the average tuition at four-year public and private colleges roughly tripled, while wages stayed roughly the same, making higher education expensive not merely for the poor but also for everyone except the wealthiest among us.[28]

One reason that price has risen is that we have switched the burden of attending college from the state to the consumer. The consumer is covering a larger part of the costs of higher education. I will write more about this shift toward thinking about higher education as a private responsibility rather than as a public good, but we need to recognize that today's students graduate with much more of a debt burden than those of my generation. Whereas in the 1960s and 1970s, students were able to earn four-year degrees from public colleges and universities with only a modicum of debt, that is no longer the case. In 1970 to 1971, US students incurred $7.6 billion of debt to fund higher education. In 2012 to 2013, US students borrowed $110 billion in student loans.[29] Customers are searching for a cheaper alternative and cannot find any.

This spells trouble for one segment of higher education: the small, private liberal arts college. These institutions are historically susceptible to small-market pressures. At institutions where tuition counts for virtually all of the revenue, a drop of ten students in enrollment, especially if the slide is constant, can have serious consequences. Regional institutions of unexceptional standing that were once considered safe, relatively local spaces for parents to send their children, are now seen as a luxury. Public colleges may be expensive, but they still cost far less than the average private college or university. New York's recent free-tuition plan is a good example of a policy, if it becomes a trend, that could cause turbulence for those institutions most susceptible to market pressures.[30] We might see one hundred or so small private colleges collapse.

Time to Degree

When I buy a book on Amazon, it arrives in a matter of days. When I shop online for a new shirt, I am disappointed when I learn it could take as much as a week to arrive. If the Wi-Fi at the coffee shop is slow and takes a minute to transfer my message, I will find another place to drink my cappuccino. Writing letters today seems quaint. Speed has become a commodity that we all value in the twenty-first century.

Except in higher education. Students apply in the fall, and a year later, they set off on their academic career. Four years later, they only have two more to go! Graduation rates for the majority of undergraduates earning bachelor's degrees are closer to six years, for those who even graduate. Unless, of course, they are at a community college and have to transfer to another institution that won't take their credits. So, maybe they have a half decade—or more—after the first two years of community college to finally graduate. And then, of course, at institutions where more than half of the students are unprepared for academic work in writing and/or math, they have to spend some time—perhaps just five or six months—taking courses that prepare them for college since their high schools did not.

Acknowledging this reality, the National Center for Education Statistics calculates the graduation rate for first-time, full-time students at six years by default. Even then, only 60 percent of students who started college in 2010 finished by 2016.[31] The average time to degree completion among the 60 percent of students who completed their bachelor's degrees was 5.1 years.[32] For associate's degrees, which should take two years, the average time to degree completion was 3.3 years.[33]

Students walk off the high school stage in June, then wait three months for college to begin. They make it through the first semester of college and have a nice two- or three-week holiday awaiting them, and then another week or so in the spring, and finally the end of the first year arrives and they get another summer break. How wonderful! Except it isn't. The leisurely academic pace exacerbates problems rather than solves them. Students need a speeded-up tempo for learning that more accurately reflects the twenty-first century rather than the agrarian nineteenth century.

The academic year is framed by the same tempo. On my campus, it is dangerous to walk down the main walkways on Monday through Thursday mornings around noon. Everyone is zipping hither and yon to grab something to eat before they go to their next class. On Fridays, I could roll a bowling ball down those same walkways and not hit anyone. Faculty and students don't like those Friday classes!

It is useful to note that some institutions have attempted to embrace full-year academic calendars. Community colleges, especially in urban areas, frequently have active summer sessions, and the state of Florida has required every undergraduate enrolled in a public university to earn at least nine credit hours during a summer term, prior to graduation.[34] However, these policies are usually the product of an overburdened system where exponential increases in enrollment make summer semesters necessary to relieve capacity issues. Full-time faculty grumble about teaching during the summer, and the classes get handed off to graduate students or contingent faculty who are happy for additional income.

Imagine if other businesses operated in that manner. Would we want airlines to be more crowded because the airline has decided—without consumer agreement—that they are not going to fly on Fridays? Or how about if our local convenience store decided to close in the summer because the cashiers had better things to do? Or what if the auto repair shop told me that he would do the routine check-up on my car and I could get it back in a month or so? I do not think we would settle for those time frames in any of these examples, so why do we accept it in higher education?

Obviously, a classroom and an auto repair shop are different. The fellow who works at my local convenience store is different from my colleague who is in the office next to me. At the same time, our sense of time in the early decades of the twenty-first century is certainly different from the 1950s for all of us. Why wouldn't we adapt our academic schedules, just as other businesses do?

Teaching and Learning

I recently talked with a college junior whom I mentor at a local area college, and he told me about the PowerPoint presentations that his computer science professor puts online. He said the professor uploads them after every lecture. The PowerPoint slides were so good that nobody went to class. "Nobody?" I asked. He laughed because he knew I was referring to him, and he nodded. "Well, I make about half of the lectures, and I sit in the front just like you told me to do." I asked how many students were absent. In a class where eighty students are registered, no more than twenty typically show up, except for exams. My mentee said he expected to get an A-minus in the class.

This sort of behavior has been the norm for years, particularly in large lecture classes. Another student told me that attendance in humanities classes on her campus were even worse. She was referring to the general education classes that students had to take. Everyone gets As and Bs, she told me, so students do not see the need to attend class.

What's going on? Clearly, the classroom experience is not particularly enjoyable to students—intellectually, socially, emotionally—if they feel attendance is unnecessary. It's unnecessary, presumably, because grades have not fallen in response to absenteeism, and students can still find their way to the finish line. What do they learn? We know that employers are unhappy with the lack of job skills of recent graduates. And we know that those who seek further degrees—master's and professional degrees and doctorates—encounter the same sort of pushback from their faculty as high school teachers hear when they send their charges off to college. Faculty feel students are unprepared. We are pushing the problems up the educational ladder rather than solving them when problems arise. We know from a raft of reports, articles, and books that what students learn in college is negligible. Those who arrive unprepared, depart unprepared—or drop out. Those who arrive prepared are not that much more prepared after they finish.

Our concern should not be simply that they have not learned vocational skills to make them more employable. When we return to the social learning component that I raised earlier, we also find that students are not substantially more engaged than when they arrived. Studies indicate that the development of critical thinking has been marginal, and the result is college graduates who are not ready to be socially engaged in a project to improve democracy.[35]

Working Conditions

A variety of changes have occurred on United States' campuses that have made them decidedly better. Although we have a long way to go—and I do not wish to minimize the challenges of anyone who finds themselves marginalized—campuses are more diverse today and generally more welcoming for many students, faculty, and staff. Campuses in general are also more environmentally friendly today than they once were. Town-and-gown engagement has largely improved.

If we acknowledge improvements, then we also have to recognize where the working conditions have gotten worse. I'll elaborate in a later essay, but the discrepancy between a president's salary and that of a new assistant professor has never been greater. The perks and amenities that members of the board and senior administrators have with regard to health care and a whole host of sought-after goodies—from parking to football tickets—have never been greater. While senior administrators and board members travel business or first class with unlimited travel funds, faculty at many universities are forced to compete for miniscule institutional funding for the one conference that they may be fortunate enough to attend.

Colleges and universities have largely outsourced an array of services because they are able to remove individuals from the payroll and hire companies that will pay people less and give them fewer benefits. The result is that we have a cleaning staff who comes to work at 3:00 a.m. during the school year and then is laid off during the summer when the students and faculty leave. Institutions could not care less about the working conditions of those who are the poorest paid on campus. These cost-saving measures would be easier to take if, at the same time, we did not see the president's private limousine, the provost's dining budget, and the membership in exclusive clubs that the deans and other senior staff obtain to ostensibly run after wealthy donors.

The working conditions of faculty have also radically changed. Tenure was once the norm, and now it is the exception. In my own school of education, roughly 80 percent of the faculty were tenure track and 20 percent were part-time and adjunct faculty when I started. Now those figures are reversed. The result is that we no longer have a financially secure workforce able to weigh in on a variety of issues that confront us without fear of retribution, and the changing cast of characters creates for an unstable workplace culture. Without the protection of tenure, and without a full-time workforce, the ability to say that academic freedom exists, or that shared governance is healthy, is a canard. Workforces always have to change, but the movements we have seen over the last generation have largely been in response to perceived crises, and they have not improved the academic workplace for either the workers or society. Budget cuts, and costs in other areas, have led to fewer tenure track faculty, stingier health benefits, and less of a retirement package.

These issues are also related. Someone may write an article about the enrollment crisis and focus on a downturn in enrollment for small liberal arts colleges, as if the downturn is an isolated issue. In actuality, though, it has a lot to do with faculty costs, online education, and for-profit higher education. What boards choose as important issues has a great deal to do with the seemingly inexorable rise in college costs. Consequently, I will move back and forth in these essays, trying to help you think through the multiple issues that face higher education.

Getting Higher Education's Groove Back

Many of us in higher education do not want to recognize the challenges that I've just enumerated. We continue to act like what worked yesterday will work tomorrow, even with the pandemic that hit all of us. It won't. In part, this book is to help us think through some of the most pressing problems that we confront and consider how to get our groove back. I am not saying that the end is near, but the status quo will not work either. My intent is to put forward the various challenges that exist to help you think through these issues and how they relate to one another and then come up with your own decision. Rather than compile a higher education cookbook with recipes for reform, I put forward the various ingredients that go into the entire menu of higher education so that we might then decide how to create a better postsecondary restaurant. I can't cover every single topic that confronts us or this would be an encyclopedia. I have, however, tried to cover the major issues, and hopefully the back and forth will help us think through them. There's no magic to having forty-nine essays—they are simply the most important topics that we face today, as we move forward, post-COVID-19. If I wrote the book ten years ago, we likely would not have discussed microaggressions; if I update the book in ten years, a few topics may drop off my list and others will pop up. Just as in real life, these topics are not linear; they occur in tandem, and their relationships frequently overlap.

Remember my young friend who skips his computer science class? His older brother does also. As he said to me one day, "The classes are boring, and they're all recorded, so I can watch them on my phone in my room." I countered that there was more to a class than simply learning the material and he agreed, saying, "I always go to office hours. I like to talk to the professor. I also like to listen to the questions other students have." He admitted that he could fast-forward through the material he found easy, and he could pause at parts that were difficult. What he did not like was sitting in a class of three hundred students and having to cover material in two hours that he could do in one.

How should we think about my young friends' course-taking patterns? The bottom line is that they get good grades, so why make them sit in a large lecture class? Why not accommodate different learning styles? Why would we think making students sit in a class just like they did twenty years ago—jeez, fifty years ago—is good pedagogy? We've got to get with it: focus on learning outcomes and present material in a way that enables individuals to engage in a manner that meets their learning needs.

I have two quiz questions for you:

1. Name the three best football coaches in the United States.

2. Name the three best college presidents in the United States.

I'm betting readers will find an easier time naming three great football coaches than even coming up with the names of three college presidents. Therein lies the problem. We presently lack college presidents, regents, or faculty who can make the case for higher education in the public sphere. Instead, we have presidents of grounds and buildings or fundraisers; people who build buildings and raise money but fail to speak on the major issues of the day that confront our students and society. Bill Clinton once said, "There are objective reasons that huge numbers of Americans are confused, angry, frustrated, and afraid." He continued: "In that environment, the proper response is relentless explanation."[36]

Relentless explanation. I like that phrase. People need to understand what we do in higher education and why our work is worthwhile. Instead, we usually come across as whiners trying to get some scraps from the legislature, or as condescending experts. No wonder our reputation is sinking. I once hoped that a group like the American Association of University Professors could make such a case, but they are more like shop stewards than intellectual leaders. Unions need folks to lobby for their interests, but lobbying for pension plans is entirely different from making the case for higher education in the public square. Before we make that case, I want readers to understand the panoply of issues that confronts academe. All of these issues can be overwhelming because we face so many—and that's precisely the way it is on our campuses. Topics come and go, they have competing analyses, and how to solve one problem will create issues in another area. What I'm trying to do, then, is enable us to think through the various topics so that we are better prepared to handle them.

We need to explain what we do, why we do it, and how we're changing to meet the needs of the twenty-first century. Actions speak louder than words, but in the communication age, words are pretty darn important too. And right now we don't have a single spokesperson who is able to be relentless in explaining the critical significance of higher education for the future welfare of our democracy.

Nick Saban sure could make the case for 'Bama football, though.

Ok, so you flunked the quiz question. Here's an essay question for you: Make believe that we do not have a higher education system in this country but that we have just decided to create one. What should it look like?

Do you think we would create the crazy patchwork quilt that we have today? I hope not. I'd like us to consider the following topics as we create that new system.

Mastery of Knowledge

Let's eliminate *terms* and *credits*. Let's figure out what students need to learn. Whether they learn it in five weeks or fifteen weeks is irrelevant. If we can agree on a specific skill set that students need to have, then, when they have accumulated that skill set, they can move on to the next level, and eventually graduate. Academe has dipped its toes in the water on this matter. For example, Western Governor's University, a nonprofit university founded in 1997 by thirteen US governors who each committed $100,000 in seed money, allows students to accelerate through programs if they can draw on previous work or educational experiences—or simply devote more time to the completion of their degrees.[37] In 2013, the University of Wisconsin created a Flex Option that has a similar philosophy. Under the Flex Option, students pay a fixed rate for an "all-you-can-learn term" that lasts a specified period of time (e.g., three months or an academic year).[38] Colleges and universities throughout the United States offer online degrees, but we do it begrudgingly and with a good deal of cynicism. It is that kind of foot-dragging that brings down traditional companies when new innovators (think the software industry) rise up to disrupt the status quo.

Eliminate Transfer

Students should move from twelfth to thirteenth grade much like they progress from eleventh to twelfth. I am betting this simple shift will create a significant increase in higher education. Similarly, all community colleges should be related to a four-year institution, or not at all. If students say they want a four-year degree when they have finished two years, then they move on to the third year. They do not transfer from one place to another. If students simply want a certificate to gain a specific skill set, then they go to a community college.

Demand Transparency

We should clarify learning objectives and ensure that the prospective student knows how many individuals learn the material, graduate on time, understand how much debt has been incurred, and know whether students end up employed. Keep it simple. That's the knowledge consumers want to know.

Reduce Duplication

Let's acknowledge that distribution requirements are political trade-offs by faculties and departments and are not optimal for learning. Have the faculty determine what they believe their students need to know, and then offer a finite set of courses that provides various learning experiences. What students need to know can vary from institution to institution; I do not believe in some grand scheme (except when it comes to the mastery of basic skills). What I want to see eliminated is what we currently have: course-taking patterns based on how early a student was able to register for a class.

Reward Faculty

I mentioned earlier that faculty in all types of institutions are given greater rewards for research than for teaching, and we have fewer tenure track faculty. In some instances, part-time and adjunct faculty are superb hires. But hiring should adhere to a schema, rather than a lack of funding, to hire tenure-track faculty. Figure out what faculty need to do, and then reward them to do it. Some institutions will continue doing research. But I am betting that the vast majority of institutions would focus more intently on teaching and learning and figure out ways to reward individuals for teaching, rather than for writing an article or two.

Prepare Students for Life in a Democracy

Although job preparation and learning the skills necessary to attain a job is certainly important, so are the skills needed to participate in a democracy.

The advent of social media and advances in technology have brought into question what "facts" are. Students not only need to be encouraged to be involved in civic life, they also need to have the ability to delineate between factually correct and fake data. They need to be involved in the great discussions of the day and able to communicate their views from an informed standpoint. They need to understand the parameters of structural racism and why Black Lives Matter. I am less concerned about the views a student holds than I am about the ability of an individual to function in a democracy based on accurate information.

Some people see the issues I'm suggesting here as a revenue problem—we simply need more revenue. Others see it as a structural problem. And still others see it as a cultural conundrum.

What we need is a public discussion about our hopes for the country and how higher education fits into those hopes. Rather than consistently whining that we need more money or that people should just give us money and leave us alone, we need a creative discussion that delineates the issues and foments a public discussion about how we might get our groove back. I hope this book will jump-start that discussion.

CHAPTER 2

Canaries in the Academic Coal Mine

The Twenty-First Century Idea of a University

The Idea of the University, written in 1852 by Cardinal John Henry Newman, is one of those books that many know about, but few have read.[1] The book is 428 dense pages. Newman was an Anglican who converted to Catholicism, a conservative who was liberal, a man of letters, a voluminous author and essayist, and one of the nineteenth-century's greatest writers.

It should not be surprising that a religious person penned a book about the purpose of the university. Newman spent his life considering his beliefs and how he wanted us to live our lives. He lived in the era of Darwin, when science was seen as an opponent of religion. Newman would have none of it. He argued that science and religion were compatible and that the purpose of a university was to discuss, debate, and argue about differing opinions. Artistic truth, Newman thought, was organic and incapable of scientific analysis. Scientific truth functioned through logic. He was entirely comfortable with the coexistence of both, and he sought supremacy for neither. Newman's purpose was religious: to do good work and to find in the daily acts of life a way to believe in, and ultimately conduct life with, God.

Newman believed the university was one of the main staging grounds for figuring out the puzzles of life. The university was important because it enabled growth and development. Newman thought everyone needed to engage in moral reflection through an intense examination of one's self and one's beliefs, but also through discussion in communion with others. He reacted against doctrinaire statements about papal infallibility and beliefs handed down without being examined. Because he questioned so much, he was constantly in trouble with the church. The pope, other cardinals, priests, and the press disliked his questioning but ultimately came to respect his intellect and his conviction that to find truth, we had to question our own—and others'—beliefs.

Newman was trying to create a university for Ireland. Even though he was a Roman Catholic, he believed that all of science must be taught alongside theology. Theology, he argued, "was a branch of knowledge." He made a distinction between the humanities and sciences but argued that both were essential to function in society. Perhaps most importantly, he passionately believed that simply training individuals for a skill was a debasement of the human spirit. He argued presciently that studying the humanities should not be the reserve of the wealthy, but for everyone. He was arguing against the utilitarian ideas of John Locke and trying to move Catholicism toward a more protean conception of knowledge and liberty. His faith was strong enough that he felt that different ideas, or contradictory ideas, should not be shunned or banned, but instead debated.

The university was the locale where students were not indoctrinated, but instead afforded space to think about competing ideas. Ultimately, each individual should be able to come to his or her own decision, argued Newman. He rejected the orthodoxy handed down from Rome and said that if any place in the world should be a location for thoughtful discourse, it should be the university.

There is, of course, much to disagree with in a philosophical tract written in the nineteenth century. Newman's text does not consider women at all, and he writes of "savages" who lack the knowledge he hopes people learn in universities. Despite its limitations, Newman's vision of what we should be doing in the university remains relevant today. He demanded access to learning for all people that had been previously reserved for the elite.

What might his ideas portend for our postsecondary institutions in the twenty-first century? We are not going to do away with the need for students to be trained for employment, a topic I will take up in the next essay. Newman, however, points to the vital role of the university as a locus for individuals to come together to engage with questions of identity, self, community, and society. And if anything, the twenty-first century presents us with a greater need than ever for the university as an intellectual commons.

We always have struggled to have productive conversations with people with whom we vigorously disagree, but today it appears harder to cross differences than at any time since I have been in the academy (starting as a long-haired college student in the 1970s). Almost daily, examples pop up on social media where someone makes a provocative comment or an errant statement, and the campus erupts in protest. At Yale University, an administrator was recently removed for a review she posted on Yelp about a restaurant.[2] At Evergreen State College in Washington, another professor was told to stay away from campus because he had disagreed with an argument that had been put forward about racial equity.[3] At the University of Maryland, a professor was pilloried because he posted a statement critical of the secretary of education for the Trump administration.[4] Sensitivity can be a good thing: we ought to be aware of our language and how what we say may hurt or harm another. All too often what occurs, however, is not that a speaker becomes more aware, but instead that the intellectual commons is abandoned. People fear speaking out and disengage.

A classroom, our common physical and virtual areas, and the institution itself ought to be a place where we are able to debate, argue, and ultimately understand one another. Why are we failing to nurture such a community? One answer is that our presidents do not see this as one of their roles. They are managing budgets or off raising money. Our senior administrators are part of a bureaucracy that sees its segment of the institution but is unable to grasp the entirety of the place. And, most distressingly, the faculty seem to have largely given up their communal role in favor of self-preservation. I get it. As I elaborate on in a later essay, there are fewer tenure-track faculty; part-time or adjunct faculty do not have the luxury to worry about the larger institution. And because there are fewer tenure-track faculty, those of us who remain have more to do. All of us worry about smaller salaries, fewer benefits, and deteriorating working conditions.

If we want higher education to get its groove back, however, we are not going to succeed if we simply focus on structural issues such as who reports to whom, or assume that our worries will be over if we just train the faculty to be more adept at online teaching, or get more funding from the state, or better train and prepare our graduates for employment—though these things are important. Ultimately, what will get us out of our current morass is building community.

In the nineteenth century, Cardinal Newman advocated for the university as a space where we might argue and debate important ideas, and that need remains today. However, we need to consider the conditions that make such discussions possible, and prior to doing that, we first have to agree that such conversations are necessary and welcomed.

Is Higher Education an Aging Industry or a Hot Commodity? Or Both?

When I was a junior in high school, my high school guidance counselor, Mr. Wildman, called me into his office, and we discussed where I wanted to go to college. He gave me a list of institutions he thought might be viable, and to it, I added the institution where my two older brothers went: the University of Notre Dame. Neither Mr. Wildman nor my parents questioned my going to college. We never discussed attending any of New York's public institutions or any other public university, much less a two-year college. If asked, I could not have explained the differences between a public or private institution. We also never discussed the cost of attendance; my father was going to pick up the tab.

A friend and I traveled around the northeast, and, after a week or two, we both decided on applying to Clark University and Tufts University. I also applied to Notre Dame, and Tom applied to Emory, where he lived before his family moved north. I got into all three universities, and Tufts was an easy decision; for an eighteen-year-old, Boston seemed like a very cool place to be for four years. (It was!) I was not very different from 98 percent of my high school class. We all went to four-year private universities, largely in the northeast. Horace Greeley High School had one black student and a handful of Latinx students. We had a few students who qualified for financial aid. The decision about where to go was relatively easy for me, my parents, Mr. Wildman, and the admissions officers.

Today, the world has shifted, but we are not sure in which direction. The pandemic has upended many norms. The Trump administration's dislike of foreigners has reduced international student enrollment—a crucial revenue stream for some institutions.[5] Enrollment drops have created difficult fiscal budgets for everyone, especially private, small regional institutions. States are less able to support higher education, and donors are hesitant to make gifts as their stock portfolios shrink. And that's just with the pandemic. We have other issues to deal with as well.

On the one hand, in the spring of 2019, the Varsity Blues admissions scandal erupted, where well-heeled parents paid hundreds of thousands of dollars to get their children admitted to the university of their choice.[6] The scandal was a brilliant scam, engineered by Rick Singer, an admissions advisor to the stars.[7] For a tidy sum, he helped parents fake the SAT test scores of their children, write college essays about experiences that never happened, and list the applicants as playing a sport, such as water polo, that they never played. Surprise! Singer's applicants were remarkably successful. Although the scam was limited to a few hundred parents, the accounts made national headlines for weeks because children of the rich and famous were involved, and the story exemplified yet again how the rich are different from thee and me.

The tale also highlighted the centrality of higher education for traditionally aged students. Parents were willing to pay literally hundreds of thousands of dollars and commit crimes to get their kids into a prestigious college. Subsequently, those institutions that were targeted have put measures in place so that their admissions systems are not compromised in the future. Those same universities also quietly pointed out that they must be doing something right if parents were paying so much to get their kid into the university.

On the other hand, we frequently hear that the end is near as another college closes its doors because it can't meet its enrollment targets. The gloom-and-doom tales of woe have been around for a while. My dissertation advisor, Lewis B. Mayhew, penned a book titled *Surviving the Eighties* that said it all.[8] In the 1980s, some people prophesied that, because of demographic declines, colleges were sure to fold. They didn't. In fact, tuition kept going up. The doomsayers' accounts were challenged by analysts who said that there were sure to be ebbs and flows, and if an institution just waited it out (and hired a new dean of admissions), things were sure to turn around. They did.

Until they didn't. When the Great Recession hit in 2008, a variety of factors seemed to come together to create long-term structural problems. The recession dramatically reduced institutional endowments of private institutions, as well as state subsidies to public universities. Many of the criticisms I am discussing in this book reduced consumer confidence in higher education. For-profit higher education produced a boomlet, and, by inference, poked holes in the nonprofit academic wall. Even when the for-profits faced severe attacks (which I'll discuss in a subsequent chapter), the criticism of the nonprofits struck the consumers' nerves.

The recession also reduced family budgets. What was once a foregone conclusion became a thorny problem. The assumption that a family's son or daughter should go to the small regional college an hour or two away from home became a luxury. Perhaps the kid is better off just going to the local four-year public? Or perhaps start at the community college?

Numerous states also faced a downturn in enrollment at their public universities even before the pandemic. In 2017, the University of Montana-Missoula had a headcount of 8,958, a 30 percent decline from 2011.[9] It was not alone. The public universities in Alaska, Hawaii, Idaho, and New Mexico, among others, have also experienced substantial declines in enrollment.[10] A great deal of the decline pertains to demographics. Sustained smaller high school graduation rates over time eventually come home to roost. Public universities often have thought that their "customers" came to them; they didn't need to market their product to their customers. In fact, words like *market* and *customer* were anathema to some of us.

In a study I did a few years ago, the differences between for-profits and public institutions were evident by simple phone calls. The for-profit admissions team was respectful, energetic, and optimistic. They answered all of our questions and showed remarkable follow-up to close the deal by proffering admission.[11]

I'll discuss later the problems with the eager beaver method of admissions, but the flip side is also illustrative. The public institutions were lethargic, nonresponsive, and unhelpful. They repeatedly said to look at the website and had no follow-up.[12] We can point out the deceptive practices that the for-profit sector has shown. At the same time, it's useful to acknowledge that many, but not all, public institutions do not invest in recruitment.

International and out-of-state students also have created issues. Many public and private universities have used students from another region as a cash cow. The University of California, for example, has publicly justified the increased enrollment of out-of-state students by saying such students add to the diversity of the institution. The University of Southern California has prided itself on its international enrollment, largely from China and India, so that it might claim the mantle of a global university.

Both the University of California and the University of Southern California, of course, are masking the real reason why they admit these special groups of students. The University of California institutions have an inflated cost of tuition for out-of-staters, which helps them balance their budget, especially as the state has reduced its support. The University of

Southern California gets full freight from its foreign students and doesn't have to provide them with grants or scholarships. The problem for all public universities, however, is this: just as some parents hesitate to send their children to a private regional institution, they now pause at spending so much not only on tuition but also for travel to another state. Just keep the kid home. And the Trump administration's unrelenting demonization of immigrants has made international students feel less welcome, so a downturn in foreign students to the United States has occurred.[13]

Threading the needle of college admissions has become that much more difficult. The result is that it's fair to say that enrollment is in flux and business as usual is out the window. Those institutions that are most at risk are small, private, regional colleges with small endowments and very little margin for error. Faculty often do not recognize the problem because they teach their classes no matter what (which is another sort of problem). If I had twenty-eight students five years ago, and today I have twenty-one students, I don't really notice any problem. I still meet my classes, grade my papers, and probably welcome that class discussions can be richer with fewer students. I am still working just as hard for twenty-one students as I did with twenty-eight. The college president and provost recognize, however, that they have a problem. An institution that admitted nine hundred students five years ago, but today has 820 students, brings in less revenue but maintains stable costs.

Nathan Grawe has written a smart, dispassionate book that points out how high school graduating classes are going to continue to get smaller.[14] I don't think enrollment is destiny, or we're in a perfect storm, or the end is near. Institutions adapt. Women's colleges became coeducational in part because they needed more bodies in seats. Part-time students and adult students were welcomed in order to balance budgets. And, of course, when my competitor institution dies, those students may come to my institution.

Clayton Christensen's prediction that approximately half of all higher education institutions are going to close within ten to fifteen years is certainly attention-grabbing—and ludicrous, even with the pandemic. Christensen first made his infamous prophecy in his 2011 book entitled *The Innovative University*.[15] We're almost ten years into his prediction, and it is still nowhere close to materializing. To wit, a handful of small liberal arts colleges with fewer than one thousand students, a lack of online programs, and/or a deep dependence on tuition for more than 85 percent of their revenue have closed in recent years.[16] Some states, such as Wisconsin and Georgia, have consolidated public colleges and universities partly to reduce expenses and partly due to population declines in rural areas.[17] But Derek Newton, writing for *Forbes*, has undertaken a deeper examination of Christensen's claims and found the following: "In the 2013–14 year, there were 3,122 four-year colleges according to the Department of Education. In 2017–18 . . . there were 2,902—a drop of about 7% over four years. That could be disruptive. But numerically all of school closures . . . were four-year, for-profit schools, which fell from 769 in 2013 to 499 in 2017—a drop of 270. Of all the colleges, at all levels, that have closed since 2013, 95.5% of them were for-profit institutions."[18] As a result, Newton concludes that "the real Christensen disruption story is that the schools [for-profit institutions focused on career-ready skills] he thought of as predators have turned out to be prey."

Nevertheless, during a 2017 Higher Education Summit sponsored by Salesforce.org, Christensen maintained, "If you're asking whether the providers get disrupted within a decade—I might bet that it takes nine years rather than ten."[19] These claims of imminent massive disruption for higher education have led to much hand-wringing by some administrators who fully buy into Christensen's theories—and incredulity from others who have taken a second look at the statistical trends. As an example of the latter group, the president of Alfred University, Mark Zupan, even challenged Christensen to a $1 million bet that half of all traditional universities would *not* fail or merge by 2030.[20]

My guess is that we will see a downturn as our most financially vulnerable institutions close their doors. According to the National Center for Education Statistics, there were 1,689 private, nonprofit institutions and 1,626 public institutions during the 2017 to 2018 academic year in the United States.[21] During a recent five-year period from 2014 through 2018, 129 private, nonprofit institutions closed, and only eleven public institutions closed.[22] All of the public institutions that closed were voca-tional schools with fewer than 800 students.[23] The pandemic has created additional problems, but most observers of higher education expect that about 250 small colleges will close within the next few years—a far cry from Christensen's prediction.

Among those survivors will be the institutions highlighted in the Varsity Blues scandal. To be sure, scam artists always can figure out the next scam. We can improve our admissions policies and try to stop the next Rick Singer, but our admissions systems are like squirrel baffles. We put bird seed in the feeder for the birds, and we see those darn squirrels climbing the feeder to munch on the seed. We put a baffle on the bird feeder to stop them. We succeed—for a while. And then the next Albert Einstein squirrel figures out a way to get to the seed, and we try to invent a new baffle. We will create baffles so we can't get scammed with college admissions too, but I'm waiting for the next scam artist to figure out a way to help rich parents aid their children.

If there is a plus side to the Varsity Blues scandal, it is that it exposed even more how college admissions policies are tilted to help the rich. No poor students were nabbed in the scandal because their parents couldn't afford paying someone a quarter of a million dollars. Poor kids play by the rules. We attack affirmative action in public forums, yet we look the other way with legacy students simply because their parents attended the institution. We create rigorous rules about how all candidates should be treated equally in college admissions—except when the applicant has a parent who donated to the institution or has a friend on the board. What Varsity Blues has done has brought a searchlight on how we admit students; although I wish the scandals hadn't happened, the ensuing spotlight has been good for all of us.

Similarly, no one wishes a pandemic on any society. However, the pandemic seems to have hastened the demise of the most vulnerable institutions. Again, no one can celebrate an institution's closure, but from an ecological standpoint, in an ecosystem of more than 4,000 institutions, the closure of some institutions is to be expected over time. Species grow or shrink; some change, and some will die.

Why For-Profit Higher Education Grew

The norm when discussing for-profit higher education is to cordon it off into a discrete chapter as if it is a momentary aberration and a recent arrival on the postsecondary scene. I interweave a discussion on for-profits with the rest of higher education because they are not a momentary aberration. They have a long history. For-profit higher education has been part of US higher education since the founding of the country. In 1784, a lawyer named Tapping Reeve opened a for-profit law school in Litchfield, Connecticut, building on his experiences as a tutor at Princeton University and training his brother-in-law Aaron Burr as a law apprentice.[24] Throughout the nineteenth century, nearly every major US city had boutique "commercial colleges" that trained students in practical subjects, such as bookkeeping, stenography, and banking.[25] At the end of the century, as many as five hundred commercial colleges were in operation throughout the country.[26] Until the 1970s, however, for-profit colleges and universities (FPCUs) were an insignificant part of the postsecondary ecology. Many of them were trade schools. In some respects, they were community colleges before community colleges existed. They taught people a trade, and the consumer paid a fee. Any of the trappings of traditional institutions were absent: traditional faculty largely did not exist, students did not receive degrees, and the curriculum made no pretense of engaging students in critical thinking. The best of the for-profits ensured that the student mastered a trade such as plumbing, typing, or welding.

The other distinctive part of for-profit higher education institutions is that, since their inception, they have been run by a great many flimflam artists. A. J. Angulo's insightful *Diploma Mills* provides a history of for-profit higher education that highlights how, since the Revolutionary War, "those with an entrepreneurial spirit could take on apprentices or open an FPCU with the goal of training the next generation of attorneys and physicians without much in the way of external oversight."[27] The result was that a group of con artists entered the postsecondary scene with outlandish claims that made the con artists wealthy while their customers gained little. The federal and state governments largely stood on the sidelines and watched colleges come and go with virtually no oversight.

In spite of this, certain areas of study became more professional, such as the legal and medical fields. These professions drifted away from the for-profit sector and into traditional higher education. The nonprofit public and private sector schools also turned to regulating themselves through accreditation. For-profit entrepreneurs know how to adapt, and rather than hire traditional faculty or seek accreditation and normalize their operations, they simply turned to new markets with the same methods that had been successful in the nineteenth century. Their fortunes waxed and waned throughout the first half of the twentieth century. At times, government oversight threatened their survival; at other times, they adroitly worked the system and tapped into state and federal monies.

In the 1970s, the for-profit world changed. At that time, John Sperling, founder of the University of Phoenix, was a tenured faculty member at San Jose State University. By happenstance, he started working with adult firefighters and nurses who had associate's degrees but wanted bachelor's degrees. When Sperling approached the leaders of San Jose State to help these potential new students, the administration found little need to accommodate him. Neither the administration nor the faculty was interested in serving an adult clientele who wanted classes at a convenient time and in a convenient location. These adults could not take classes during the day because they had jobs. They did not care about going to a campus, and they certainly did not need a dorm room. Voila! To avoid the California regulatory and accreditation agencies that would likely block his new institution, Sperling relocated to Arizona, where a different accreditation agency might be amenable to his entrepreneurial ideas. The University of Phoenix was subsequently established with eight students in 1976. After expanding to a second city (San Jose, California) in 1980 and adding online programs in 1989, the university went public in 1994 with around twenty-five thousand students.[28] As they say, the rest is history.

The strength of for-profits is that they are trying to meet the needs of the customer. Courses are offered in convenient locations at convenient times. Classes can be taken all the time, without pausing for the Christmas and summer breaks of traditional academe. The strategy, at first, was to meet the needs of the customer–student.

Although the for-profit industry had been a blip on the postsecondary screen, once other entrepreneurs saw that federal funding was available and there was a lack of regulatory control, the gold rush began. Beginning in the 1980s and continuing through the first decade of the twenty-first century, the for-profit sector was the fastest growing component of the higher education world. It went from barely 1 percent of the total enrollment of postsecondary students to approximately 12 percent at the turn of the twenty-first century.[29] What enabled this enormous growth?

One irony of the for-profit sector is that, as public institutions have had to rely more on private fundraising, for-profit higher education has moved in the opposite direction. Virtually none of the FPCUs engage in private fundraising or receive revenue from research. Although some students can afford to pay the tuition out of their own pockets, the vast majority of income derives from student grants and loans. If the federal and state governments no longer provided grants and loans for students, the for-profit sector would shrink back to a blip on the postsecondary screen. Thus, the most capitalist of postsecondary institutions is also the most socialist of enterprises. They survive—and thrive—at the public trough.[30]

The business model of FPCUs is easy enough to comprehend: find more customers and the company will have more profit. The way to find more customers is to create them, rather than try to compete with the traditional sector. Upper- and middle-class high school students—or their parents—have likely been thinking about college throughout their high school years, so FPCUs targeted first-generation, low-income students, most of whom were adults.[31]

Part of this marketing scheme is admirable. Just as Sperling was trying to serve a clientele that the traditional sector either did not want or would not accommodate, the for-profit sector went after individuals who had given little thought of going to college because they thought they could not afford it. I will consider in a later essay the shortcomings of traditional institutions' inabilities to adapt to first-generation students, but there is something admirable about for-profits ostensibly trying to create opportunity for students who are likely stuck in minimum wage jobs by providing a college education.

Unfortunately, many for-profits engaged in marketing practices that had little to do with helping the underserved and a lot to do with enriching the owners of the FPCUs. The result was that for-profit institutions worked with students to apply for federal loans and grants, which then enabled the students to tap into state loans and grants. Again, there is nothing inherently wrong with an organization helping a customer work through confusing paperwork. I am sure many of us would like our health-care providers and cable companies to walk us step by step through confusing application forms.

The for-profits, however, engaged in practices with their customers—many of whom had very little financial literacy—that encumbered them with enormous debt. The consequences were fourfold. First, new students did not fully comprehend what they were getting themselves into and ended up dropping out without anything to show for their effort. The institution generated revenue through the tuition the student paid, but the student accumulated debt. Second, whether students dropped out or completed their degrees, many were saddled with enormous debt. Third, students frequently thought that they would automatically earn their way into high-paying jobs and instead found themselves back where they had started in low-wage positions. Students who thought they were being trained to be chefs found jobs as dishwashers. Students who thought that the wages of a yoga instructor or beautician would enable them to enter the middle class discovered that they were still unable to pay their bills. And fourth, when students defaulted on their loans and declared bankruptcy, the government was left to pay the bills to the for-profit institution. The customer was screwed, and so was the taxpayer.[32]

The for-profits were extremely savvy about pricing structures. They left very little money on a federal or state table. They also were adept at finding new clientele. They marketed to individuals in groups who rarely received encouragement to attend higher education but who were eligible for receiving grants and loans. Veterans in particular were targeted for recruitment.[33]

The for-profits had two kinds of defenses when I spoke with them. On the one hand, they had a common refrain that every industry had a few bad apples. Of course there were mistakes, claimed those in the for-profit sector, but they were the exception to the rule, not the rule. Yet, Senator Tom Harkin of Iowa, after an extensive investigation of the for-profit industry, concluded that the problem was not a few bad apples, but the entire orchard. The for-profit industry did not help itself by its inability to police its own. In my many conversations and meetings with various groups involved in for-profit higher education, I never heard anyone state that egregious violations had occurred. Instead, they always claimed that regulation was a problem, but they seemed unable and unwilling to either ensure the orchard was ethically healthy or sanction those few bad apples.

On the other hand, for-profit apologists often explained that of course their dropout rates were high. They were educating people who were harder to educate than those students who went to Harvard or Stanford. Such a claim had a degree of merit. Institutions are likely to have higher or lower completion rates based on the academic backgrounds of their students. But if an accountable institution is going to take a chance on a high-risk student, then it has to have the structures in place to support that student, and the for-profits were woefully lacking in such structures.

By the end of the Obama administration, the boom days of the for-profit sector were over, or at least in abeyance. Donald Trump, however, had his own for-profit university and saw very little of concern with its functioning and outcomes, even though Trump University mirrored some of the worst mistakes that had been uncovered in the industry.[34] Indeed, when one investigates the history of for-profit higher education, we find that the problems that ran rampant at the start of the twenty-first century were largely the same that plagued for-profits in 1900. The only difference is the industry is better organized today, and it is unwilling to admit any malfeasance. What ought to be done?

We have a capacity problem in the United States. As I have mentioned, we need more people participating in higher education, but unless we are willing to fund more public education, that will not happen.

Students cannot take on more debt, so the federal and state governments need to provide more funding for students to attend public and private nonprofits. But I do not see that happening either. I used to believe that the for-profits could fill seats when the public sector was unwilling or unable. But without a more vigorous regulatory framework on federal and state levels, I am no longer optimistic that the problems of the past won't be repeated in the future.

"It's None of Your Business." "Yes, It Is!"

Many years ago, I was at a friend's party in Massachusetts in the early summer. When she introduced me to her friends, someone asked what I did, and I simply said, "I'm a teacher." My friend, and most of the party-goers, were working-class Boston Red Sox fans. The sport I know best is baseball, and I can hold my own in conversation about the strengths and weaknesses of any major league team—especially the Red Sox (and Dodgers). Over beers, we had a spirited discussion about their current travails.

When she introduced me, my friend had mentioned that I was from out of town and someone jokingly asked me, "How come you know so fricking much about the Red Sox?" I laughed and said I had gone to graduate school at Harvard; there was a slight pause. Someone guessed, "So you got like a master's degree for your teaching? What do you teach anyway?" I did not think about it and said that I was on the faculty at Penn State, that I had received my master's degree at Harvard, and then a PhD at Stanford. I laughed while telling the group that at Stanford, I'd almost learned to like the hated nemesis of the Dodgers: the San Francisco Giants. There was a palpable pause, and then the most ardent of the Red Sox fans said quizzically, "So, you're not like a teacher. You're like a *real* teacher. A professor?" I nodded and started talking about the woes of Oil Can Boyd, but the tenor of the conversation had changed. I had gone from a guy who could drink beer and talk about baseball to a "professor."

For much of the history of the United States, the professoriate and the US college and university have held a vaunted reputation. A democracy has no hallowed grounds. Our academic institutions are among the oldest organizations in our country, and there is (or at least was) a sanctified air about them. People cared about higher education, but what happened on campus was slightly mysterious.

Universities were where smart people did things, though what they did was not entirely clear. Professors didn't work with their hands but with their minds; they taught their charges so that they too could work with their minds. For the first time in the twentieth century, individuals from the lower and middle classes began to realize that academe was not merely the preserve of the wealthy few but might present an opportunity for their kids as well. In a democracy, education has played a central role—in myth and fact—in enabling people to move out of poverty and into the middle class.

The play *A Raisin in the Sun* is Lorraine Hansberry's searing portrait of racism in the 1950s. At the end of act I, Walter, the husband and father of the poor black family, thinks he has come into some money that will make him wealthy and enable them to move into a house. In a long soliloquy to his seven-year-old son in the family living room where the boy sleeps, Walter dreams of better days and says to the boy:

> And I'll pull the car up on the driveway—just a plain black Chrysler, I think with white walls, no black tires. More elegant. Rich people don't have to be flashy. I'll have to get something sportier for your mom, maybe a Cadillac convertible to do her shopping in. And I'll go inside the house and your mom will come downstairs and meet me at the door and we'll kiss each other and we'll go up to your room to see you sitting on the floor with the catalogues of all the great universities in America around you. All the great schools in the world! And—and I'll say, all right son—it's your seventeenth birthday, what is it you've decided? Just tell me where you want to go to school and you'll go! Just tell me what you want to be—and you'll be it! Yessir! You just name it, son, and I will hand you the world.[35]

Walter's heartbreaking comments echo what many thought about higher education throughout the twentieth century. Academe was a ticket out of poverty. Although the cost of college might be a stretch, anyone could do it if they worked hard and planned for it. Until recently, virtually all surveys looked on higher education favorably. Lately though, the favorability of higher education has begun to change. People have begun to wonder if the cost of higher education is worth the price of the ticket.

Professors always have been suspect in a country where intellectuals are not valued. But we have not been disdained. Instead, we have been granted the benefit of the doubt because we were perceived to be doing a public service: educating the young. By the time I went to Tufts University in the 1970s, the suspicions and doubts about academics had turned from an occasional criticism to a constant critique. The protests in the 1960s, the vociferous clamor against Vietnam, and all the subsequent demonstrations seemed rooted in the minds of the era's college students. These students seemed to have turned against the values that their parents believed in and had instilled in their children. The faculty were the culprits, claimed some, and as with any constant drumbeat of criticism, over time the critique took hold.

What those of us in higher education never really learned was that our innate drive for contemplation also created a perceptual problem. I have long maintained that a higher percentage of academics are introverts than the average in the larger society. Regardless of the discipline we choose to study, we often need time alone to think through the challenges of our work. The surprise registered by my friend's friends was that a professor knew the ins and outs of baseball as well as (or better!) than they did. The perception was that academics did not speak, think, and act like regular people but instead lived cloistered from society.

Faculty saw themselves as the arbiters of learning. If students got an A, then they were good students, and those who got Bs and Cs were less good. If a student graduated summa cum laude, then obviously the student was highly regarded by the faculty. The curriculum was the prerogative of the faculty, and outside interference was not welcomed. Any sense that the curriculum was linked to actual learning for jobs or that grades in a class suggested the student would be prepared for the world of work was largely absent. Over time, the administration helped determine the priorities of the institution. Since the 1970s, the role of faculty in shared governance has decreased, and the power and authority of the administration has increased. For those not involved in academe, however, the nuances of university governance were lost. The message remained the same: those at the college knew what was best, and we should just trust them about what they said. Scheduling, the tempo of a term, how classes were taught and graded, all revolved around faculty determinations. The same message largely held true with regard to how states configured budgets for public institutions. The university submitted the budget, and perhaps there was a bit of fussing about the specific amount of revenue to be provided, but what an institution wanted was largely what it got. The specifics of what an institution wanted was largely left up to the faculty and administration. The message was, "We know best," and for quite some time that assumption went unquestioned.

Part of such an assumption made sense. If someone delivered a quality product, and the cost for the product was within the budget, then why argue about the intricacies of how much money was needed to develop the product? Why question the judgment of a master craftsperson?

The answers to such questions are manifold. John Sperling provided one answer based on the extended assumption of Walter in *Raisin in the Sun*: lots of people wanted a college degree, but the faculty made taking courses virtually impossible by offering classes at inconvenient times and locations. Students also began to move back home when they graduated from college because jobs were no longer plentiful. Add to these concerns the persistent drumbeat that faculty were out-of-touch snobs who indoctrinated students with left-wing rhetoric, and the conditions were ripe for a change in the way society viewed academe.

For most of the twentieth century, we'd been saying to those outside of our ivy-covered walls, in effect, "It's none of your business what's going on here—and you probably would not understand anyway." The response finally came back, "Yes, it is our business, and we do understand what's going on, and we are concerned." One consequence was that state legislatures no longer approved an institution's budget without careful oversight. Indeed, what has come to be known as performance-based funding became a policy focus of many state legislatures. The assumption was that money should still go from public coffers to public institutions, but there should be strings attached: "I will give you X dollars if you achieve Y outcomes." Such a logical proposition made intuitive sense, but ultimately had very little empirical validity.[36] It's extraordinarily hard to link what is learned in a classroom to what will be needed in the workplace—especially when individuals no longer keep one job for life.

Another corollary was the rise of for-profit higher education. Regardless of the questionable practices that for-profits engaged in, the initial push for their expansion came from the perception that traditional higher education was not functioning in the best interests of the customer: the students. All of these activities resulted in higher education finally recognizing that it had a product to sell and that the customer would make judicious choices. When classes were offered in convenient locations at convenient times, students would choose that institution even if it meant they had to pay more. The initial rhetoric about the student as customer was met with pushback from those of us who thought we were doing something more than selling a product. But a downturn in revenue forced institutions to become more customer friendly. On the one hand, we often hear about colleges that build climbing walls and cascading rivers to attract students, while on the other hand, there is criticism that we are still not responsive enough to the customer.

What's an academic to do? In part, we have to constantly assess our environment, and that environment has changed. The changes all revolve around the transformation of higher education from a public good to a product in a co-marketplace.

"Good" Public Goods

The essays in this chapter pertain to the idea of higher education as a public good, who gets to decide the nature of the public good, and who gets to decide if the public good is actually bad or ineffective.

The *public good* is a deceptively simple term with numerous different meanings and interpretations. Traditionally, *public good* has been used by economists to signify something that is both useful to the public and available to all members of the public. Public goods have two characteristics: nonrivalry and nonexcludability. If a good is nonrivalrous, its use does not diminish the availability of the good to others. If a good is nonexcludable, individuals can use the good regardless of whether or not they pay for it. The clearest example of a public good is national defense. When the country spends money to defend the country, as an individual, I am protected as well as everyone else in the country. Utilities are another example of a public good: when a state provides potable drinking water to its citizens, everyone enjoys the water, not just an isolated few.[37]

A theory of a public good always meets social reality. If national defense is the clearest example of a public good, the assumption is that no individual should bear greater cost for the good than anyone else. But while the cost of protecting individuals against nuclear attack may be the same for the individuals in the continental United States, surely the costs rise when the residents of Guam need to be protected as well. Although, as an American, I will be defended against a nuclear attack (because defense is a public good), I am potentially less vulnerable to such an attack if I lived in Guam rather than New York City. The costs of providing pure drinking water may be equivalent in much of a state, but there are rural areas where reaching individuals will be more difficult and costly. Should individuals in rural areas be faced with higher costs or forgoing the service entirely? In those cases, it would not be considered a pure public good. The privatization of public goods suggests that if a good costs more for one individual, then that person should bear the cost, rather than the public.

Some individuals pursue private goods as an alternative to public goods. For example, police officers are a public good. They exist to protect everyone, not just a privileged few. If I do not feel secure, however, I may decide to buy a security alarm, hire a security company to watch my house, or live in a gated community with a private security system and my own security guards. Whatever I pay for private security is a private good. The good is confined to my house or gated community; simply because I enjoy the service does not mean anyone else does.

When individuals decide that a public good is insufficient for their purposes and consequently turn to private goods, there are two policy-related ramifications. First, the perception and/or the reality that a public good is ineffective—that it is a "bad" public good—has the consequence of decreasing support for the public good.[38] Second, there becomes an increased demand to make private goods more available to the public. Any public good receives fiscal support from the state, and that support derives, in one way or another, from tax revenues, such as general individual taxes, taxes on business, or taxes specifically earmarked for that good. This system works on the assumption that the community members support the public good and are willing to pay a portion of their income for that good. A municipal bond that will increase taxes to upgrade highways, school buildings, or subways is an example of a vote that the citizenry makes to support a public good. Increasingly, however, individuals argue that they are unwilling to pay for goods that they perceive to be ineffective. Conversely, if those public goods do not meet the needs of the citizens, forcing them to buy additional services, they might seek some form of direct tax relief or indirect tax support through a credit on their tax form.

Nowhere has the debate of public goods been more vociferous than in the domain of education. In line with the idea of public education, the United States has assumed that a right to an education extends to everyone—whether they are male or female, rural or urban, black or white, rich or poor. In part, the Supreme Court's decision in *Brown v. Board of Education* pertained to the denial of a public good to a particular race of people. The Supreme Court ruled that "separate but equal" negated the concept of a public good.

Throughout much of the twentieth century, a continuous debate revolved around Catholics who desired to send their children to a parochial school. Why, they asked, should they support public education while paying for their child to attend another school that provided a religious education? Insofar as the Catholic child was not taking up a place or using resources in the public school, should not those monies that the public system saves be used to support the Catholic school? The argument was that the educational public good pertained to individuals, not to institutions, and that it was the individual citizen's decision about how to enact that public good. In effect, Catholics were paying twice for their child's schooling; they sought to change the rules. The response to this argument, of course, was that Catholic parents *chose* to send their children to private school. They were welcome to send them to a public school supported by public monies. A strict separation of church and state required that no public funds be given to religious schools.

The vaunted Master Plan of California paralleled the idea that any students who wanted a higher education could have one for free; like clean drinking water, access to a postsecondary degree was considered a public good. If someone wanted to go to a private college or university, that was his or her right—but a public option existed.[39] By way of Cal Grants, students who attended a private institution could get a grant, but the bulk of the cost would be borne by the students.

The debate over individual resources, parochial schools, and private postsecondary institutions did not initially revolve around the inadequacy or ineffectiveness of the schools and universities but instead focused on two issues: (1) the additional services that a particular segment of society desired and (2) that individuals should be able to choose whatever type of institution they want to attend.

Detractors have asked why we must pay for a public good by way of tax dollars if it is ineffective. Some will suggest that a college education is strictly about the job skills one needs in the workplace, and if public education does not do that, then why ought tax dollars be spent on it? Why not simply let individuals pay out of their pocket for higher education? The necessity of public funding for national defense seems clear to these critics, since an individual cannot create an army or protect him or herself against nuclear attack. But individuals can educate their children or get an education without the support of the state, the critics point out.

Increasingly, the argument shifts between two questions:

1. Should education be seen as a public or private responsibility?

2. Should support be provided to institutions or individuals?

Such questions extend to most areas where public goods exist and underscore the contested nature of the idea of public good. Some, for example, will argue that all adults have the right to use freeways if they have a driver's license; infrastructure is a public good, and all individuals should be ensured safe travel on adequate roads. But if freeways are chronically unsafe and dangerous, then a question will arise about whether individuals would be better off not paying for an ineffective means of transportation and left to their own devices. Perhaps support should not go toward the freeway system in the United States—but to some other means of individually supported transportation. The response, of course, will be akin to the argument I just made about public education. Not everyone can afford private jets. For the economic health of the country, some level of public transportation must exist. If it is ineffective, then it must be improved.

As individuals have grown dissatisfied with public education, they have advanced three critiques that suggest that education need not be a public good as it has been defined over the last century. First, insofar as the execution of the public good is inadequate, the citizenry has a right to look elsewhere. Second, a public good need not be defined and carried out in the same way for all individuals. Third, given that the contexts for the public good have changed, so too should the assumption that education needs to remain both *public* and a *good*.

It is important to note that the definition of a public good has changed over time. A century ago, the public good of national defense did not consider the possibility of a nuclear attack. Only twenty years ago, terrorism would not have registered in a manner that it now does. Similarly, although citizenship education might have been a prerequisite at the turn of the twentieth century—and could have counted as a public good—many today will argue that no such need exists. We have a smaller percentage of immigrants than we did a century ago; we have many more families that are second- and third-generation Americans; we have many more students with high school degrees.

What remains unresolved is how society should deal with those who cannot afford a private good that was once a public good. Some will argue that such a concern has less to do with the definition of public good and more to do with the position of the state vis-a-vis particular rights. Homeless shelters exist for those who cannot afford a home of their own. Public monies being spent for homeless shelters have never implied that all individuals have the right to a home based on the principle of a public good. Clearly, such an assertion defies my initial definition. Further, most students of public goods do not suggest such an expansive notion of the concept.

How a society defines a public good changes over time. Fire stations, for example, were once private; individuals contracted with different companies. If a family contracted with one company, and their neighbor's house started to burn, the company would protect the family's house but not their neighbor's. Over time, the public decided that fire stations should be part of the public good and that all citizens should be protected.

I noted earlier that public institutions, such as the University of California, are a public trust, epitomizing a state's definition of a public good. Over the last century, however, the means by which the state of California supported that public good have shifted dramatically by providing much less public support, even as the perception remains that the board of regents serves as a buffer between the state and the institution.

Other states have suggested even more dramatic action. The governor of South Carolina opined that perhaps all of the state's postsecondary institutions might go private and do as they wish; the result would be that South Carolina no longer needed to support them.[40] Virginia's major institutions are moving toward private status.[41] Colorado has considered implementing a voucher system whereby individual institutions could set tuition and fees; students would receive the bulk of public funding rather than the institution.[42] One may well debate the fiscal wisdom of such actions, but I leave that argument to others. What intrigues me in these actions are the interrelated assumptions at work regarding trust.

The first assumption is that the public, by way of the legislature, no longer trusts postsecondary education in a manner it once did. On the one hand, some believe that a college degree is unnecessary, and on the other, some distrust the institutions themselves. Of consequence, the second assumption is that if the institutions do not have the trust of the public, then they do not need to be a public good. The third assumption is that the marketplace can provide replacements, which is why we have seen the for-profit sector blossom.

Clearly, we have come a long way from the days when Newman penned *The Idea of the University*. I'll discuss later why those of us who might be thought of as traditionalists wish to maintain much of what Newman argued for in his epic. An equally compelling case can be made, however, for why customers have opted for for-profits, even with their shady business practices. At a time when consumers prefer to shop online and bookstores are a vestige of the past, colleges and universities may seem antiquated and out of touch. Globalization and technological revolutions have raised questions about the age-old quandary about the role of the individual in the US community and how much of an obligation individuals have to one another.

CHAPTER 3

The Kids Are Alright—No, They're Not

John Dewey, Meet Mark Zuckerberg

John Dewey, perhaps the preeminent educational philosopher of the United States, has had worldwide import as a progressive intellectual. He moved teaching from the realm of the rote introduction of ideas and/or memorization to what we today might call *critical pedagogy*: the involvement of the learner in reflective learning. The dichotomy of teaching strategies is not always clear-cut—sometimes one *does* need to memorize information to proceed—but how we position the learner helps define how we decide what a teacher should do. If the memorization of text is critical, or the view is that the learner needs to learn truths, then the instructor is akin to an all-knowing sage.

I have played that role. Many years ago, as a young Peace Corps instructor in Morocco, I was told that a surefire way to silence a noisy class was to quote the Koran: "The Teacher is like the Prophet and you must respect Him." I certainly needed to call on that phrase more than once to quiet my noisy charges, but the statement reflects what I've come to think of as the anti-Deweyan perspective. The Teacher-As-God—or at least the Prophet—makes the instructor the vessel for the transmission of knowledge.

Dewey opted for an alternative that I have tried to model in my classrooms. Rather than assume the stance of the proverbial know-it-all, I believe the teacher's job is to engage learners so that they are able to come to their own definitions and particular ideas—which is also what I'm trying to do in this book. Sure, there are correct answers on math tests, but rather than focus only on the correct answer, the instructor wants to see how the student arrived at the answer. For a young Peace Corps instructor, that meant conversational methods rather than recitation, and, of course, students were not prepared for that kind of teaching. In some respects, to be the reciter-in-chief is an easier role to play than one who needs to engage learners in a group activity where knowledge is created and shared rather than transmitted.

If we accept a Deweyan framework, then all sorts of logistical problems arise. Seminars are more likely to be the pedagogical tool rather than the lecture, so that students might engage in discussion with the teacher and one another. Seminars call for small classes rather than large lecture halls. Classes are likely to extend over a long timeframe so that student ideas might evolve and students might get to know one another. Teaching is decentered: the focus is more on teaching *students* rather than teaching *content*. Instead of chanting terms that need to be written down or memorized, the instructor must become familiar with the learner as well as the subject material. Examinations are more likely to be essay responses to questions, rather than true-false tests with predetermined answers. Rather than a summative mark at the end of an exam, the instructor likely needs to provide substantive feedback throughout an essay. Indeed, grades themselves are less likely to be the evaluation of choice; instead, a formative response might be employed.

The philosophy that one needs to enable dialogue so that students can become critical learners is diametrically opposed to simple skill development. Some years ago, for example, I wrote a book about curricular design and did a series of case studies, one of which was at Reed College in Portland, Oregon. "Reedies" were very clear about the purpose of what faculty taught and students learned. Reed taught classes such as Spanish and Introduction to Acting not so that a student simply learned a skill but so that they might gain an expertise that enabled them to learn about a particular idea. The assumption, for example, was that reading *Don Quixote* in Spanish would be a richer learning experience than reading it in English. They would never train students simply for a skill that led to a job such as a translator or, God forbid, an actor.

The trade-off of jobs versus critical reasoning, or citizenship, or engagement, or whatever one wants to call it has bedeviled educators for most of the twentieth century. The governor who says the state should fund engineering but not dance, computer science but not anthropology, is not saying anything new.[1] He's just found a provocative way to bifurcate vocational education from critical thinking. Dewey rejected the idea that education should be nothing more than training for the workplace. As the job market has constricted, however, there is increasing urgency to prepare students for some sort of employment when they graduate. The false notion that faculty are radicals trying to indoctrinate students with a left-wing ideology takes the idea one step further by suggesting that schooling should be little more than preparation for the world of work.

Dewey's ideas were widely admired not only in the United States but throughout the world.[2] He was one of the most widely admired citizens of the United States, and he was even honored by the US Postal Service with a thirty-cent postage stamp in 1968.[3] The staying power of his work has been impressive in an age when fads come and go with head-spinning speed. I have long noted that if we were able to transport Dewey to a college classroom today, he would likely not be particularly surprised. Although an early twentieth-century researcher would find how one does contemporary research and disseminates it revolutionary, the teacher would most likely find one of two teaching modes—the lecture and the seminar—that were prevalent in Dewey's time. Dewey might be depressed that his form of teaching has not become pervasive, but he would not be surprised to discover any new techniques. The way we teach today is not that different from a century ago.

People have called for, and expected, a revolution since I was in graduate school many years ago. The faculty have been remarkably resilient and consistent in resisting change. But perhaps a change is coming now. Mark Zuckerberg likely does not see himself as either an acolyte or opponent of John Dewey, but he and others (like Bill Gates) are on track to revolutionize teaching. The pandemic and then the force for racial change also has forced higher education to rethink teaching and learning.

When I was an undergraduate, I did not think very much about what I was going to do after college. In retrospect, I had a very fuzzy idea about the world of work. But I was not worried about work itself. I assumed there would be work. Compare that attitude with students today who start to strategize during their first college year about what they need to do to get a leg up on the competition for a job. As I noted in the previous chapter, this is also why for-profits, in part, have grown. They sell themselves, rightly or wrongly, as a vehicle for finding a job.

Until recently, students also pretty much accepted the established pace of academic life. There was a clear delineation between being at school and not being at school. The summer was meant for many things, but it had little to do with staying on campus, and it certainly did not mean that classes at some other campus were in the cards. College implied four years, give or take a semester, and classes were either lectures or seminars similar to what Dewey would have condoned. Class readings were bought at the bookstore in the form of books or reading packets.

In the era of iPads and iPhones, what once made intuitive sense no longer seems logical. If individuals can complete all the requirements we ask of them in two years, then why should they not be able to graduate? Why not read everything for class the way we read everything else? Why not take classes the way we watch a series on the web or on Netflix: incrementally or binged in one great gulp over a long weekend? If I can order books so easily on Amazon Prime, then why is registration for class such an arduous process? If I check a catalogue, buy a fancy suit, and get it delivered to my house in seventy-two hours, then why am I applying to a college in November and not hearing whether I've been admitted until April—and even then, I might not be really sure about financial aid until mid-summer?

I am not sure how Dewey would respond to all these structural changes, but we need to recognize that I am speaking of more than simply stylistic advancements. This is more than moving from a chalkboard to a smartboard, more than switching out the overhead projector for PowerPoints. Pedagogical structure intrudes on intellectual purpose. If reflective dialogue is a central component of progressive education, then I think most of us may worry that what occurs online makes it harder to enable such engagement.

Neither Newman nor Dewey saw education as utilitarian. Recall what James Baldwin said: "The purpose of education is to create in a person the ability to look at the world for himself, to make his own decisions, to say to himself this is black or this is white, to decide for himself whether there is a God in heaven or not."[4] Nowhere in this statement is there the idea of learning for the purpose of gaining an advantage in the job market. Must we, then, choose the convenience and speed of twenty-first-century technology and forego the kinds of conversations that Dewey said were necessary for a democratic society to have with its young? Or do we stick with a critical framework that resembles classrooms embedded in structures that functioned quite well a century ago? Can we have our intellectual cake and eat it too? Can we not we agree that these structures need significant upgrades but that we must not jeopardize the experience that Dewey enshrined for the classroom?

That Pesky Problem of the First College Year

The student graduates from high school with all the pomp and circumstance that goes into the special event, wiles away the summer waiting for college to start, heads off on move-in day, meets other new students, and makes acquaintances with his or her dormmate. The initial excitement then turns into all sorts of different feelings. Somewhere between week one and week eight the student goes home and eventually drops out for a year or two, or perhaps forever.

Or perhaps the student stands on the stage at high school graduation with every intention of moving to the next level of education, but never makes it to academe's front door. Or the student sits in the exam room for mid-terms only to find that memorizing the material was too confusing; the all-nighter that everyone pulled is not working for this student, so the student simply walks out of the room and heads back home. Or the student actually makes it to the end of fall term, wishes the others in the dorm all the best, and makes it home with the intent of returning, but when January comes around, finds out that staying home was not so bad after all and decides not to go back.

What gives? Why would students who successfully graduated from high school and earned admission to a postsecondary institution not make it to January of their first year? We know that various benchmarks matter: the probability of actually getting a four-year degree rises substantially if a student makes it (a) to the front door, (b) to mid-terms, (c) to the end of fall term, (d) to the beginning of spring term, and (e) to the end of the first year.[5] Each of these points are signposts along the way that suggest the student will graduate.

Remember when a college's president would assemble the new first-year class for a lecture at the start of the year? The president would likely intone, "Look to your left and look to your right. One of you will not be here in four years to graduate." The stern warning had no dates attached, and the invocation by the president suggested that the burden of retention lay on the student's young shoulders. The assumption was that the dropout was someone who partied too much, did not attend classes, did not do homework, received bad grades, was placed on academic probation, and had to leave the institution.

Virtually everything about such an assumption is wrong. The burden of retention should be mutually shared by the individual and the institution. Students largely leave not because they are placed on academic probation but because of nonacademic issues, such as a lack of what many call *college knowledge*, or because they are facing financial difficulties, or they find that college is not what they thought it would be.[6] The more we focus on the timeframe between high school graduation and the start of sophomore year, the more likely we are to ensure that individuals will also stand on the stage for their college graduation.

There's very little magic about what needs to be done to increase student retention. The problem currently lies with the handoff from high school to college, the initial messages (or paucity of them) that a student receives on arrival, and the culture of the first year. The first missed opportunity is what I think of as the hand off. As soon as commencement is over, the high school breathes a sigh of relief, while the college or university begins to think about how to prepare for students' arrival at the start of fall term. Those students who are in the middle or upper class—and whose parents have gone to college—are likely to engage in formal or informal college preparation activities during the summer. Their parents might pay for them to take a refresher course in a subject or have them take the proverbial trip to Europe, which will acquaint them with an array of information that will inform their initial foray into college life.

The first-generation, low-income student life is different. The students will need to earn money over the summer, so many end up bagging groceries at the local supermarket. Many of their friends will not be going to college. They will know few, if any, individuals who have gone to college, so they will not know what to expect or how to prepare. The pandemic only made matters worse insofar as many students completed their high school years in absentia.

Consider, for example, an individual who has never traveled abroad. When I have taken graduate students on trips to Asia, some of them have never left the United States and have traveled on vacation by airplane very little even within the United States. The result is that, for a one-week study tour, they pack enough bags for a multimonth tour around the world. They are not sure how to prepare, so they take everything they could possibly want. The same is true for students who may not have even visited the campus where they will be going. They cannot envision what to expect—and why should we expect that of them?

The first mishap, in the parlance of those of us who study college readiness, is that they "melt" away.[7] Here, we have students who had the qualifications to be admitted and planned on attending when they graduated from high school; three months later, we discover they never made it to the starting line. What happened? Some students can't handle the confusing messages they receive from the college or university, especially pertaining to financial aid. When financial literacy is low, students can't tell the difference between a loan and a grant and do not know that missed deadlines can cause them to lose the funding that enabled them to attend college. Other students find that their friends have jobs that give them cash to go out on dates, buy a car, or help the family meet their expenses. College is ephemeral and foreign. Why not stay home?

If I'm having a dinner party, I may give the person who does not show up a call to see if he or she is OK. I also may double-check with everyone a day or two before the party to ensure they are still coming. When I initially invite them, I may find out if they have any dietary needs or allergies I need to know about so that I am adequately prepared. Why do we not do the same preparation and follow-up with incoming first-year students?

We need to keep students engaged over the summer and not only prepare them cognitively but also equip them with the college knowledge skills that can give them a heads up about what they are getting themselves into. Fear of the unknown often disadvantages students who could otherwise succeed in college, but they need support structures that are often absent or inadequate.

On the one hand, many students need support to improve their writing and mathematical skills. They likely attended schools that had a dearth of advanced placement classes and may not be adequately prepared for the challenges of academic life. A summer away from academic work compounds the problem. The handoff from high school to college needs to be smoother and uninterrupted. Unfortunately, what happens now is quite the opposite. There is no handoff or transition, especially at second-tier institutions. Places like Stanford University or the University of Southern California know that it is to the their social and economic interest to get involved during those crucial summer weeks. They offer summer orientations, bring parents to campus, or provide seminars for students who may need extra help before the school year begins. Second-tier (and third) public and private institutions often do very little for students over the summer, and those are the institutions that are most likely to have students who need help and advice.

This involvement will cost additional monies from one coffer or another, which I'll address in a later chapter. But if we take seriously the earlier arguments about public goods and the twenty-first century idea of a university, then what I am suggesting is not a nicety—another climbing wall for college slackers—but a necessity, not only for the students who will benefit but for society at large as well. We need more college graduates to grow our economy.

Once students arrive on campus, they need more culturally relevant engagement. Native American students, for example, often feel as if they are a dot in a sea of foreign faces. African American and Latinx students feel marginalized and ignored. They are underrepresented as students and on the faculty. Their learning improves when culturally relevant activities are intertwined with their coursework.

College also should provide the conditions that enable students to discover their likes and dislikes and to take risks—not only to succeed but also to fail. There is a robust literature that talks about the support structures needed to enable college success. But students need to know that these support mechanisms exist and that there is no stigma attached to using them. If a student does not understand that having health care means that a visit to the health center to diagnose a cold and get medication is free, then the student will not avail of the service. Similarly, if students feel that it is embarrassing to acknowledge they need help with their writing, or worse, they are experiencing anxiety to the extent they should visit a counselor or therapist, then they will not seek help.

There is a great deal of extant literature that details what is effective for staying in college. However, I am troubled by strategies that have little, if any, empirical backing and virtually no cost-benefit analysis. We know, for example, that joining either academic or social clubs can be beneficial to a student's first-year success.[8] There's not much evidence that a club that pays for students to travel to Europe over the holidays offers benefits that outweigh the costs. Similarly, we have little indication that the exorbitant, multimillion dollar outlays sunk into student-centered facilities (such as the recent $85 million renovation of Louisiana State University's recreation center) and other amenities improve retention—or even increase student enrollment.[9] Instead, state universities that once prided themselves on accessibility and frugality now charge massive student fees every year in response to a perceived desire for amenities. According to one study, student fees have risen by 95 percent at public four-year colleges and by 61 percent at private colleges since 2000.[10] In an environment where students are frequently compelled to leave college due to debts of $1,000 or less, these sorts of hidden costs have a deeply harmful effect on college completion.[11]

If we accept that making it to the start of sophomore year matters a great deal, then why would we not focus resources and energy on activities that are proven to strengthen students' cognitive and noncognitive learning? Most colleges know, for example, that intensive writing before the start of the first year will better prepare students for first-year writing, give them added confidence about their skills, and help them get oriented to new friends and the campus.[12] However, many institutions only provide these writing classes online and have no valid way of assessing whether the enrolled students' writing has improved. We also know that dual enrollment programs that enable high school students to take college classes (and earn college credits) improve the likelihood that students will be ready for college and complete a postsecondary degree.[13] Even better, classes taken under dual enrollment are sometimes free for the student, depending on state and district policies.[14] Nevertheless, many parents and students are unaware that such programs are available at their high school, and the programs that exist are poorly publicized.[15] Moreover, we have strong data that shows summer counseling can ameliorate "summer melt," an event where recent high school graduates who are accepted to college fail to enroll.[16] We can do a great deal more to solve that pesky problem of keeping students engaged and enrolled during their first college year.

Let's Get Real about the (Lack of) Importance of Attending Class

After receiving my PhD in 1984 and then undertaking a two-year postdoc in Boulder, Colorado, I became an assistant professor in 1986. In the fall of that year, I taught my first class on organizational theory in a room that held about twenty people. The class was composed of beginning and intermediate doctoral students. In the fall of 2017, I taught my last two classes at the University of Southern California. The room also held about twenty students, and the students were beginning and intermediate PhD students. In thirty-four years, what has changed and what hasn't? Perhaps more importantly, which of those changes have concerning or unfortunate implications?

What's Changed

Certainly, the accoutrements of a class have changed. I no longer hand out reading packets, because many students read their books on their laptop or iPad. PowerPoint, videos, YouTube, and live video chats have replaced the overhead projector and slides. Smart classrooms enable desks to shift back and forth into various formations, and chalkboards are rarely seen anymore. Students used to hand in written assignments on paper; I typed up voluminous comments and attached them to their papers, then I handed them back at the end of the next class. Students now submit papers online; I embed comments and return them to the students electronically after the conclusion of the subsequent class.

In the culture of today's classroom, I have to be far more careful about my words and actions than thirty-four years ago. I have never allowed any form of harassment or unacceptable behavior in or outside of the classroom, but the language and actions we use today are under such a microscope that I refrain from casual compliments that might be misconstrued, and I second guess myself all the time.

When I began teaching, I was told always to keep my office door open so that I was never behind closed doors with a student. Over time, however, that became difficult. Working with PhD students is a great experience, but as anyone who has written a dissertation knows, the experience can be emotionally draining. During office hours, I've worked with a number of students who've broken down in tears or admitted wanting to give up. These students have understandably wanted privacy, as well as uninterrupted time with me, without someone else barging through the open door with a quick question. The result is that more often than not my office door has been shut while I have been at the University of Southern California. Nothing has ever happened behind closed doors that I would be ashamed of or afraid to have someone else see. But today's faculty members risk rumors and innuendo, so these days I make sure to keep my door open at all times.

Student perceptions of the literature have also changed. The sense of immediacy today means that articles written only a decade ago seem old to individuals raised on "breaking news." Classic texts, such as those written by Émile Durkheim or Max Weber, may be tolerated because they are understood to be classic, but articles written in the 1990s—which may come to be considered classics someday or are simply important for the section I am teaching—are frequently frowned on by students trained to privilege what is new. The internet has also made it easier for students to rely on informal articles and texts that lack scholarship. The result is that students often cite the *Huffington Post* but do not regularly peruse new academic journals in the library the way I used to in my graduate school days.

Indeed, they—and I—rarely go to the library, other than to find a quiet place to work on our laptops. The library was once a regular destination in my campus peregrinations, and now I may only go there once a semester. When I started teaching, my students needed library skills to find the various texts that lay hidden in the bowels of the building; now they need to understand how to navigate the internet and how to store the articles they read in a manner that will help them when the time comes to write an article or their dissertation.

What's Not Changed

The structure of my class has not varied much, albeit the pandemic moved classes on-line. The class is a seminar that begins and ends at a particular time and runs for the semester, roughly fifteen weeks. If the class lasts for more than three hours, then we take a break for ten minutes in the middle of the class. The readings for the class are extensive, and I tend to vary them by about 25 percent each time I teach the class. These variances are based on feedback from the students or my own investigations that suggest an additional text would be useful.

I prepare extensively for every class as if I have not taught it before and have lesson plans that I update every summer and then a week or two before each class. I reread the texts in 1986, and in 2017, and every year in between. The class is a seminar. Students have occasionally teased me that my favorite question is, what do you think? The material we cover has less to do with reaching the right answers and more with thinking about how one responds to an article based on one's belief about the world.

The students also work hard. Over time, students have learned that my classes are not what we used to call a *gut*, or an easy-A class. Because classes largely involve a discussion of the readings and enrollment is limited to around twenty-five students, it's hard for a student to fake it. The result is that they have to read a great deal, and they also have a great many writing assignments.

I do not assign letter grades to writing assignments. From time to time, the lack of a grade has caused one or another student a degree of anxiety. Instead, I provide numerous comments, and I have told students if they want to find out how they are doing for a grade, they should come and speak with me. I avoid giving grades because I want students to concentrate on the elegance of their language in conveying their arguments and on how to improve their writing. The grade is far less important than the content of my feedback. The vast majority of my students have gotten As and Bs; rarely have I given a student a C, which reflects the mores of the academy during my tenure as a teacher.

How Today's Classroom Is Different from Yesterday's Classroom

Although the structure and technology of my classes have been updated to reflect the times, my courses have not changed much intellectually, and I am essentially the same instructor I was when I nervously walked into that first class so many years ago. And yet, academic teaching—and of consequence, learning—has changed during my tenure in academe. Large lectures are more prevalent today than when I began. Dewey would be bereft! A student at a large public university like the University of California, for example, is likely not to take a class with fewer than seventy-five students until junior year. Some will say that distance learning begins in the fifth row, and there is a great deal of truth to that glib comment.

Large classes might be fine now and again, but there ought to be a pedagogical reason why such a class is reasonable. As an undergraduate, I took a drama class with two hundred students where the professor lectured on one play for one hour, three days a week, for one semester. Professor Ritchie was a marvelous actor who was able to enthuse his class with a love of plays by the way he had constructed his lectures. We probably would have lost something if the class were run as a seminar. He needed a stage to perform in front of an audience. The vast majority of lecture classes, however, are not pedagogically determined.

The result is that far too many of our entry-level courses are large lecture classes. Today's lectures are frequently recorded and, along with PowerPoints, uploaded to a server that students can access and download. To try to accommodate a class of four hundred students, graduate students may teach breakout sessions of "only" fifty or sixty students. What's the result? Attendance at the class has become superfluous, so students skip it.

As with the brothers I mentioned earlier who also skip their classes, the vast majority of students I have worked with are not slackers. They take their education seriously, and they hope to learn enough to get good jobs upon graduation. Therein lies the problem. Why should they attend class if they can get the lectures online at a time that is convenient to them, in a format that allows them to fast-forward, and as one student said, "skip the boring parts"? For most of these students, college is about skill development: learning what they need to know to land a job.

After students started telling me that they skipped classes, I sat in on a few of their lectures to see what the course was like. What particularly surprised me was that rooms that should have had three hundred students had half that number or fewer. In my own class, if students were absent, I always enquired about them. I told students to let me know if they were not coming to class so that I did not worry. If I am bothered when one of my students fails to attend a class, what must it be like for an instructor who shows up to lecture and finds one hundred students are MIA? When I posed this question to a few instructors, they seemed unperturbed. They all said their notes were online, so they understood why a student might skip a class. When I asked deans and provosts if they knew about what was going on, they all sheepishly admitted that they did.

I will consider online education in a later chapter, but what are we to make of in-person classes that students routinely cut? The solution depends on an institution's philosophy on the purpose of education. If we remain true to the Newman–Dewey idea of learning as the development of critical thinking skills, then it's vital to engage students in the way that I try to foster in my own classes: seminar-style classes where all students are expected to attend, with accommodations for technological advances.

On the other hand, if teaching and learning is about skill development and little more and if students are not offered the opportunity to take seminars, then we need a radical restructuring of the curriculum to make learning as efficient as possible. It seems absurd to perform the charade called "class" when everyone knows and accepts that students consider attendance voluntary, including the teachers and administration. Why perpetuate a fraud? I am not claiming students learn nothing or that teachers do not impart wisdom. If students gain from the written class notes and PowerPoints what they could otherwise learn sitting in a gigantic lecture hall, then we had best dispense with the credit hour and simply focus on learning outcomes.

What's Going on Outside of Class

Although we focus most of our efforts on what happens within the classroom, students spend the majority of their time outside of class. The lives of commuter and part-time students frequently have very little to do with the goings-on about campus. Full-time students who live on campus could ostensibly enjoy many activities such as lectures by prominent intellectuals, community outreach programs, and student support groups that are offered by the institution, but they frequently avoid participation for one reason or another. The question for us—whether we are campus leaders, parents, or students ourselves—ought to be, what sorts of outside activities might stimulate learning and enhance the learning that occurs in the classroom? There obviously does not have to be a direct symbiosis between a classroom and every external activity, but far too often, I have observed no obvious connection between the extracurricular activities offered for students (whether full-time, part-time, or commuter) and their academic studies. The problem is only compounded when we take online learning into account.

Why should out-of-class activities matter? One reason is to offset the reduced role of coursework itself. In an influential book entitled *Academically Adrift*, Richard Arum and Josipa Roksa point out how learning activities have diminished over time. Students do less homework, read less, spend less time talking about assignments, and have fewer demands placed on them in class.[17] My own experience aligns with these findings. I have often thought that students and faculty have an unstated compact. The vast majority of college students earn As and Bs.[18] Does that mean we are teaching exceptional students? Nope. The compact seems to be, "If I do not make you work too hard, then you will not ding me on my Rate-My-Professor page as a 'ball-buster.'" Students skip classes because they can. But what is happening outside of class?

The current state of out-of-class activities compounds the problem. The vocationally minded worry that today's students are often unprepared for the workforce. Although vocational education proponents lament what is not learned in class, a similar concern might be made about out-of-class learning. With notable exceptions, such as Northeastern University's internship program where students have jobs off campus that are related to their on-campus learning activities, not enough students gain a sense of the world of work and the world of civic engagement. An undergraduate education should, in part, enable students to gain an understanding about the variety of jobs that exist for degree holders. It should also give students the experience that will make them attractive to potential employers and give them a sense of what sorts of responsibilities exist for individuals living in a democracy. Far too often, students graduate from college with the dimmest idea about which careers might interest them and lack the skills to pursue these careers in any case. They have never done volunteer work and think that sort of engagement is only for do-gooders.

We have long had proxies for determining quality, and I have been one of them. I write a letter for a student, as an endowed chair at a prestigious university. The potential employer sees my own qualifications and concludes, "Well, if Tierney at the University of Southern California says she's one of the best students he's ever had, then I guess we should hire her." Employers might have glanced at cumulative grades for a candidate, but since everyone earns As and Bs, that no longer means much. A professor's letter used to be the gold standard—until it was not.

Two problems arose. First, job opportunities dwindled. Suddenly dozens of candidates were applying, all of whom had sterling letters from guys like me. Second, many employers had grown wise to the fact that a candidate might have received a top-notch letter even though the candidate lacked basic writing and numeracy skills. A buyer's market reflects the economy that now exists. The disconnect between what a letter-writer wrote and what the employer discovered suggested that alternative criteria was needed.

I fully recognize that a candidate's resume is just as much a proxy as my letter of recommendation. We will never be assured that what candidates have accomplished determines how they will perform in the future. Nevertheless, employers now tend to look for an array of criteria about what a student has accomplished outside of class during his or her college years. Working as a bagger at the local grocery store, or a barista at one of our ubiquitous coffee bars, may have met the immediate economic needs of a student. But it will not do very much to convince an employer that the candidate is qualified for a position at a tech company or engineering firm. An internship at a tech company or engineering firm certainly seems more relevant.

The second problem with out-of-class learning activities has to do with the more humanistic side of learning. I appreciate that my humanities-minded colleagues may express discomfort with my suggestion that students should focus more on job skills when they are outside the classroom. They might argue that there are an array of critical thinking skills that also could help a student in the pursuit of employment. I fully agree. I am not particularly interested in getting into a tired argument about cultural literacy or trying to develop a checklist about what should be included on a "great books" list. I'm entirely fine with students developing a diverse set of learning experiences. What I find disorienting, however, is that across the board, today's students have little cultural literacy. Sure, they may not share my specific taste or interests, but what does it say when many students have never attended a musical concert or play, when they haven't taken part in any type of cultural organization different from their own culture, or when they are not conversant on any number of current social, economic, or political issues?

Similarly, students are not encouraged to get engaged in their local communities. Any number of internships could be developed that will generate more well-rounded students who are better prepared not only for the workforce but also for democratic engagement.

Why is it that college students are not more involved in learning experiences that equip them either vocationally or culturally? It's easy to blame the students. We can say they spend too much time on their smartphones and that they are more obsessed with popular culture than any previous generation. I do not think, however, that such a critique is accurate, fair, or useful. Sure, students spend more time on their smartphones than my generation spent watching TV. But if we know anything about the technological innovations of our lifetime, it is that they have radically changed how we conceptualize and utilize time.[19] We all multitask in ways that were unthinkable a generation ago. We want instantaneous information. If an earthquake happens five time zones away from me, and I have friends there, then I instantly check Facebook to ensure they are safe. We track our children's whereabouts as they leave home, get on a bus, travel to school, and enter the classroom. Part of these activities speak to our own twenty-first century, post-9/11 fears, but they also occur because we have technological capabilities we've never had before.

We might think that these capabilities have expanded our social universe, but we fail to recognize that they have also altered it in ways that impoverish us. Anyone who innocently sits down to check Facebook, then looks up ninety minutes later wondering where the time went knows of what I speak. In a culture of instantaneous gratification, how we find time, or make time, becomes a challenge unto itself. Where children once had long summer days or afternoons playing outside or reading books, they now have lives consumed by texting their friends and posting to social media. The result is that when I ask someone if they have read about a particular problem that has deep, entangled roots in Middle Eastern history, the person has no knowledge of the event—or the time to learn about it.

Unless we make it happen. When I teach, I work assiduously on structuring the class with regard to learning not only the objectives and outcomes but also the structure and pacing of the class. Although any good teacher will improvise based on student comments or the mood of the class, the vast majority of quality teaching is not extemporaneous. Meanwhile, our out-of-class learning experiences are one giant improvisation. To be sure, those of us who attended college in the 1960s and 1970s like to fondly remember all-night BS sessions where we solved the problems of the world (often enhanced by one or another drug). I am not suggesting that students need to lead regimented lives that leave little space for downtime. All too often, however, we educators leave extracurricular engagement up to individual students without attempting to integrate it with classroom learning.

When I speak with first-generation students en route to college, I encourage them to get involved. I suggest they join an academic club, participate in a social club, and attend cultural and sporting events. Unfortunately, students who have never set foot on a campus often do not know how to begin. How does one choose from the potpourri of events? We have an odd dichotomy where, on the one hand, we try to compress classroom learning to enable students to accumulate credits and graduate sooner. On the other hand, when it comes to out-of-class activities, we have no idea what sort of learning we want for our charges. Why would we not want our students to have a holistic experience that melds classroom learning with what takes place beyond it?

Ironically, the challenges that confronted us a century ago are still with us, albeit in different registers. The ideas of Newman and Dewey remain current, and the tension between vocational training and humanistic critical thinking is still central to the conversation about what a college education should entail. Not all institutions need to march to the same drummer: a community college student learning to be a plumber should have different curricula than the student training to be a physician or foreign affairs officer. What should tie our learning experiences together, however, is a demand for integration between in-class and out-of-class learning. We need to recognize how the modalities have changed and, with them, our expectations of what we expect from individuals as students and then as entrants to the workplace.

CHAPTER 4

Safe Spaces, Trigger Warnings, and the Contours of Diversity

America's Love Affair with "Merit"

The United States has long had a tension between individualism and communalism. On the one hand, we celebrate the idea that an individual in a democracy who works hard, is ambitious, and is determined will find extraordinary success. On the other hand, democracy assumes that we are all connected; we provide a hand to those in need and come together to support one another when times are tough. These ideas need not be incompatible, but we have made them so over the last century. We also have long mythologized both concepts. Films and literature have engaged in the trope of the West as a frontier where individuals fought adversity and created their futures for themselves. A war, or more recently the events of 9/11, inevitably get framed as collective calls to action: "We are all in this together."

The more recent discussions about the individual and communalism have tended to revolve around government regulation. Ronald Reagan ushered in the idea that if government simply got out of the way and let the individual do what Americans do best, then the United States would be able to achieve greatness. What stymied progress, from this perspective, was the government telling hardworking Americans how to lead their lives. A more benign explanation was that those who supported government intervention were well intentioned, but mistaken, because government intervention would limit individual liberty. Those who cleverly defined the term *nanny state* believe that the government should have no say in whether I want to drink huge sugary sodas or wear a seatbelt. The government should not interfere with my right to ride a motorcycle without a helmet. For these folks, the idea of a public good is anathema, and at the far end of such a belief is the libertarian notion that government should barely exist.

At the other extreme are the communalists. From their perspective, the definition of public goods should be expansive. Those who harken back to the 1950s for the sort of tax structure where citizens pay three times as much in taxes as they do today are the communalists. Public goods require individuals to contribute to the community. Big Gulp sodas should be taxed, and warnings should be put on salty foods. Health care should be made available to everyone regardless of their individual ability to pay. Communalists believe the state should provide shelter and food for the homeless, while individualists believe such help is in the province of religions and charities funded by donors who choose how to spend their money.

Although individualists have begrudgingly accepted the notion of public higher education, how one gets admitted to an institution remains a subject of debate. Individualists oppose affirmative action, believing it is unfair for colleges to consider race, gender, or class when admitting students. They believe that individual merit should be the only deciding factor: that what should be done is simply to evaluate one individual's credentials against another's and then determine, in objective fashion, who merits admission to the academy. Objectivity is valued, and preferential treatment is disdained—except when it comes to the children of alumni, otherwise known as legacies, or if a student is especially skilled in sports.

Many of us have problems with a merit-based viewpoint. Studies have shown, for example, that how a reader views the same letter written by a man and by a woman frequently will privilege the male. A student with a Latinx-sounding name is less likely to be chosen for a job than someone with an Anglicized name.[1] There are any number of areas where conscious and unconscious biases call into question the idea of objectivity in decision-making areas such as college admissions.

We also need to recognize that social ideas are based on the socio-historical milieu in which the idea is situated. In the early twentieth century, for example, elite universities like Harvard and Yale first began the practice of legacy admissions so that the children of alumni, who were predominantly Protestant, would receive preferential treatment during the admissions process. During the 1960s, however, Jerome Karabel has shown that elite college presidents began to behave like "intellectual investment bankers," eschewing legacy admissions in favor of "meritocratic admissions."[2] In 1907, the School of Dentistry at my own institution graduated its first black student John Alexander Somerville. When he first enrolled, all of the white students protested. Even after Somerville argued that he simply wanted to earn a degree and that he deserved to be admitted because his credentials were similar to everyone else's, the white students insisted that a black person did not deserve to attend the University of Southern California. Somerville persisted. The dean at the time said that Somerville merited admission based on his application, and if the white students had a problem, then they could leave the institution. Somerville ultimately graduated first in his class.[3]

Thus, merit in the early twentieth century was in part a vehicle for overcoming prejudice. By the late twentieth century, the argument for merit had been turned on its head, and it is now viewed by some as a way to exclude certain groups—Asian Americans and Anglos—rather than expand opportunity. For instance, Abigail Fisher, a white female, twice fought a US Supreme Court battle against the University of Texas in 2013, claiming that the University's consideration of race in the admissions process was a violation of the equal protection clause in the Fourteenth Amendment.[4] In a more recent legal challenge, Michael Wang, a young Asian American, contended that Harvard's approach to affirmative action attempts to balance the racial demographics of each incoming class and is therefore illegal.[5] How do we judge the worth of another individual or a group, and by what metrics?

These questions turn on our understanding of the past and a determination about how we should make decisions for today. Colleges and universities are not only arenas where we are able to wrestle with difficult ideas; they are also communities where these ideas get worked out every day. How we teach, what we do outside of class, what we might expect or demand of one another, all speak to the tensions we face along the individual–communal spectrum. An individualist conception assumes that I should be able to say anything and have a free-wheeling discussion without limits. The communalist has a quite different interpretation: standards have to be imposed so that we all are safe. The challenge, of course, is not merely what those standards are but who gets to determine the standards—and what to do when someone disagrees.

When racism came to the fore in 2020 yet again colleges and universities began to reckon with their past. Confederate statues came down.

Names on buildings of individuals who were racist or sexist were changed. Another push began to make the ranks of the faculty and student body to be more representative.

In this light, microaggressions get studied, defined, and debated in a classroom, but microaggressions also occur—or they do not—in that same classroom. Microaggressions are commonly defined as "brief and commonplace daily verbal, behavioral, or environmental indignities, whether intentional or unintentional, that communicate hostile, derogatory, or negative . . . slights and insults."[6] We currently have the most fraught environment that I have seen in the last thirty-five years. Conversations are harder inside and outside of the classroom. Individuals are less willing to raise questions or disagree with someone, which seems to have less to do with an individual not trying to offend someone and more to do with the fear that a speaker's words will get the individual in trouble. The pity is that we are not thinking through these thorny issues; instead, we are just trying to avoid them.

Students of color who long felt unwelcome on campus through large and small slights now wish to highlight which words and acts can and cannot be said without causing harm to the students. Women document a history of marginalization and abuse and will no longer sit still. The LGBTQ community demands visibility. The disabled are unwilling to put up with buildings that exclude them because of lack of accessibility. Intolerance will no longer be tolerated—but how we define *intolerance* is up for grabs. How might we live among one another without excluding some and silencing others?

Safe Spaces for "Snowflakes"

In today's political discourse, conservatives have had a remarkable ability to use language that puts their opponents on the defensive. The tactic is largely to demean and belittle, but in doing so, they also tend to win the argument. The use of the term *snowflake* is a perfect example. It is unclear when the term *snowflake* precisely entered daily discourse, but it was commonly used as far back as the early 1860s, when an individual opposed to the abolition of slavery in Missouri was called a snowflake.[7] Obviously, the modern propagation of the term has a completely different meaning. The current usage is frequently credited to Chuck Palahniuk; in his popular 1996 novel *Fight Club*, the primary antagonist Tyler Durden states, "Listen up maggots. You are not special. You are not a beautiful or unique snowflake."[8] Who wants to be labeled a snowflake, something fragile and able to melt away in the noonday sun? The language we employ helps frame the argument we are having. Unfortunately, when we employ terms like *snowflake*, it's impossible to have a meaningful discussion that extends beyond name-calling.

When I was in graduate school, I was still a closeted gay man. At one point in an anthropology graduate seminar at Stanford, we were discussing interviewing in difficult situations. A friend in the class spoke up about the privilege she felt as a white middle-class woman when she was interviewing poor women of color. She thought her interviewees were sensitive about what she thought about them, and she was trying to figure out ways to appear more supportive. "These are good women," she stated, "They're not like drug addicts or criminals or homosexuals." In the flash of a second, a fellow student—a friend—had lumped me in with drug addicts and criminals. And homosexuality was probably worse, since one might recover from drug addiction or criminal behavior. I was apparently a lost cause.

I remember the class did not miss a beat; we all understood precisely what she meant. The professor did not stop the conversation. No student questioned the comment. Instead, there was a very lively discussion about interview strategies the student might employ. I had been able to hide my identity, so no one looked at me. The rest of the class was just a blur for me. I could not listen, concentrate, or speak. I simply waited for the class to end so I could flee. The students in class did not process how our language impacts the way we see the world and the other—certainly an irony for a discussion about interviewing.

That comment has stayed with me for more than thirty years. Whenever I have mentioned it to any closeted gay individuals of that era, they have their own stories about being emotionally frozen and terrified of people finding out. In addition to being painful on a personal level, the comment was also a missed opportunity. An enlightened instructor—and this professor was one of my favorites—might not have scolded the student, who was unaware she had said anything wrong. And yet, it was certainly an example of what many of us think of as a teachable moment. What differentiates "us" from "them?" What makes activities so despicable that we define not just the act but the person as "bad"? What's wrong with drug addicts, or criminals, or homosexuals?

By the criteria of those who have coined the term *snowflake*, my reaction to the student's comment means I was just being too sensitive. I shouldn't have let the student's slights get to me. Or I should have spoken up and argued my position. Grow a spine, some might say. What the snowflake-callers do not understand is that arguing about a characteristic that is fundamental to one's identity, especially in a group that has shown little sensitivity, is quite different from arguing about organizational theories, rational choice theory, or any number of other topics. I may vociferously disagree with your stance on climate change, but that doesn't mean I'm claiming that part of your identity is flawed, even criminal. In 1984 in the United States, in many countries today, and even in many states in this country today, to speak openly about being gay is to risk hearing people say, "Based on my beliefs, you should go to prison," or "You will go to hell," or "I would never let you around my children." Further, people still risk physical violence or the denial of services simply because of their sexual orientation.

The point of learning is not to avoid controversy, despite the con-flict-averse attitude in many classrooms today. To a certain extent, I do not want us to feel safe, if safety means we avoid difficult conversations. In a linguistic sleight of hand, I want students to feel safe enough so that they might feel unsafe. We need classrooms where students are able to take risks and speak openly about difficult topics in a respectful manner, with the goal of achieving communion with one another through dialogue. To do that, we all need to feel vulnerable, not simply the gay kid who is struggling with coming out or the only black student in a class who feels out of place.

I had to give a series of lectures at the University of Virginia shortly after the Nazis marched through the campus and town. I spent a few days interviewing individuals to write a brief report about the climate of the institution. One undergraduate African American student at the University said that he had been at home in another part of the state when the events transpired. He said that watching the Nazis march across campus on TV "scared my mom and dad. They did not want me to come back." What parents would not worry for their child's safety in such circumstances? Another student, a young white woman, said sincerely, "I have lots of questions about black people. I grew up in an isolated town; we are all white, so I do not know very much, and I'd like to learn, but I do not want to ask cheesy questions. I do not know how to go about it."

Both of these students and their compatriots deserve safe spaces on their campuses. No one should have to worry about their physical safety. We also need an environment where a student can honestly ask "cheesy" questions if they are posed in a respectful manner. What might such a classroom look like? How might we define feeling unsafe that respects and honors individual opinions without marginalizing any individuals? What might that anthropology classroom of mine have looked like if it had been a safe space to feel unsafe?

If a professor has a dialogical relationship with a class that is based on respect, then a comment like the one that I had to confront will be embedded in a culture that assumes understanding across cultural and intellectual borders. Individuals certainly can have strong opinions, but these comments need to be couched in a language of respect. At the start of a semester, a professor might acknowledge that we come together out of respect for one another and with respect for one another's opinions. Our aim should be not to agree with everyone, but to make space for each person's standpoint and opinion.

In this framework, the professor is perhaps best considered not an authority who dispenses knowledge but rather a guide who is able to adapt the class based on the suggestions and comments of the students. Students feel free to point out when the professor has erred, and they are not afraid to voice sentiments that contradict the professor. In such a classroom, we need to acknowledge the legitimacy of individuals' identities, and we also need to be able to work out quite thorny issues. In my anthropology class, the professor could have challenged or framed my friend's comment about homosexuals as horrible people. There are students today who come from a fundamentalist religious background and still believe homosexuality is a sin. I am concerned that religious students often feel marginalized. Should their viewpoints be respected as well? Yes.

The professor might have asked my friend to take a step back and question her position with regard not only to the individuals she was interviewing but also to anyone she might interview in the future. What is gained by labeling someone a deviant? Rather than cast aspersions on the other, the goal is to achieve understanding.

To take the point one step further, consider how I framed good versus bad earlier. I felt silenced because I had been compared to criminals and drug addicts. But for all I knew, the fellow sitting next to me was a recovering addict and the person on the other side of me had spent time in jail for a crime. What I had done in that moment, unknowingly and reflexively, was say, "I'm not them! I'm good, not bad!" In a more open classroom climate, we might have been able to process the original comment more fully so that the discussion was enhanced rather than shut down.

The point is not to put people on the spot. I would never have responded if the professor had asked, "I'd like to know how any homosexuals feel about that statement." We should not place those who lack privilege in the position of being translator-in-chief, a guide to the neighborhood, so to speak. The goal, then, is that we approach a classroom in a manner that accepts we are all learners who require respect and understanding. We all have something to add, and something to learn, in conversations, and if we approach learning in this manner, then the sorts of problems I've highlighted here will be lessened.

The Imprint of Microaggressions and Trigger Warnings

A decade ago, *microaggression* and *trigger warnings* were not terms that many faculty or administrators employed. Today, these terms are commonly discussed and debated, and policies have been developed around them. While the terms are sometimes used in similar contexts, they actually have distinctive meanings. Microaggressions are commonly defined as "brief and commonplace daily verbal, behavioral, or environmental indignities, whether intentional or unintentional, that communicate hostile, derogatory, or negative . . . slights and insults."[9] Microaggressions in higher education are a concern among those who worry about the unspoken comments and assumptions that minoritized and other underrepresented groups are compelled to endure. Meanwhile, trigger warnings are intended to "notify people of the distress that written, audiovisual, or other material may evoke."[10] Professors, in particular, feel increased pressure in recent years to include trigger warnings next to any material in a syllabus that might cause distress among students. The common thread between the concept of microaggressions and trigger warnings is an understandable concern about individuals who might not be able to participate in the classroom or campus life due to an environment that is perceived to be hostile or unwelcoming.

Assume I enter my class and the students are waiting for me. One fellow sits in the back of the room with his arms crossed, wearing a baseball cap. The cap is emblazoned with the words "Make America Great Again," or MAGA. Toward the front of the room, a woman wearing a hijab sits with her eyes looking down and her hands crossed. I ignore the students' clothing choices and proceed with my class. After class, two students ask to speak with me. One says that he felt threatened by the MAGA hat; the other says that she felt threatened by the hijab.

If we contextualize each student's experience, we highlight the challenges of determining how to define microaggressions and trigger warnings. The life experiences of undocumented students who fear deportation for themselves and their family because of President Trump are obviously different from a middle-class white student who is angry about the president's policies but faces no immediate threat. Students who believe that all Muslims are terrorists because of what they watch on Fox News is different from an individual whose parent died in the World Trade Center on 9/11.

Even those who call others snowflakes might acknowledge that some texts or some images may indeed be a trigger for some students. A survivor of rape may be uncomfortable with a graphic portrayal of rape in cinema or literature; at the least, one might want to alert this individual to what is in the text. What an instructor might think of as an even-handed discussion about the events surrounding 9/11 might also trigger memories and images of the building falling for someone who was there.

At the same time, any number of seemingly neutral actions can trigger an unpleasant memory. For over a decade, I have used a text in a class about the ins and outs of interviewing. Part of the text discusses interviewing survivors of domestic abuse and focuses on how to depart from a standard interview protocol. The text is not about domestic abuse and has no quotes from abuse survivors. Nevertheless, one student later told me that although neither she nor anyone in her family had suffered domestic abuse, she found the text triggering. She said she was in tears after reading the text.

Where do we draw the line? How do we draw the line? On the one hand, those who call others snowflakes assume there is no line or that only in the rarest of circumstances might a professor need to forewarn students about a discussion or text. On the other hand, my friend's comment in our anthropology class might be thought of as a good example of microaggression that occurred in an educational environment and impeded learning. There could have been no warning because the student simply blurted out the statement. The challenge, of course, is that because the idea of microaggression is a relatively new term, how one understands it and what one does once it is found are not yet clear. Some might argue that wearing a MAGA hat is a microaggression; others might suggest that even a discussion about the meaning of the hat could foster microaggressions if the conversation is not handled in an appropriate manner.

From a scientific standpoint, we do not yet have enough empirical evidence to ascertain exactly which speech or action would be considered a microaggression and how it impacts learning.[11] We have a great deal of narrative evidence, however, that microaggressions exist and impede learning when they occur.[12] Individuals may learn how to adapt to such slights, but they are clearly placed at an educational disadvantage in ways that other students are not. The discussion that occurred in my anthropology class after my friend's comment may have been useful for the rest of the class, but I heard none of it since I was so busy processing her comment and my relation to it.

As mentioned at the outset of this chapter, we generally think of microaggression as any statement or occurrence that brings injury to an individual based on one's identity—race, ethnicity, gender, sexual orientation, religion, disability, and the like. Sometimes these statements come as a back-of-the-hand compliment: "For someone like you, you've done great," or "I have to hand it to you. I never thought you'd be able to do it."

At other times, perhaps frequently, the slights are unintended. I used to work with a fellow who put in a lot of effort to appear comfortable working with a gay man. Every time he saw me, he'd comment on my clothes: "Nice shirt!" or "Wow, I love those slacks," or "That coat sure looks sharp on you!" Over time, I realized he made sartorial comments only to me—and alas, my clothes were frequently not so sharp. In effect, he saw a gay man and reduced me to clothes because being concerned with fashion is a stereotype of gay men. To be sure, his comments were less offensive than that of my anthropology classmate, but some would still see them as a form of microaggression. By cordoning off conversations—speaking about budgeting to some people and clothes to another—we risk privileging some and reducing opportunities for others.

What might we do in a classroom or campus setting to enable our students to feel comfortably unsafe? What do we do when an unexpected statement or action in class is considered hurtful? Most faculty are not particularly adept at recognizing what a microaggression is; we need to begin by developing sensitivity to not simply the material being covered but also the learners being taught. There is no magic potion for teaching faculty to care about students, but an engaged classroom begins with the assumption that what we say and do in and out of the classroom impacts learning. A reflective professor not only plans for the upcoming class but also thinks about the events of the class that just occurred and how students might have interpreted the messages they've heard.

Compacts need to be created with students at the outset of class about what they expect from one another. Some of these expectations may be simple requests about not eating in class or arriving to class on time. This is also an opportunity to clarify expectations that pertain to microaggressions and trigger warnings. But what about the fellow with the MAGA hat? One might argue that someone should not wear a garment that makes another person uncomfortable. Fair enough, you might say. What do we then do with the student whose gay flag T-shirt makes a Christian student feel uncomfortable? Or the woman wearing a hijab? If a fellow student had a parent die in 9/11 and is uncomfortable, then should we ask her to appear in class without Islamic clothing? There are no automatic answers, and these issues can be very different from one another based on the viewpoints of those who wear the clothes and those who see them. Some will think of a MAGA hat as a political statement, whereas the hijab is an integral part of a religious practice. Others will be unable to differentiate politics from belief. We can sanitize a classroom and campus—no decorative caps, no T-shirts with messages, no religious clothing, and such. But such actions stymie conversation rather than provoke learning. It's precisely the wrong message to send and would probably not help us avoid controversy in any case.

We need to be able to deal with these issues on a careful, deliberative, case-by-case basis. We need to take seriously the concerns of students and others when they claim that a microaggression has occurred or that a text or event has triggered the individual into feeling psychic or physical pain. The reflex response from critics when I make such statements is that the classroom ought not be one long therapy session. The rest of the class has material to master, observe many; we ought not sacrifice learning the material to help calm someone's nerves.

I disagree. I do not believe that a classroom or any learning experience will occur if we only focus on the material at hand. We can chew pedagogical gum and walk intellectually at the same time. Indeed, an engaged class where students are able to confront one another openly, without fear of rejection or intimidation, is more likely to enhance than impede learning. Even if we do not yet have complete empirical evidence about the pervasiveness of microaggressions or their measurable impact on learning, we know that they exist and that they influence learning. Why don't we approach teaching and learning in a manner that seeks to affirm one's identity en route to learning the material at hand rather than try to make believe that what we say inside and outside of class does not matter?

Of course, there are moments and actions that go too far. Sometimes an individual's sole purpose is to disrupt, rather than engage in, learning. A member of the alt-right who walks onto campus dressed in a Nazi uniform and wearing a swastika is certainly not interested in learning algebra. We need to think through how to handle these sorts of actions and individuals as well. The challenge is always context and interpretation. As I noted earlier, a trigger warning usually is thought of as words or actions that trigger a painful memory for an individual. A soldier who suffers from posttraumatic stress syndrome or a survivor of sexual assault may encounter triggers in a classroom by a reading or a comment. Generally, however, we have not assumed that a trigger warning is generic—readings about homosexuals placed in concentration camps are not triggers for all homosexual readers. The challenge today is to work our way through these meanings so that we improve the learning environment for all individuals but do not unnecessarily limit conversation and thoughtful dialogue on difficult topics.

Demands versus Conversations

Shared governance came about in the early twentieth century. The term is imprecise, and of consequence, its articulation is equally imprecise. The assumption is that the board of trustees, the administration, and the faculty all share in governing the institution. How one defines the "share" varies from institution to institution and changes over time. The sharing is also very personality-driven. Some presidents regularly consult with the faculty, and others try to keep them at arm's length. A unionized campus has a different definition than a nonunionized campus. Boards, as I discuss later, have tremendous differences between them.

In general, academic governance has frequently been ridiculed either as a genteel debating society that accomplishes little or as a fiercely political legislature that quarrels over the most microscopic of issues. There is certainly a degree of truth to both points. I appreciate administrative frustration at the sluggish pace of decision-making. Although most faculty I know work extremely hard, much of our work is deadline free. We conduct research and write papers at our own pace. To be sure, those of us who are grant active have reports to write and time frames to accomplish tasks, but academic life is entirely different from the pressure cooker of offices, where one or another task must be accomplished by 5:00 p.m.

Governance for the faculty is particularly time insensitive. A committee writes a report for the senate on teaching effectiveness, the senate discusses it and sends it back to the committee or sends it to another committee, and then a final report reaches the senate at the end of the academic year. No work occurs over the summer, and a new group of senators look at the report in the fall with fresh eyes and have concerns, and the work begins anew. Although the work is not generally earthshaking, the topic is important, and it is one that the administration hopes will be decided in a matter of weeks, rather than years. Ultimately, the senate reaches something approaching consensus and passes the legislation along to the administration.

The first article I published, as a graduate student at Stanford, was the result of a year-long ethnography of the faculty senate.[13] I called the text "Governance by Conversation." The title certainly was not intended as a compliment, but I thought of it as neutral: an observation of a social fact. Over time, however, the title might be viewed as both a criticism and an artifact of a bygone era. Individuals always have bemoaned academic decision-making's pace, but the tempo of life has picked up while our governance structures have not. Taking the summer off seemed like a logical step in an environment where campuses closed down from June until Labor Day. Today, in an environment where we struggle to meet the payroll and competition from many sectors has intensified, such downtime seems foolish, if not dangerous.

Coupled with the determination for expedited improvements is the changing nature of discourse. "Governance by conversation" as the norm has shifted to "governance by demand." The strength of the idea of a conversation is that we are able to discuss issues; behind that idea is the assumption that we will ultimately reach a decision. There is also a genteel belief that by creating a framework around which different personalities can air every conceivable opinion and angle of an issue, we'll reach a fully informed consensus.

Obviously, such a goal invites any number of criticisms. At times, I thought I should have titled my article Governance by Filibuster because the disagreement of a lone professor can stymie a vote simply by the ability to talk and talk. Consensus might be good for the majority, but it also might be seen as a way to silence those on the margins who feel compelled to go along with the majority. Consensus also has the potential to cordon off controversial discussions, since there will never be agreement. Why discuss a topic if no one agrees on the parameters of the problem at the outset?

Critics of shared governance and academic decision-making generally have not yet presented a viable alternative. As with many issues, we are able to point out the shortcomings of academic decision-making. We might argue for the pokey pace of decision-making to be speeded up or for closer adherence to Robert's Rules of Order to stymie a filibuster, but these are matters of degree, not kind.[14] All of our actions occur in a larger sociocultural web that frames how critiques are articulated and addressed.

The result is that we have refashioned governance by conversation to governance by demand. Rather than assume that individuals can sit down and discuss issues, we have moved in the opposite direction. Administrators are prone to move unilaterally for a multitude of reasons—including a desire for rapid change, a perception that quick decision-making will impress influential constituencies, a hope that the move will go largely unnoticed for a period of time—and faculty and students then publish demands in response. More often than not, the demands are linguistically hollow. An ultimatum announces that if demands are not met, consequences will ensue. But administrators generally know that really, what the demand writers are saying is, "I'm mad as hell!" and that they can simply wait out faculty or students until the holidays roll around or the summer begins.

This is not to suggest that unmet demands are a victory for administrators. For those of us who lamented governance by conversation, the replacement by government by demand has only made matters worse. The challenge for those of us who are trying to think through quite thorny, controversial issues pertaining to microaggression, trigger warnings, and other similarly heated topics is that precisely at a time when we need thoughtful, nuanced conversation, we find ourselves faced with demands. And for faculty who do not wish to court controversy, the response to demands is to try to avoid the issue entirely. Keep your head down, and do not say anything that will get you in trouble.

This attitude is anathema in an environment where the search for truth is our primary undertaking. If we hold the search for truth as a core value, then we at least have the lineaments of how to proceed in confronting events that roil the campus. Rather than keeping one's head low, or making a plaintive plea—can't we all just get along—we need to welcome earnest disagreement and questions from our community.

When the Nazis marched through the center of the University of Virginia's campus and ultraconservative speakers sought to disrupt UC Berkeley's campus, many of us were unsure what to do. However obnoxious and vile such events are, I suspect that the larger failure for a university is its lack of planning. The University of Virginia was unprepared. UC Berkeley spent hundreds of thousands of dollars on preparations to ensure that there was no violence, and they avoided a calamity. A case can be made that a racist march or racist speakers can be allowed if every step of the event is carefully considered and planned. As I'll elaborate in the essay on academic freedom, I do not like the costs we must pay for these sorts of events, and the sight of Nazis marching down any street moves us away from a microaggression to a macroaggression. If there are events that merit trigger warnings, then skinheads goose-stepping is example number one. I do not think, however, that banning such marches gets us very far. Bullies are not going away, and we need to stand up to them rather than try to silence them.

Events within a classroom can be just as conflict laden. One white professor playfully opens class by singing along with any song a student decides to play; one student plays rap where the verses repeatedly employ the N-word. The professor sings along. Another white professor uses the N-word repeatedly in class as a pedagogic tool. Some students walk out of the class. It is the norm in these sorts of situations to turn to legalities to determine right and wrong. Should the professor be sanctioned and removed from the classroom? Should the professor be allowed to say whatever he wants because he has academic freedom? These are scenarios in which dialogue—where we honor one another's subject position, where we are able to reach some sort of communion about what bothers us and what gives us joy—is key to fostering community on campus.

Does the professor have the right to use the N-word in class for pedagogic purposes? Probably. Is it a smart, strategic move that furthers understanding in the class for everyone? Probably not. Should we engage in dialogues that make us uncomfortable? Absolutely. Can we have the dialogues in classrooms where trust is lacking? Absolutely not.

CHAPTER 5

Students as Customers

Universities as Amazon (or Whole Foods)

I ordered two books this morning on Amazon Prime. I thought about waiting until we returned to our second home in Santa Fe, New Mexico, because Garcia Street Books is located next to our favorite café. We like walking to the café, ordering expresso, reading, and then wandering next door to leaf through some books. I have said to friends in Santa Fe that I feel like I am keeping the bookstore in business given how many books I order. My friends, all of the same age, agree with me: they buy books there as well. But when Amazon came into existence, I stopped having the local bookstore order books for me that weren't in stock, since even then I could get the books delivered to my doorstep faster than Garcia Street could get them to me. And nowadays, it seems absurd to buy books from Garcia Street when Amazon is faster, cheaper, and more convenient. When I am in Los Angeles, I also use Amazon Prime. The books are always less expensive than in a bookstore, and they come right to the house, frequently within twenty-four hours.

Everything I have just written is likely old news to you. Who doesn't use Amazon, or at least know about it? Who likes to jump in the car—especially in a city like Los Angeles—fight traffic, search for a parking space, enter a mall to buy a necessity, and then reverse the process? Done repeatedly, the cost of gas, parking, and time easily exceeds the cost of an Amazon Prime membership and lacks the convenience.

The same point can be made about Uber and Lyft. Driving to the airport, parking, waiting for the parking lot shuttle, and hauling luggage around used to be a necessity; most of us could not afford a limousine, and taxis are slow and frequently less than spotless. Uber and Lyft changed everything. They arrive within minutes, the cars are clean, the drivers are friendly, we get left off steps away from the terminal, and the cost is half the price. The added advantage of these car shares is that they also work like a game, so we can spot the car's location and track it as it makes its way to our pickup point.

We like the convenience of getting our products delivered to our house at the click of a mouse. Although many of us bemoan spending so much time in front of our various screens, very few individuals miss the way we used to shop, get to the airport, and do any number of other pre-internet activities.

I still go to Garcia Street Books because I enjoy having a cup of coffee sitting out in the courtyard soaking in Santa Fe's sunshine and then moseying over to the current fiction section at the bookstore. I enjoy seeing what the owner's "hot picks" are for the month. I enjoy deliberating if I should actually buy that book on the biography of John Stuart Mill or if I have too much to read. (I do; I still bought it.) And therein lies the aspect of shopping that Amazon can't provide: we go to some shops for the experience.

When Whole Foods came on the scene, it provided a more curated shopping experience for those of us who enjoy cooking (and eating!). Whole Foods is a niche grocery store focused on high-quality organic foods. With prices much higher than local supermarkets, it quickly earned the nickname Whole Paycheck. But it offered a shopping alternative to those customers who valued having a wide variety of gourmet and organic food options and who were willing and able to pay for it.

Some businesses have been successful at transforming to the new economy, and others have not. Perhaps the newspaper industry is the best example of a product that refuses to die even though it appears to be on its last legs. Hundreds of newspapers have gone under as consumers have migrated to social media. The *Los Angeles Times* has gone through five owners over the past several years, and each owner has tried a new business model that has failed. The newspaper used to arrive with a thud on our driveway; now it's so thin that I am afraid it might blow away with the wind. Because I rise early, I start reading the *Los Angeles Times* online then go outside for the print copy and pick up where I left off. What's that about? Why do I need print anymore? In part, I relate reading a newspaper with the past enjoyment of reading the paper and drinking a cup of coffee in the morning. And yet, as iPads have gotten stronger (and my eyesight has gotten weaker), it's actually more convenient to read texts online.

The newspaper's text is "old news," too, by the time I read it. When I start reading the online version, I first check the latest news to see what's happened overnight. *The New York Times* is even more clever since it sends me updates throughout the day in a manner that many readers will find useful, almost addictive. For most of us, print versions of a newspaper are redundant at best. We get our messages from so many places in the twenty-first century that *The New York Times*'s slogan, "All the news that's fit to print," seems like a message from a bygone era—and good riddance to that era.

Sure, there are additional issues that arise with the range of purveyors available today. The labor practices of many newcomers on the scene have been egregious. Large companies have gotten tax breaks so that they were able to drive down their prices and drive their competitors out of business. "Fake news" is an issue for those who only read from a particular source. It can be difficult to separate news from opinion. Marketing has a way of tracking my every click, and the result is that I am fed news stories based on my past reading and browsing, which means that I am more likely to agree with the article rather than have it broaden my knowledge base or intellectual horizon. Nevertheless, while we may take issue with aspects of the new digital media platforms, very few of us would be willing to go back to what once was.

The same is true with music. Record stores, and then CD stores, were ubiquitous. The way we not only bought our music but also found new music: first on the radio and then at the store. Pandora, Spotify, and other providers have entirely changed how we consume music. Spotify broadens my musical horizons, podcasts make standard radio programming seem antiquated, and streaming services mean I have many more choices for watching movies and shows. These innovations bring up various questions that need to be debated, but we cannot recapture the past. We're not going back. Consumers like what is fast, cheap, and convenient.

So, what's with higher education? We seem to be stuck in the record-to-CD phase. We make changes, but they are not as substantive as any of the industries I have just outlined. Perhaps there is good reason for our recalcitrance. Newman and Dewey certainly never looked at their students as customers. A generation ago, I edited a book *The Responsive University*; one of the authors Ellen Chaffee wrote a chapter on the student as customer, and we received a great deal of pushback from Dewey's disciples.[1] She argued that the faculty were too often at the center of the enterprise, when it should be the students at the center. The assumption was that we had introduced the marketplace to an arena that should be exempt from marketing gimmicks. It was as if we had pissed in the sacristy.

I get it. The most business-like of postsecondary enterprises—for-profit higher education—has shown the multitude of problems that can arise when we treat higher education strictly as a market. At the same time, I suspect that our foot-dragging with regard to change is more than a principled stance about the nature of education. I imagine that newspapers, CD stores, food emporiums, bookstores, and any other number of industries might not have changed if they did not have to, or they did not see an opportunity.

What, then, is keeping higher education from undergoing the dramatic changes that need to take place? I do not think a case can be made that the students-cum-customers prefer the convenience of Amazon but drop their preferences when it comes to higher education. It's entirely possible that the Whole Foods experience is preferred by some postsecondary customers and not others, but even at Whole Foods there is a convenience factor that frequently does not exist on our analogous Whole Foods–like campuses. That is, some students will want a traditional campus experience, whereas others will not. But even that traditional experience will have been updated in ways that students now expect. When I went to college, registration was a daylong event where we stood in long lines in the gym to register for classes. Now, students register online at their convenience before school begins.

Some of the changes we have made have kept pace with demands. Although critics allege that upgraded fitness centers and similar amenities are a luxury, at some institutions, that's exactly what the customer expects. Smart classrooms, updated libraries, and improved technical facilities and labs are all examples of our colleges and universities trying to keep pace. The pace, however, pales in comparison to what we have seen in numerous other businesses.

We still have great trouble inventing new models of delivery and new products for these customers. People have touted some form of online education since I was a graduate student, and the online experience still has not measured up to what takes place in the classroom. Amazon or Uber or any number of new industries are not poor seconds to what currently exists—they are improvements on what exists, and that has generally not been true with regard to dramatic changes in higher education. I also do not believe, however, that we have tried to reinvent higher education. If anything, we are trying desperately to hold onto what we frequently think of as an academic utopia when students learned at the feet of wise pedagogues. We know, of course, that the student body was once comprised of white students, male students, and able-bodied students. We know that a particular version of society was taught to our students. We wax nostalgic about higher education's past, when in reality it was far from being a utopia. Why, then, do we not think about new institutions that might enable not only better delivery systems but also a better product? What, or who, prevents us from envisioning and enacting a dramatically different postsecondary experience?

The Lords of the Manor: Faculty

Today, the overwhelming portrait of faculty in media and literature is as privileged buffoons. We are either radical leftists intent on indoctrinating our students, or we are fusty old-fashioned people who have no sense of the real world because of our work and because we only occasionally come up from our laptops or out from our libraries for air. The caricature is easy to make and hard to erase. Recall the example I provided where people paused at a party when they discovered I was a member of a university faculty, rather than *just* a teacher.

We also have no sense of time; we are not in a rush to change anything. One January, I received an email marked urgent from a faculty senate president who asked for an emergency meeting of past presidents to discuss a pressing issue. He asked if we might be able to attend the meeting—sometime in April. In another example, the California State University system proposed to change its remedial coursework for the system. The measure was put forward in September for the next academic year—a year away—and the faculty union complained that the proposal was rushed.

The perception of many has been that only special people get to attend a university, much less teach at one. A young friend was recently admitted to a doctoral program; the acceptance was a remarkable achievement for someone who grew up desperately poor in another country and who was raised by a single mother who only had a fifth-grade education and made $9,000 a year. When he told his mom he was going to get a doctorate and explained he was not studying to be a doctor, she simply concluded: "More school? Get a job."

I recall my time in graduate school when I read night and day because I felt I did not know anything. One day after I had gotten up at 5 a.m. but never left the house, a friend said, "It must be nice not to have a job." She was not criticizing me so much as observing that compared to her 9 to 5 job, my work seemed like a luxury.

And it is—for some of us. It is not necessary to delve too deeply into the psyche of academics, but for many tenure-track faculty, the ability to spend night and day reading and writing about a topic we have chosen to study is a privilege. I have never once thought during my thirty-year career that I wished I was doing something else. Of course, we grapple with feelings of intellectual inadequacy, and the vast majority of us will never be rich. Yet all in all, academic life is a remarkable privilege that has its own perks.

Compared with other fields requiring advanced degrees, the salaries of academics are often unimpressive. I do not know anyone who likes faculty meetings. Too many people work to the point of exhaustion. The tension in classes that I discussed previously can be upsetting. College campuses, however, are generally physically delightful places to work, and, for those of us who enjoy young people, fun. We set our own hours, however long they may be.

We also help frame what happens on the campus—or we used to—and therein lies part of the problem. I know very few faculty, especially now, who come to campus every day. In a city clogged with traffic, such as Los Angeles, coming to campus more than three times a week is excessive. All individuals have different temporal rhythms, but faculty are the rare exception who have the ability to frame their work around those tempos. I'm a morning person, and I teach in the mornings; I have a colleague who does her best work late at night, and she rises around the time I am ready for lunch. Her classes are in the afternoon.

The result is that much of what happens on campus revolves around the convenience of the faculty. Those like me who are morning people will have classes between 9:00 a.m. and noon; some of us prefer short, one-hour sessions, and others like longer classes two days a week. Some individuals like one long class so they can focus on their research the rest of the week. We may have mildly accommodated our students' needs; by and large, however, the faculty see themselves—and are seen—as the lords of the manor.

Obviously, a great deal of that perception is false. Indeed, throughout the pandemic we had multiple examples of faculty bending over backwards trying to stay in touch with their students. Virtually all faculty turned on a dime to offer their classes on-line in the spring of 2020. The clearest misperception has to do with the transformation of the faculty from tenure track to nontenure track. Tenure-track faculty are a shrinking percentage of the overall faculty, and with that downsizing, faculty have a smaller say in the affairs of the institution.[2] Shrinking budgets, and an increase in nonteaching activities, have increased an institutional focus on ways to generate revenue. One key tactic is through pedagogical activities, even though we are spending less revenue on teaching as an overall percentage of the budget. The result is that virtually every institution has looked at online courses as manna from heaven, and faculty, mostly nontenure track, also have started offering classes at times that are more conducive to the students, rather than offering classes that meet the whims of the professorate.

When students are customers, then the seller—a.k.a. the faculty—is forced to move away from the bookstore model, opening and closing at the convenience of the owner, toward something approaching Amazon. The result is that, today, we see many more courses offered in the evening, on weekends, and in the summer than we saw a generation ago. There ought not be any *dead* time for a classroom that could be generating revenue. Efficient airlines are those that keep their aircraft in the air; when planes are on the ground, the airlines are not earning revenue. The same might be said of classrooms.

Campuses also are trying to diversify the student body with regard to not only race and gender but also individuals who may not have thought of themselves as college-goers. The average student age is going up because academe has realized that adult students are a vast untapped market. Creating new markets is a standard for any business, and when students are customers, then colleges are businesses.

The other part of the university being a business creates dilemmas.[3] When I place my order at Starbucks for my latte with nonfat milk and an extra shot, I am extremely clear about what I expect. It's not only that I expect the latte delivered to me in a timely manner. I also expect the taste to be what I have come to expect. I do not want it weak; I do not want it lukewarm; I do not want it served without foam.

How does that translate on a campus? A student does not simply pay to take a course. The expectation of a customer is that the learning will be commensurate with the outcome, and the class will meet the customer's expectations. The result is that students expect As for a grade, which, in turn, will move them along so that they will graduate on time and get a job after commencement. Such expectations highlight the challenges (some would say shortcomings) of the idea of students as customers. Despite the many flaws that may exist in a grading system that is at least in part subjective, individuals cannot assume that simply because they pay for a course, they should earn an A grade.

A market analogy only goes so far. Campuses should be more responsive to the needs of students. If learning is commoditized, however, then the product is not real learning, but rather a hollow credential. The challenge, of course, is that learning is not simply a one-way transmission from the knower to the known. Further, good grades do not guarantee that students will land the jobs they expect. The market may constrict and make jobs harder; the individual may not interview well. The fact is that the product cannot be a high grade that ensures a good job. We need to think about how to change our lordships, somewhat, but not eliminate them for our own ideas of the university. At the same time, we need to think about alternatives that make creative use of the metaphor of a market.

The Parameters of a Good Idea:
For-Profit Higher Education

As I alluded to earlier, although for-profit higher education has always been in the postsecondary ecological system, over the past twenty years, the growth has been remarkable. Neoliberalism has created an environment where market-based policies and organizations are encouraged. When a particular type of organization accounts for less than 1 percent of the market share, it can be ignored. When that organization becomes the fastest growing sector in the market, accounts for 13 percent of the market, and has its clientele incur nearly 50 percent of all loan defaults, it deserves to be investigated.[4] Higher education is in a peculiar situation. I have argued that students should not be treated only as consumers. At the same time, colleges and universities do compete for students. Until recently, for-profits have done very well in this competition. What I explore here is the rationale for their success and then, in the next essay, question their success.

Although many of us enjoyed bookstores once we made it to them, not too many people liked taxis. Indeed, in the late twentieth century, large (but cozy) bookstores were popping up all over the country because savvy booksellers thought they had figured out what the customer wanted—places to sit and sip a cup of coffee while they thumbed through the latest James Patterson novel. Borders, at one point, was one of the fastest growing companies in the United States—and then it collapsed.

Taxis faced very little competition. The rich could order a limo to get to the airport, but for daily travel, all of us were pretty much stuck flagging a taxi if we needed transportation and did not want to drive. In some cities, such as Washington, DC, the costs were mysterious since the taxis did not have meters; in others, like Los Angeles, taxis usually had to be called because the distances between individual houses are so vast. Whether taxis arrived when we needed them was a crapshoot. There were baffling surcharges added to a bill for one reason or another, and the cars were inevitably less than shipshape. I've had taxis where the windows didn't roll down and the air conditioning didn't work, and I've had taxis where the windows didn't roll up. I've had taxi drivers who kept the windows down since they didn't want to turn on the air conditioner, and taxi drivers who've begrudgingly turned on the air conditioner at the lowest level after I've begged.

Is it any wonder that companies like Uber and Lyft came into existence? I appreciate that today's taxi drivers are facing decreased wages because of increased competition. I realize that they now need to work even longer hours because they are making less money. I also am aware that companies like Uber and Lyft have spent more on their lobbying efforts than Walmart or Google to get legislation that favors their companies. I completely agree that the wages these upstart companies pay their workers is much less than what taxi drivers have made. Taxi drivers have to undergo drug tests to ensure passenger safety, and so should drivers for Uber and Lyft. Drivers are employees and should receive health benefits. In many instances, these companies have circumvented safety rules and regulations and hired drivers who should not be working for the company; they treat them as casual workers or contractors when they are not. What I have never heard from taxi companies, however, is an acknowledgment that they were Uber's enablers. Uber only came into existence because taxis allowed them to by turning out a crummy product.

Unfortunately, I haven't seen any improvement in taxi service in the time since I've started taking Uber or Lyft. Taxis are barely clean jalopies compared to their competitors. I can hail Uber and get a car within minutes; I still keep my fingers crossed when I page a taxi. Uber drivers are friendly and talkative; taxi drivers act like they could care less about me—the customer.

And therein lies the connection to higher education. For-profit higher education institutions grew exponentially not only because they lobbied Congress. They were clever about ways to avoid onerous rules, and they figured out strategies to create loopholes. They bought off some members of Congress. But traditional higher education is the taxi association. They pointed out for-profit misdeeds rather than acknowledging that the for-profit colleges and universities (FPCUs) had a point.

The growth of industries is an amalgamation of different organizational strategies that try to take advantage of current environmental conditions. Borders bookstores grew because they figured out a market niche; they simply did not anticipate Amazon and did not know how to adapt. Starbucks had much the same idea as Borders, but it also has continually updated and altered its initial plan. I once could only get coffee there, and then breakfast items were added, and now I'm able to buy a whole array of foods that appeal to the type of customer who wants a cappuccino with a sprinkle of cinnamon. The result is that I'll find panini and sushi for sale; I won't find the sort of hot dogs the local convenience store sells that sit on the burner for hours on end. Customer preferences matter. Customer preferences also change. Starbucks doesn't have a competitor like Amazon to deliver coffee to our door, but at some point, it will face competition and the question will be whether Starbucks is able to adapt.

And sometimes, an entrepreneur creates a new business where the customer was not waiting for a better product. I always liked coffee, and I always liked books, so cafes and bookstores were favored locations for me once I reached high school. Back then I, like everyone else, knew nothing about the internet, but once it came into existence, it was indispensable.

The for-profits are not akin to the internet, but they took advantage of what the internet had created in ways that traditional postsecondary institutions disdained. They offered classes at convenient times (such as in the evening and on weekends and in convenient locations such as shopping malls). They also capitalized on what many customers disliked about traditional colleges and universities. On the one hand, as I noted, the lords of the manor arranged times for their courses that were convenient to them, but not to the students. On the other hand, many customers, even those who lived literally blocks from a campus, never thought that the college had anything useful to provide them.

For-profits were the academic equivalent of Uber. They saw what existing customers did not like about their experiences and changed them; they saw an opportunity to bring in new customers who never thought about using the traditional company, and they saw an exponential rise in revenue. How did they do it?

The lords of the manor claimed their time and place for their courses. The for-profits realized what many customers wanted and offered classes in the evening or on weekends. Classes began as soon as the applicant applied and was admitted, rather than applying in November and waiting to hear something in April and then waiting again for classes to start in September. Classes didn't stop during the summer and only briefly stopped during holidays, such as Christmas. Working adults wanted a degree so that they could earn more income; the faster they got their degree, the better, so what would be the point of a long summer vacation?

Many students did not need a campus. What they needed was convenience. Just as the main response to the question about parental school choice was frequently found to be that parents wanted the school close to where they lived and worked, what mattered to FPCU customers was a classroom where they could park for free and did not have to drive out of their way. There's a reason that FPCUs have classrooms in shopping malls and near an exit ramp of a freeway. Traditional faculty like me would harrumph if we had a class in the evening next door to an Arby's on the second floor of a mall. FPCUs did not create classes with faculty like me in mind; they created them with the customer in mind and then found teachers who could do what needed to be done. And, for the customers of FPCUs, places like Arby's afforded an opportunity for a quick meal before heading home.

Indeed, people like me not only would not want to teach at the times and locations the FPCUs have chosen; the FPCUs would not want to hire me given my focus and outlook. FPCUs come down squarely on the side of vocational learning. They are less interested in the philosophical aspects of learning and undoubtedly disagree with the intellectual frameworks created by Newman or Dewey. They want to enable their customers to get a job, and to that end, they've taken the decisions about what goes into a course, how to develop curricula, and where and when to offer classes out of the hands of the faculty. Academic freedom at an FPCU is absent; it's not something to be debated because such discussions do not exist. Teachers are fired at will. If there is a downturn in the course, then the instructor will not be asked to teach again. A colleague who taught a business class at an FPCU frequently went straight from his day job at a law firm to the shopping mall where his course was offered. He usually wore a business suit. One week he had been on vacation and came dressed in a sport coat, dress shirt, and jeans; he was warned not to dress so casually ever again. No one would ever tell me what to wear to campus, but FPCUs have a model of what they want, just like Uber has a model for the kind of vehicle they want their drivers to have to pick up customers.

FPCUs analyzed the weaknesses of existing organizations, overcame those weaknesses, and then saw ways to expand their market share. When online learning became available, rather than hem and haw and worry whether the pedagogy was up to snuff, they saw it as another way to expand their customer base. The goal of the FPCUs was always similar— enable students, either refugees from the traditional institutions or new ones—to gain employment upon completion of their coursework. What could possibly go wrong with such a model?

The Flimflam Man Reexamined:
For-Profit Higher Education

Broad brushstrokes that paint an industry in a bad light also have the potential to taint those who adhere to a strict code of ethics. As I noted earlier, the generalization about the for-profit industry had to do with orchards and apples. By the end of the Obama era, the Congressional hearings and press about the for-profit higher education industry was unrelentingly bad. The fastest growing higher education sector in the late twentieth and early twenty-first century was now the fastest shrinking. What happened and why?

We know that the for-profit industry always has had a checkered history. For more than a century, the promises that for-profits made did not sync with reality. For-profits were profitable for the owners, less so for those who earned a degree that led to a career. In the 1970s and 1980s, Congress looked into the sector and enacted a variety of measures to assure compliance, which were then modified or simply undone by subsequent administrations. They banned recruitment strategies that rewarded recruiters with incentives for bringing in more students. In the 1992 Higher Education Act, they stipulated that for-profit institutions needed to rely on 15 percent of revenue that did not come from federal grant, loan, and work-study programs.[5] The assumptions behind such proposals were that body counts were not an ethical way for an institution to attract students; an institution should not live solely on federal and state largesse when its purpose was to make profit.

The for-profit sector has an enormous lobbying arm, and it was able to weaken the legislation or simply eliminate it.[6] The result was that, by the turn of the twenty-first century, recruiters received enormous bonuses when they met or exceeded the goals that had been set for them. Unqualified students were unwittingly admitted to programs for which they were unprepared. The students might have had little understanding about what the program entailed, what specific opportunities awaited them at the conclusion of the program, or how much the program cost. Some students found after a few weeks that the coursework was not to their liking or too difficult, and they dropped out without understanding that they had accrued tens of thousands of dollars of debt simply by registering for the degree. Still others completed the program, but their financial literacy was low; they then discovered that their new job paid $20,000 a year, but they were $100,000 in debt with enormous interest rates.

By 1998, the 85–15 rule changed to 90–10.[7] This new rule enabled for-profit institutions to subsist on an even smaller amount of private dollars to thrive. And when the institutions recruited veterans, they did not have to meet any rule. If the federal and state governments no longer provided financial aid, both private and public nonprofit sectors would undoubtedly face enormous challenges. The for-profit sector, however, would simply go out of business because there was no more money to be made.

From time to time, I have supported the for-profit sector. As I discuss in the next chapter, when I look to the future, I see a capacity crisis with regard to qualified workers for certain degrees. We need more people participating in higher education. I also am a critic of many of the practices of traditional private and nonprofit higher education. I do not see public colleges and universities, in particular, responding in a manner that enables significant reform. If my assumptions are correct, then the for-profits can play a meaningful role: there is a great deal to admire in institutions that put the needs of the students ahead of others. Offering classes in convenient locations at convenient times ought not be extraordinary, but when the FPCUs did so, they were acting out of the norm. Many students also want training that is efficient and more vocational than humanistic. Again, we might quibble about the nature of the curriculum, but I appreciate that someone who wants to learn how to be a plumber or a computer technician develops those skills and finds gainful employment.

Unfortunately, the for-profits took a good idea and let it go bad and then were unwilling to own up to their problems. They essentially tried three strategies when confronted with the evidence. Their first effort was aimed at the generous public willingness to forgive the occasional transgression: "Trust us" was their refrain. For-profit advocates were antiregulation; they believed the market should decide if a product was good or bad, rather than bureaucratic regulators. This argument warrants careful thought. If I go to a restaurant and receive bad service, then I am not likely to go to the restaurant again. We do not need the government intruding between buyer and seller claims the antiregulator. Or do we?

Obviously, if we move the analogy from a waiter providing bad service to the food being bad, we have a different issue. If the food is spoiled, and people become ill, then for many of us the government has a role. The government has the authority to recall tainted meat, for example. The question is, what kind of regulation would be suitable for the for-profit industry?

When confronted with exceedingly low completion and graduation rates, the FPCUs pulled out their second strategy: the for-profit sector had higher percentages of low-income, first-generation students, as well as above-average representations of African Americans, Latinx, and military veterans as students. "Of course the dropout rate was high," claimed the FPCU apologists. "By regulating the sector, is the government really going to preclude opportunity for those who had been shut out of traditional institutions?" This strategy, too, had a compelling ring to it. The traditional sectors had not done enough to enable poor students' passage through college, and the participation rates of Latinx and African American students remained well behind those of their Anglo and Asian American counterparts. Why criticize an industry that was trying to do good?

If we use the analogy of the health-care industry, however, we see the absurdity of the claim. If a poor neighborhood neither has a clinic nor a hospital, then clearly those citizens are poorly served. One conceivable solution might be to allow a for-profit clinic to operate in the neighborhood until the traditional sector gets its act together. But the costs might be so high that no one can afford to go to the clinic. Or patients who visit the clinic might become sicker after their visit than they were before. Some might even die. We would never knowingly allow a clinic to serve patients if we knew that its remedies were snake oil that made people ill.

A health clinic is a useful analogy here because the market does not usually operate in every aspect of one's life. We do not buy and sell romantic partners. We do not pay for the privilege of going to church. And we traditionally have thought of some services as a public good.

Indeed, the fight over health care revolves around the profit motive, but even Republicans want to ensure a modicum of regulation. I cannot simply walk into a neighborhood and put up my shingle saying Tierney's Terrific Therapy and expect that I will not face penalties and fines. I must have a license conferred by the state. And my license should be revoked if I provide fraudulent care. A replacement for inadequate service is not always an improvement. The replacement could be worse.

The final defense strategy of FPCUs relates to the earlier ones: "Sure we're bad; so are they." Indeed, some traditional institutions have low retention and graduation rates. Dropout rates are particularly high for students who need remedial coursework in the community college sector.[8] I appreciate turning the spotlight on low graduation rate institutions to understand what they are doing (or not doing) to improve. However, the fact that someone else is not doing well is not a valid excuse to also underperform.

The problem with the for-profits' argument is also that students do not simply fail. A student gets a loan from the government, and the student has to pay that loan back, or go into bankruptcy, in which case the government has to pay off the loan. When students leave a community college, they do not depart with more than $50,000 of debt. They do not have to declare bankruptcy. They do not force the citizenry to pay the institution that caused the failure because it is owed tuition. And if we go back to Senator Harkin's analogy, we also are dealing not with an apple or two, but the whole orchard.

So what do we do? Do we give up and set fire to the orchard? The challenge of for-profit higher education returns us to the underlying theme of this book: what do we want a college education to be, who should provide it, and who should pay for it? From a purely communitarian perspective, a college education would be largely free and provided by the public sector.[9] We might revert to some version of California's vaunted Master Plan that stipulated free college for any Californian who wanted an education and was qualified. If higher education is a public good and the provider is the state, then the private nonprofit and for-profit sectors will have limited roles. If a state agrees to the idea that it should offer postsecondary courses, then presumably the regulatory role of the state will also be significant. Clearly, a consistent line of thinking runs from the assumption that the state has a vested interest in offering free, public education to the idea that the state must protect its citizens from unscrupulous practices.

For all of my adult life, however, we have not believed that the state should provide free public education; we have moved in the opposite direction and assumed that individuals should incur a greater and greater proportion of the cost of their postsecondary education.[10] I suppose there's something to be said for consistency, because we also have downplayed the regulatory role of the state with regard to food and drugs, environmental protection, gun control, and higher education. The Trump administration has been particularly consistent in the belief that consumer protection should have a minimal role for the government, particularly in education.[11] Recall that Trump University had its own problems with the same issues I have outlined here. Under oath, former managers of Trump University stated that the institution "relied on high-pressure sales tactics, employed unqualified instructors, made deceptive claims and exploited vulnerable students willing to pay tens of thousands for Mr. Trump's insights."[12] After making the same rationale that others have used and I outlined previously, and then claiming that all the allegations were false, Trump made an out-of-court settlement with those who were defrauded. The university has been shuttered.

We are on the horns of a dilemma. From my own vantage point, the for-profit industry should only be allowed to flourish if there can be reasonable regulation that ensures that past malfeasance has been eradicated. A healthy for-profit industry with customers who are well served and happy with the product they have received should have a place in a capitalist country. Unfortunately, such regulation is unlikely to happen anytime soon. The result is that the rampant disregard for consumer protection will lead to greater costs for the customer and the taxpayer. The educational interests of neither the students nor the citizenry will be well served. One might think that in a system that does not cover the costs of education as a public good, we might at least provide rigorous consumer protection. The result is actually the opposite. Indeed, when the for-profits were encouraged to put forward their own thoughts about regulations during the Obama administration's hearings, they declined. The takeaway from my own work with the for-profits is that some very good people work in for-profits, but the overarching profit motive has taken a good idea and made it unworkable.

CHAPTER 6

Tear Down That Wall

From High School to College

College for All?

In the sixteenth century, Henry IV of France supposedly was the first to promise, "I want there to be no peasant in my realm so poor that he will not have a chicken in his pot every Sunday." Herbert Hoover went a step further in his campaign for President of the United States in 1928, announcing that he wanted not only a chicken in every pot but also "a car in every garage." Except for the vegetarians and vegans among us, the goal of a chicken in every pot seems like a laudable aspirational goal. In the first part of the twentieth century, the goal of car ownership for everyone seemed like a remarkable aspiration. A century later, however, we are seeing a drop in the number of young people who own a driver's license.[1] Millennials are prolonging car ownership compared with previous generations, reflecting changing consumer tastes, and today, in response to a chicken in every pot, we'd probably ask where the chicken was raised and if there were alternatives to chicken.[2]

Nevertheless, Henry IV's and Hoover's aspirations seem to speak to attempts to expand public well-being. How that aspiration gets acquired and enacted may be based on one's philosophy. All politicians claim to support the idea that individuals should have health care, for example, but hold very different opinions on the degree to which the individual and the state are responsible for paying for that health care. And one is not entirely sure what the consequences are for the individual or the leader when the public finds out that some have chickens in pots, cars in garages, or health care, and others do not. The environment also frames the possibility for achieving one's aspirations. Shortly after making his claims, Hoover faced the Great Depression and was booted out of office.

Aspirations, of course, also could be foolhardy or mistaken. "I want everyone to eat a chicken everyday" seems absurd since a chicken is a great deal of food, it is probably not good for you, eating chicken every-day would get boring, and it would be bad for the environment (not to mention chickens). "I want everyone to drive a Rolls Royce" seems farcical to anyone who knows how much such a car costs. And not all of us want to drive such a gigantic gas guzzler. However varied our aspirations are, they need to be in sync with societal understandings of what everyone wants—but does not have. And how one achieves a goal is up for grabs, even if we all agree that it is an enviable goal. Who will pay to turn a goal into a reality?

Governor Edmund Brown of California put forward a quasi-aspira-tional goal with the Master Plan of Higher Education. Any Californian who wanted a postsecondary education could get one, and the state would pick up the cost. There were a few catches. California put forward a tripartite system of community colleges, state universities, and elite research uni-versities—the University of California (UC) system—that offered graduate education. The community colleges would be open access, and the others less so. Nevertheless, whoever attended the institutions would get a free ride. The word *tuition* was not even in the lexicon for California; students might have some fees assessed to them, but fees were for materials, activi-ties, and events, such as club sports, not deemed central to taking classes. The costs of the basic infrastructure for the postsecondary system would be borne by the state. If there were not enough classrooms, then the state would build more campuses. If there were not enough faculty, the state would hire more. The goal was to make California the best-educated state in the country. The Master Plan served as a model for decades about how to increase access to higher education and highlighted the role of the state in educating its citizens.[3]

The plan was far from perfect. Not surprisingly, the poor, African Americans, and Latinx were overrepresented in the community colleges; the upper classes and Anglos, and later Asian Americans, were overrepresented at the UC institutions. Over the last fifty years, numerous problems have arisen regarding capacity and cost. But it's worth pausing to admire the refreshingly broad aspiration of the individuals who drafted California's

Master Plan: the commitment that every Californian high school graduate who was able to benefit from college could attend a college or university. California became the first state or, indeed, governmental entity to establish this principle of universal access as public policy.[4]

At the time, the plan was extolled for its ambition.[5] In many respects, the goal was a continuation of the United States' love affair with education. As I noted, Horace Mann in the early nineteenth century called for universal primary education that would be free. During the Civil War, we enacted legislation for free public higher education in land-grant colleges. By the time we admitted states to the union in the twentieth century, we required that public schools be available through high school. In the 1950s, we coined the word *dropout* and created laws that required students to be in school—and all of this schooling was covered by the state.

We now inhabit a different world. The logical next step from Horace Mann's initial call is the idea of "college for all." California's Master Plan may not have gone so far as to proclaim college for all, but it was moving in that direction for those of us who are education enthusiasts. To go from the idea that individuals had a spot in higher education if they desired to the assertion that everyone should go to college was not a very big leap. But that idea has come under withering criticism and analysis. What happened?

The tax structure in the state of California collapsed and made free higher education impossible. The national conversation about enabling more students to go to college has run into conservative arguments that the economy does not need more college graduates. Even moderate and liberal think tanks do not envision a vocational need for everyone to attend college. The Public Policy Institute of California, for example, predicts that the state needs more people getting some type of postsecondary training, but acknowledges that even by 2030, fully 30 percent of jobs in California can be filled by those with a high school degree.[6] The result is a large chorus that says the aspiration of college for all is misplaced.

From my own perspective, the concerns of the vocationalists are valid. I have seen no studies that say we need 100 percent of our high school graduates to go on to a postsecondary credential or degree. Most of the studies I have seen suggest that we should aim to provide somewhere above 60 percent of high school graduates with some form of postsecondary credential or degree.

We also have come a very long way from the idea that a postsecondary education should be free. If we were to make college free for everyone, in a manner akin to what the California legislature did in 1960 with the Master Plan, the costs would be enormous. The only way we could enact such a plan would be to have crippling tax increases or to enact a progressive tax code akin to what existed in the 1950s.

The real challenge, however, involves the decision of who goes to college and who does not. As I mentioned earlier, when conservative economists argued that too many Domino's Pizza delivery drivers have college degrees, they were pointing out that we need fewer college graduates. If college is only about vocational training, then they have a point. When making the determination about who goes to college and who stays home, my guess is that these economists' children will go to college. Let's also acknowledge that the assertion "we neither need nor can afford more college students" is being made precisely at the time when more first-generation, low-income youth of color are entering the system.

When I attended Horace Greeley High School in Chappaqua, New York, in the 1970s, there was no discussion about whether to attend college. The question was *where* to go to college, and growing up in New York, none of us really thought about attending the State University of New York system. We were all going to a private college or university. Today, we speak a great deal about college preparation or college readiness, whereas in the 1970s, those terms were assumed—that was what high school was for.

But there are many more reasons for a college education than simply getting a job. Cultivating the life of the mind and preparing for the critical role of participation in a democracy should also be central concerns. From this vantage point, we need more people participating in higher education, even if the cost is prohibitive. But who should decide who gets to attend a postsecondary institution? And whose obligation is it to pay for that education?

College for Some?

Newman's *Idea of a University* had a sweeping vision of academe's purpose.[7] However, he never addressed whether he envisioned everyone attending university. Governor Brown's Master Plan opened the door for mass higher education, but the individuals behind the California Master Plan never really envisioned all high school graduates obtaining a four-year degree. Part of the problem is that we have historically linked higher education to wages. I appreciate the humanists who point out the need for higher education to play a more critical, contemplative role for our citizens, but the overwhelming commentary about higher education is that it enables individuals and society to remain competitive.

I do not see us decoupling education and earnings anytime soon. The challenge, of course, is that if US society paid workers an equitable salary, then we might return higher education to the more humanistic framework that Newman advocated. Unfortunately, income disparity continues to grow rather than shrink.[8] The result is that how one works his or her forty hours a week makes a significant impact on one's earnings. People would not be so desperate for their children to go to college if what we used to think of as working-class jobs afforded entry into the middle class: the ability to buy a home, raise a family, and plan for retirement. We do not live in that society. Unless there are significant social changes beyond the scope of this book, my guess is that higher education is going to remain a hot commodity for making individuals' resumes more competitive.

Margaret Spellings, a former secretary of education and president of the University of North Carolina system, has usefully pointed out that "we live in an age when yesterday's abstract knowledge is tomorrow's practical necessity."[9] We tend to forget that, just over a half century ago, less than 50 percent of US citizens older than twenty-five had a high school diploma, whereas today it is around 90 percent.[10]

Other countries handle matters very differently from us. Brazil has a very large for-profit sector, for example, and the public universities are hard to gain entrance to and are largely elite.[11] Germany sorts students into career or university tracks immediately after primary school.[12] I am not suggesting that either model is correct but simply wish to point out that a country's philosophic stance about what we want a public good to be is open to (re)interpretation and definition.

Here is our dilemma. The workforce is changing as dramatically as at any time in the last century, and there is little to suggest that it won't continue to change. The larger economic environment has made working harder and longer a norm, rather than the exception. We have to change what we think of as a postsecondary education. It's likely that many, though not all, individuals will need some sort of training after high school. This could shift from a standard four-year degree to an array of postsecondary options that are greater and more successful than what exists now. When we factor in that there are obvious discrepancies across class and race, we need to recognize that the problems—or perhaps more optimistically framed as challenges—that have confronted us throughout our history are as significant as they always have been. Let's consider, then, what we expect of our high schools in terms of college preparation.

Preparing for College

In moving from eighth grade to ninth, some students make a choice: not whether they will go to high school, but where. Some might choose a charter school, or a private high school, or a school that focuses on the arts. Most of us, however, simply move from our local public middle school to the local high school, and those who were our classmates in eighth grade are right there in ninth grade. The structure of the day and our classmates remain relatively the same.

Once we are in high school, we move along from grade to grade. True, some students drop out, and few others fail to pass their grade and have to repeat their level. The overwhelming majority, however, simply progresses as if they are on an escalator. Students may have a choice or two about what kind of course they want to take, but the overall architecture of their academic year is not questioned. No one asks a student in eleventh grade, "So are you going into twelfth?" or "Where are you going for twelfth?"

At Horace Greeley High School in Chappaqua, New York, we had a version of the escalators in twelfth grade as well. No one asked us if we were going to thirteenth grade: the question was, where? The path forward once students reach high school in places like Horace Greeley is relatively straightforward. Their parents and older siblings are likely to have attended college. The guidance counselors are aware of what the plan is from day one of the first year. In the academic lingo, we have a great deal of "opportunity hoarding" in these sorts of schools, where parents function as a college concierge for their children.

Most middle- and upper-class students assume they will attend some sort of four-year college or university. At Greeley, I cannot remember anyone who considered a two-year college, and less than a handful joined the military as officer candidates. We knew we were getting on another escalator because our parents, our siblings, our friends, and the neighborhood all created the guideposts for us to figure out which escalator to choose.

A large part of college preparation that enables one to get on the right escalator is not surprising. Students need to do well on an exam and write a college essay. If a student has a lousy SAT score and cannot read, write, or do arithmetic, then that kid is going to have a hard time. By no means am I suggesting that every child of the wealthy or middle class go to college, but we know that many more attend a four-year institution than their less well-off counterparts. The same may be said about institutional selectivity. More rich kids go to Harvard than the state college. The zip code where a child is born has more to do with going to college and the type of institution he or she will attend than any individual capacity that a student has. Such an observation sort of puts to rest the assumption that standardized tests are objective measures of merit that filter out the best from the rest.

The students mentored in the program I ran for over a decade were in low-income high schools that had horrible college-going rates. In my work with the students, two findings stood out above all else. First, unlike their wealthy counterparts, the students had to make a very active decision about going to college. These students got to the top of the escalator and got off. They really had no idea what awaited them once they stepped off the escalator on graduation day. Most of them found low-paying jobs; some tried a community college. A handful of others went to a four-year institution. A few of us run around these schools and try to point out: "Look! Over there! See that escalator? Go over there! It's got cool things at the top!" The result is that any students in a low-income, first-generation school or family have to make a decision that their well-off counterparts never have to even consider.

Second, in the writing program we offer for college-bound youth who attend these schools, we ask for a five-page writing sample. I do not really care what they have written, or for what class; we simply want to gauge how they write so we might be better prepared to help them in the month-long intensive writing program. Unfortunately, more often than not, students cannot give us a five-page paper they have written throughout high school, because they've never been assigned one. One need not be a specialist in testing to know that the lack of writing instruction in high school will be a serious impediment to college work.

I previously raised questions that are open to debate: (1) Should everyone who graduates from high school go to college? (2) How do we decide, or who gets to determine, attendance for college going? The problem I am raising here, however, is different. We know that there are gross discrepancies across income, class, and race. If we make the case that not everyone should go to college, how do we address these disparities across income and race?

A case can also be made that some sort of objective measures can be used to ensure that a class has some degree of academic comparability. We want some sort of academic similarity in classes—it's rarely a benefit to throw beginning learners in with advanced students. What do we do, however, when we also know that some children have parental and filial concierges who are escorting them to the right escalator and the remaining kids do not even know there is another escalator?

I do not think a shrug of our academic shoulders is enough. Those of us in higher education should not get to act like academic Pontius Pilates, washing our hands of what goes on in high schools with low college-going rates. We are not close to equitable outcomes for the poor and students of color in terms of college-going rates. Are we comfortable with economic and racial inequity? Or do we need to up our game? What do those of us in academe need to do to ensure that our schools provide a more equitable environment for their students?

College Knowledge

I once asked a young woman who was my mentee where she wanted to go to college. She said she had narrowed it down to three places: UC Berkeley, Cal State Dominguez Hills, or Los Angeles City College. Her responses surprised me because of the variability. Berkeley is notoriously hard to get into, Dominguez Hills has the highest acceptance rates of the California State Universities, and Los Angeles City College has open admissions. My mentee was a senior at a low-performing high school, and her applications were due in six weeks.

I asked how she came up with these choices. She responded: "My history teacher went to [Berkeley], and he said it was great. My brother's friend goes to Dominguez Hills, and my boyfriend went to City and took a course. I want to play soccer, so I looked on their websites, and they all have soccer teams, so I thought it made sense."

"What do you want to study," I asked.

"I want to be a cop," she said.

Compare this with my own application process a generation ago. My brothers attended Notre Dame. For more than a year, all my friends at Greeley had been speaking about which institutions we might apply to. My best friend and I did a tour of institutions in the northeast United States and visited about ten colleges and universities. My parents looked over the promotional brochures with me, and voila, off to Tufts University I went.

By comparison, my mentee had never set foot on a college campus, even though a half dozen were a stone's throw from her high school and home. She had no regular discussions about college with her friends, and she did not understand the difference between a two-year and four-year institution. She had an idea what she wanted to do after graduation, but she did not understand what she had to do to become a police officer. In academic parlance, her college knowledge was low.

Another mentee was accepted at UC Los Angeles, and I had one of my PhD students take him there. It was the first time he had set foot on a campus. UC Los Angeles was far from his home near Echo Park, where he lived in a two-bedroom apartment with his mom, his younger brother and sister, his aunt, her disabled son, and his grandparents. When he returned from his visit to the university, he sent me an email: "Dear Professor! UCLA was amazing! It was like a large garden!" And he went on to describe the wide variety of people he had seen at the University.

His college knowledge, too, was low. He lived in a largely Latinx neighborhood and went to a school that was 90 percent Latinx. For such students, campuses are foreign zones, frequently as confusing as a first-time traveler setting off to a foreign country. Most of us who study college-going have created two ways to think about college readiness: cognitive variables, like the ability to read, write, and do mathematics; and noncognitive variables, which set the stage that enables or disables cognitive learning to occur.[13]

Dropping out of high school and college are different. The end result is the same—the student is no longer taking courses—but the reasons are quite distinct. The academically challenged student moves from eighth grade to ninth grade, and the high school knowledge is not much different from what the student needed to navigate elementary school. Classes are harder, however, and no one likes getting low grades. The student drops out.

Most students who leave college, however, are not flunking. They have weak, but acceptable, grade point averages and simply drift away. For these students, it's the noncognitive variables that get in the way of learning. They cannot exactly put their finger on it, but they've found that they do not really like college. The reason their college knowledge is low is because they attended schools that did not emphasize that sort of learning.

I referred earlier to the person who had never traveled before and brought enough suitcases to last for months, even though our study tour was less than a week. Poor, first-generation students face many similar imponderables. I forget how young I was, but I know I was not out of grammar school when my parents had me open a bank account; for one of my birthdays, my father bought me some shares of stock with $100 that I assiduously followed day by day to see how much I made—really a pittance. My financial literacy bloomed in a way that it does not for first-generation students. Students frequently do not know the difference between a grant and a loan, and many have never dealt with a bank. Another student I mentored contacted me as soon as he arrived for his first year at his university; he had obtained a credit card and immediately heard from a Nigerian who was going to send him $100,000 if he gave him his deposit account number. Such luck!

Time management, how to interact with faculty who come from different backgrounds than you, and how to navigate campus life are issues all students face. The problem is that most first-generation students have not had any advance warning about what awaits them. Just as high schools could do a better job teaching students about writing and math, they also could develop a more formative framework for crucial college-knowledge skills, such as financial literacy, time management, and networking.

We want students to be able to grapple with issues in a manner that Baldwin mentioned in his "A Talk to Teachers."[14] For students to be able to wrestle with issues, and understand difference, they need experiences in high school that begin to move them out of themselves so that they are able to entertain experiences that are different from their current lives. Critical engagement is not simply the mastery of skills, and it is not something that occurs overnight. If college is to be intellectually rich and broadening, then students need to be prepared for those sorts of experiences in high school.

CHAPTER 7

Jobs, Jobs, Not Jobs

The Good Old Days:
Before Anyone Was "Academically Adrift"

What happens when prepared and underprepared students arrive on campus? What is their experience while on campus, and how prepared are they when they leave? These are simple enough questions for which we do not have very good answers. How important is it for us to have answers?

These questions certainly were not of concern when I attended Tufts University in Boston, Massachusetts. Formalized terms such as *cognitive variables* did not really exist nor had they made it into the nomenclature, and informal terms such as *college knowledge* had not been invented. A few months ago, I went back to Tufts and walked around the campus. In many respects, what I saw was not much different from when I was there in the early 1970s. There were new buildings, but students still ambled around campus and hung out in cafes, and I even saw some guys playing Frisbee on the quad. What's changed?

The vast majority of students in my region were more like me: white, middle- and upper-class students. We may have had siblings or parents who went to college, or at least someone in our extended family who had. Many, if not most, of our high school friends went to college. We were accustomed to an educational rhythm that was set in high school—a fall term with a long Christmas break and then a spring term with "ski week" in the middle and an even longer summer hiatus. During those breaks, we either earned money or took a nice vacation.

College was affordable. We took out minimal loans, and we did not really worry about how to pay for our tuition. I had a job in the university library for a few hours a week that paid a few bills, and I did work in the summers to earn money. Other than that, my dad was the bank. I did not even know the cost of college; I just knew my father could afford it. Solidly middle class, I knew that neither my parents nor I would be awash in debt when I graduated.

College curricula have gone back and forth between prescription and one that is relatively free of requirements. Although there are high-minded arguments about whether students should take classes that aim to give them a well-rounded understanding of the world or those that focus more intently on their major, the reality is that the curricula involve a great deal of horse trading. Think of it as trade agreements among countries, where the countries are departments. The math faculty claim that students need two courses to master elementary mathematics, and the humanities respond in kind, so the general education requirements are increased. The result is that there are fewer courses in the major. The romance language department chimes in that three courses are necessary to be able to speak adequately, and the sciences want their piece of the credit-bearing and revenue-generating pie. General education requirements beget distribution requirements, which create havoc in majors. Departments then argue that the university-wide requirements do not allow enough time for students to master basic competencies in the four-year time allotment, so committees then begin to shrink distribution requirements and general education courses. And so it goes.

The assumption underlying the curricula was that a standard undergraduate degree was four years, a standard course was three credits, the class met three times a week for one hour or twice a week for ninety minutes, and faculty needed to teach courses to pay for their positions. Finances were relatively straightforward. A department had X faculty that taught Y courses every term. X times Y equals the number of courses in the department times the number of units equals the departmental total credit hours times the cost per hour of a credit equals the revenue the department generated. Presumably, the combined tuition for both semesters paid for the faculty in the department. Departments generally wanted to increase faculty size, and to do that, they needed to demonstrate that their areas were popular. Faculty preferred to teach advanced classes in their majors and graduate courses, so younger faculty were made to offer the large survey courses to first-year cash cow students, reserving the smaller seminars for senior faculty.

The system largely worked. As I noted, the public, the administration, and the students and their families deferred to the faculty. When faculty pointed out the essential importance of a general education curriculum, their audiences generally nodded in agreement, and then a decade later when they pointed out the importance of the major, they nodded again in agreement. When students graduated from college, they mostly went on to live profitable lives and stayed in or moved smoothly into the middle class.

The faculty were the proxies for learning, and apparently they did a good job. Students graduated, obtained jobs, and then sent their kids to college. Higher education became a booming industry. When foreign countries stopped buying US-made goods, the opposite happened with higher education in the United States: foreigners flocked to our shores. They loved the product! We could do little wrong.

I attended college at a time when requirements were nil and course taking was a smorgasbord of delights. I took virtually no science or math courses, and I took as many literature and philosophy courses as I could. I had a smattering of history and political science classes as well, but no foreign language courses because of the very low standard one had to have to place out of the requirement. I might bemoan, looking back, that I was not forced to take Spanish, or math, or even science, but I certainly was not adversely affected once I graduated from college.

I wasn't harmed because jobs were easy to come by; we did not worry very much about what we were going to do. The only people who seemed focused in the 1970s were those who labeled themselves pre-med because they had long, grinding coursework and residencies ahead. The rest of us mostly lived for the moment. I did not really think about what I was going to do until my senior year, and by then, I had stumbled into a variety of options. I had a job waiting for me as a counselor at a homeless shelter; I had the Peace Corps waiting to send me to Morocco.

College offered fun as well as opportunities for introspection, which I suppose is what many of us think college should be. I made a bunch of friends, we participated in lots of teenage hijinks frequently involving marijuana, but we also talked a great deal about the meaning of life. At the time, I thought my referent group was large—certainly larger than my friends at Greeley High School—but, in retrospect, the circle got a touch larger, but not by much. My first-year roommate was African American;

a good friend down the hall was a Jew from Baltimore; I met someone who was homosexual (other than my closeted self, of course); I had a friend who grew up on a ranch in New Mexico. Although these individuals were out of the ordinary for me, they were not much different from my middle- and upper-class friends back in Chappaqua. To attend Tufts meant that your family was middle or upper class.

What helped me expand my intellectual and socioemotional horizons was working at the Pine Street Inn, a home for homeless men. Pine Street was a subway ride and a world away from Tufts. Most of my time was spent with the two hundred or so men who stayed there during the day and slept there at night. I worked my way up from being one of a handful of assistants to being the night manager who oversaw the floor from 3:00 p.m. to around 10:00 p.m.

I discovered the job because I wanted to earn some money and wanted to make a difference. In the two years I worked there, I learned a great deal about myself. I suppose I could say Tufts had nothing to do with the experience because I found the job through an alternative newspaper, but Tufts also enabled me to do something that seemed of no practical utility. I stumbled on an experience that helped me consider what I wanted to do with my life, and, by way of that experiment, I suppose I found something of a vocation—even though I didn't know it at the time. I had no idea what I was looking to do when I first entered the Inn on a bitterly cold winter's day. The ad simply said, "Interested in working with people," and I was. I didn't know that I would be good at my job. I learned that I enjoyed listening to people, and when I shut up, people had a lot to say.

We also worked pretty hard at our schoolwork, but we did not consider it work. There was lots of fooling around until late into the night, but virtually every evening, except on the weekends, most of us were reading for our classes or writing essays that were due. A literature major had an extraordinary amount of reading, but I took it as natural—that's what college was about, after all. I also had astonishing professors who welcomed conversations with me, even though I was by no means an amazing student. The faculty saw their job as expanding the life of the mind of their students. In-class and out-of-class experiences revolved around asking probing questions of the material and ourselves so that we might better understand the material being studied and presumably be better educated when we left academe and entered the real world.

I have gone down my collegiate memory lane because the contrast between my experience and that of today's students is so stark, even if the campuses and individuals look similar. Individuals frequently speak of the diversity of today's students, and to a certain extent, this is true. Campuses are more diverse than a generation ago, although they still have a long way to go. Students also still tend to segregate themselves by race and class. Nevertheless, they are less segregated than when I attended Tufts in the 1970s. A great deal of ink has been spilled that attributes the current worries about academe to the diversity of today's students: yesterday we did not have these problems with college readiness, remediation, and job placement, yet today we do. The implicit reason is today's students aren't like yesterday's students. There is a smidgen of truth to the comment, but the inference is problematic, and the reality is not true.

The largest differences are environmental, which, in turn, forced changes on all of our campuses. Due to advances of the internet and what has come to be called social media, today's students not only consume information faster but also expect information in ways that were not apparent or available in the 1970s.[1] New teaching arrangements are largely populated by contingent faculty. There is no longer any sense that we are learning and teaching materials that are simply for the life of the mind and spirit.

Students and their families are also terrified, for good reason, about the state of the job market upon graduation, especially given the economic fallout from the pandemic. Students are wondering about what they can do in college to better equip themselves for jobs. The experimentation I encountered at the Pine Street Inn is largely eliminated. Instead, we counsel students to find more fruitful avenues for whatever experience might count in making them stronger candidates with a bolstered resume. Whereas my work at the Pine Street Inn was to earn some money and do something different that seemed socially worthwhile, we now counsel students to be very clear about why they are spending their time on a particular activity.

There is decreasing tolerance for the structure and pace of classes and degrees because they seem to proceed at a snail's pace. Today's students skip classes with abandon, and as researchers have shown, the willingness to do homework and additional course activities outside of class has dropped precipitously.[2] We might say that there is a correlation between the faculty's diminished desire to be involved in the lives of the students and the students' decline in an interest of the life of the mind, but there is no one-to-one relationship. Faculty who are part-time may not even have an office for office hours; students are no longer in an environment where individuals around them see faculty interaction as useful or necessary. Time matters. Professors no longer hold office hours merely to have a casual getting-to-know-you kind of conversation between the student and professor; the conversation must be addressing a specific issue. Although adolescents entering higher education may have no better idea what they really want to do when they graduate, they do have more angst. They are likely to have debt from college as soon as they graduate. Their job prospects are unclear. The compression of time and the contingency of academic work has made the meaningfulness of academic life less pertinent. College now seems to many students like an abstraction that wastes one's time rather than enhances it. What can be done? There is no simple or obvious response; in the conclusion I put forward an idea or two, but really what we need is a conversation on several levels to come up with solutions.

Reading and Writing and Arithmetic

It's hard for me to remember a time when I was not reading—and enjoying it. Two elementary school experiences stand out. I grew up at a time when we got two newspapers a day—the *New York Times* in the morning and the *World Telegram* in the evening when my father came home from work. The *New York Times* was too big for me to hold when I started reading it, so I put it on the kitchen floor and looked at it as my mother made breakfast for all of us. At first, I only read the sports pages, inside the second section, so that I could talk with my brothers about who won the ballgame. My mother peppered me with questions that I did not realize was a way to get me to read, but she had me first looking at just box scores, and then the text. Eventually, I read the News in Brief on the first page of that second section, then started glancing at the front page, and eventually the entire newspaper.

In grade school, one of my friends, Michael Boyer, liked reading Tom Swift novels; he was a "Swiftie." I preferred the Hardy Boys. The brothers were amateur detectives. Reading kids' fiction is interesting when it's self-motivated. I got books as presents for Christmas and my birthday, but I also had my mom buy me the Hardy Boys series books. I loved the adventures that they got themselves into and that everything got figured out in the end.

Science fiction didn't interest me, but Michael liked reading as much as I did. We used to take books to school and keep them under our seat to read during breaks. Our penchant for reading did not set us apart or get us labeled as nerds or dweebs. We might have read more than our friends, but reading was the norm in our neighborhoods and school.

In my work with today's high school students, I find pretty much the opposite. There are individuals who have reading problems; they may be dyslexic and have trouble that makes reading work, rather than fun. In general, however, students read less, and, reflecting the times, their reading is in tidbits rather than long-form articles and books. My graduate students are less well read than my classmates a generation ago, but their reading is more varied. The volume of possible texts I can skim on my phone or iPad is a quantum leap over what was available to me as a graduate student. All of us reflect the culture of reading tweets and clicking from one text to the next and then the next.

I do not think there's much value in bemoaning a paradise lost, but it is fairly obvious that a decline in reading presages problems for the workplace. Indeed, at a time when "fake news" runs rampant, the inability to be discerning, critical readers is a cause for concern not only for the workplace but also for participation in a democracy. When students read less, they are less well prepared for the sorts of tasks expected in white-collar jobs. And if reading is problematic, writing is even more troubling. The evaluation of writing is one of the simplest and most confusing topics I have encountered. One need not be an educational psychologist to know that if students do not write in school, then they are not likely to be very good writers.

Practice may not make perfect, but no practice makes perfect impossible. Unfortunately, that is the case in far too many schools. I noted earlier that in the summer writing seminars we held for college-bound students, one requirement for admission was that they give us one five-page assignment they had written in any class during high school, and students could not come up with anything. How can we assume college readiness if students have never written a five-page paper before they arrive on academe's doorstep? While students in college-going schools are likely to have written multiple essays in high school, the reason that 40 percent of California State University's students arrive to campus unprepared is because they do not have activities that get them ready for college.

The point is not simply that students should develop basic writing habits or critical literacy, where students are able to engage in deeper learning. Students also need to learn how to express themselves in a manner that is expected in the workplace. I'm not convinced—and very few people are—that we need to suffer through algebra, geometry, trigonometry, and calculus to be successful in the workplace or in one's personal life. But, for any professional job, a student needs a certain level of writing ability to participate in professional tasks.

We do need to write a coherent sentence; not all of us need to know how to solve a quadratic equation. What's unclear is which mathematical skills a student needs for the workplace. We make assumptions based on a student's major. An engineer needs a higher level of mathematical skills than an English major. Is there not a floor for mathematical knowledge that we should all agree is necessary for the workplace? Unfortunately, the answer is no—we do not agree.

We make assumptions that students don't know what they want to do when they are in high school. We assume they know neither what they want to take in college nor what they want to do professionally. It's possible that the kid who's mediocre in algebra in ninth grade gets motivated by taking chemistry, and then math makes sense. It's also possible, however, that a bunch of us taking geometry have zero interest in the class and never will. While we might argue that the course will help us think deductively, that's a secondary effect that I'll discuss later. A high school English instructor used to have us memorize poems by saying it was "a rose in the garden in the mind." Ok, if you say so.

We tie ourselves into linguistic knots defining explicitly what we mean by college readiness, and, even more so, what students need to do to overcome those deficiencies. More often than not, our solutions have been failures. We assess that students are not ready for college and place them into remedial classes that they never escape. We send them to a community college to master the basics and then expect them to transfer to a four-year institution—except they never do. Or we conduct research and discover that the students in the remedial classes did no worse than students who were in the credit-bearing classes. Everyone ends up frustrated. The state or institution is spending monies that do not solve the problem; the faculty teach lower-level classes that they do not enjoy teaching, and the students are stuck in classes that offer neither remediation nor credit.

One irony is that high school teachers believe that about 64 percent of their students are ready for first-year college coursework without having to take remedial coursework.[3] College instructors, however, believe the inverse: they feel about 78 percent of their students are not college ready.[4] This discrepancy likely stems from a fundamental disagreement across sectors about what students need to know with regard to basic college writing and math.

Of late, as I have mentioned, there has been a great deal of criticism about the professor being the proxy for achievement. There are many good reasons why we have been criticized. Grade inflation sends the wrong signals to students and future employers. A culture of rewarding less than stellar effort—or effort rather than achievement—pervades much of academe. One reason that prospective science majors switch to the humanities or social sciences is because of subjective grading: it's hard to get a ninety on a math test with the wrong answers; it's less hard to get an A-minus or B-plus on an essay in a first-year survey class where the writing is subpar. Too many professors know that low grades create problems. In a consumer-driven culture, students complain. Teaching evaluations take a hit. The result is the temptation to give high grades because "everyone does it."

We also know that biases exist. Due to implicit bias, students of color are suspended much more frequently than white students, and they are referred to gifted programs less frequently.[5] Studies further indicate that a nonblack teacher is likely to have lower expectations for black students than black teachers.[6] Women are made to feel that they do not do as well in science, technology, engineering, and math fields.[7] Nevertheless, more often than not, with the office door closed, when I talk with a colleague about a student's work, we tend to agree. We certainly agree on evaluations where the student's work is either extremely good or extremely weak. We also are able to agree on large areas such as creativity: students' ideas and ability to express themselves. For every political decision I have seen faculty make, I also have participated in countless fair and judicious decisions about the quality of a student's work. What we have not done on a systemic level, however, is develop a standard rubric for what *fair and judicious* means.

What I am suggesting is that the concept of signaling is not so bad if faculty are willing to take seriously the task. Signaling, the idea elaborated on in economics by Michael Spence, Joseph Stiglitz, and others, suggests that if one has X, it signals something else.[8] If one has a college degree, then one must be better prepared than those who do not have a college degree. The signal, however, has come under fire in part because the signalers have been seen as flawed, if not corrupt. Signaling is not entirely symbolic. Or, at least, the symbol needs to be believed by more than those who are doing the signaling.

Ahead at the Starting Line

My father and mother were the first in their families to earn college degrees. Both of my brothers earned bachelor's and master's degrees. Those two sentences may not have predicted my career path, but they say a great deal about my anticipated socioeconomic status. It turned out to be true. Even though the economy does not need 100 percent of its workers to have a four-year degree, as I mentioned at the outset, we know that individuals who get a college degree earn a great deal more than those with only high school degrees.[9] If a college degree matters, then what makes a difference in terms of going to college? If, as the previous essay delineated, some parents will do anything to get their kid into college, what are the challenges and opportunities to getting into a college?

A first stumbling block has to do with finance. No one asks a poor person, "Are you going to Europe for the summer?" You might counter, "But poor folks could go to community college. They could get scholarships and fellowships. College is available to everyone if they want it!" True—but . . .

The previous essay spoke about cognitive variables: literacy and math skills. This essay speaks to noncognitive variables, or college knowledge: the ability to get help finding out what you don't know or what you need.

I once taught a very nervous graduate student who broke down in my office. She kept saying, "I just don't understand. I don't understand the readings." I tried to be comforting but made the situation worse by saying, "The answers aren't important. What you need to do is just ask questions about the material; then we can discuss your questions." She sobbed, "If I could ask questions, then I wouldn't feel so lost. I don't even know the questions."

Therein lies a problem for many students setting off to college: they don't have the tools to ask questions. It is clear these sorts of skills are needed to navigate entry into college and then the job market.

When I was in college, I may not have thought much about what I wanted to do with my life, but I knew that I wanted to make a difference. Making oodles of money was never a goal, and if I had made less or more money, I cannot really say whether I'd be happy, but I certainly have had enough resources to live a very nice life. I never really decided what I was going to do with my life; it just sort of happened step by step.

Today's students have to be much more strategic. Job knowledge is not unlike college knowledge or cultural knowledge. Students need to begin to build their resume in their first college year. Simply working at Starbucks to earn some money will not make someone more employable; going home for the summer, getting a summer job, hanging with the friends from high school, and kicking a soccer ball around on weekends will help pass the time, but it will not confer an added advantage when it comes to the job market.

Most colleges have perfunctory activities to help students, but they are nothing near what those who have job knowledge enjoy. A job fair may give a college student an idea about what exists, but what the student needs to do to prepare is a longitudinal, constant exercise, rather than episodic.

Students also have an unclear idea about the kinds of jobs that exist, or what they need to do to become competent in their field of interest. Students may know that if they want to be a doctor, they should be premed. If they want to make some money and are good in science, they may consider engineering. Once they land in a prospective major, however, they tend to rely on the advising system to tell them what to do. Advising tracks a student through a set of required courses and monitors the student's progress to make it to the finish line. The better institutions are able to ensure that the student stays on track and grad-uates in a specified amount of time—hopefully four or five years. It does not ensure that the student has the requisite skills and finesse to assume gainful employment upon graduation, or even that the student knows how to land that gainful employment. Those students who were like me and started to think about what to do the summer before senior year are going to be out of luck.

The result is that students get a serious case of what I think of as "resume envy." The first-year student who started to think about the specific skills and activities needed for the job market will have tried to land opportunities to put on the resume. That student will have letters of reference from professors, advisors, and people with whom he or she interned that are much more than perfunctory comments about the nice disposition the student had two years ago when he or she took a class and got an A. Summers are neither spent whiling away time on beaches or cutting lawns; instead, the summer months are spent working in increas-ingly upwardly mobile internships that demonstrate a clear trajectory of tasks, skills, and competencies.

I don't believe that being strategic about the job market means students must forfeit enjoyment in college. I love to run, and I'm very strategic about what I need to do to prepare for a half marathon, marathon, or once, an ultramarathon—for the couch potatoes, an ultramarathon is fifty miles—and I ran it in my fifties with my brother and best friend in just under eleven hours. That ultramarathon took me a year's worth of training, and I had to plot out week by week what I was going to do to make me better prepared for the race. Even now, in my sixties, I have to be strategic and forward thinking as I plan for my next half-marathon with my aging knees. Simply because I have to think about what I want to do—to understand the course conditions, the weather, and the terrain—does not mean that it's not fun. Preparing for the world of work does not have to be that different from my running plans. My main point is that people cannot just jump in the race at the last minute, or they simply won't finish. If they do finish, the race itself will be very little fun.

The other way to approach graduation and the world of work is pretty much what I did. I had no plan. I had an idea. I wanted to experience the world. I wanted to be in situations and locations that made me nervous. I wanted to face difference. I wanted to change the world. The result? I worked in a homeless shelter. I worked in a halfway house for recovering addicts. I joined the Peace Corps and lived in a town where no one spoke English. I worked at a Native American tribal college in North Dakota. I figured out I was gay and came out.

At the time, I did not know that any of those experiences would be useful for my work, much less my resume. The problem we have with college students is, on the one hand, they do not adequately prepare themselves for the world of work, and on the other, their lives are devoid of experiences that have made them reflect on the larger world and their role in it. I learned a great deal working nights in a homeless shelter and living in a village with running water for only three hours a day. The problem is that we have young adults entering the workforce who are poor in both areas, and our postsecondary institutions do very little to encourage either.

Kicking the Learning Can Down the Road

The function and application of a college education and degree remain unclear. Those who are vocationally focused say that we want students to be prepared for the workforce, in general, and trained for a job, in partic-ular. But what exactly does that mean? On the one hand, we often speak as if students are being trained for a very specific job; on the other, we acknowledge that unlike previous generations, today's learners are likely to hold multiple different jobs during their lifetime. The former suggests very specific skills; the latter generates well-intentioned bromides such as "learning how to learn."

I want to reject the idea that learning should be entirely vocationally focused, especially in college. I can wax poetic about the import of the humanities for humanities sake, but my point is that these skills enable individuals not only to find gainful employment but to participate in a democracy in the twenty-first century.

I do not think it's too much to expect that entry-level workers for blue- and white-collar jobs have reading, writing, and mathematical skills that a collective group of scholars would assess as college-level. I do not think we are doing that today, and more often than not, we are kicking the learning can down the road into the employers' laps. We have moved in the wrong direction. We have increased administrative and external authority and decreased the number and roles of tenure-track faculty. And we approach employability as a structural issue, rather than as a cultural one. A structural response develops measurable outcomes and assumes that learning can be tied to objective tests, and students will follow the lead. I don't think it works that way, and in any case, our assessments are haphazard, perfunctory, or so confusing that they are unusable.

An organization is a culture where individuals come together and either agree on goals or perform instrumental tasks. Faculty can come together to engage one another in discussions not only about what ought to be learned but also about how they intend to work together to ensure that learning objectives are monitored in formative fashion by formative feedback with one another and the students.

When we reduce a college education to instrumental learning, we not only misunderstand how to educate today's learners, but we also short-change society and the workplace. I am not making a simple-minded call for a return to general education but rather for us to focus more intensely on primary and secondary impacts of learning. I mentioned earlier that as an instrumental skill, individuals do not need algebra and geometry. However, studying geometry develops a skill that may provide direct help to those pursuing jobs in the sciences; it also helps nonscience learners think about deductive logic. Such reasoning will be helpful in numerous tasks, not only in the workplace but also in one's personal life. The fact that this is secondary does not mean it is a waste of one's time. Similarly, students might be asked to read a novel by Gabriel Garcia Márquez not because the information from the book can be directly applied to a job but because the ideas have the potential to generate conversations about fundamental themes like collaboration and the role one takes in a community.

We also have to move aggressively on incorporating particular skills into our activities. Statistics helps students weigh various topics and issues that are commonplace in the workplace and one's life. Financial literacy is critically important, but we think of it as a component of college knowledge that students might pick up along the way, rather than assuming it's necessary for any individual entering the workplace. The ability to write in different registers is necessary to function in multiple workplaces.

We are missing the opportunity to make our institutions central to resolving some of the most pressing issues in a democracy.

CHAPTER 8

The Cost of Free Speech

Understanding Academic Freedom

For over a century, academic freedom has been front and center as a primary totem of the academy. Permit me to review ever so briefly the well-worn territory about the genesis of academic freedom.

As US research universities first developed during the late nineteenth century, a sizeable number of US graduate students studied in Germany. When they returned to the United States, they were interested in importing the German ideas of *Lehrfreiheit*, or "the right of the university professor to freedom of inquiry and to freedom of teaching, the right to study and to report on his findings in an atmosphere of consent," and *Lernfreiheit*, "the freedom to study, to intellectually wander where one's ideas take them, without institutional or governmental interference."[1] The ideas did not immediately take hold. The US university of the late nineteenth century was still largely dominated by the institutional president and the board, who, in tandem, enjoyed considerable freedom to make unilateral decisions on behalf of the institution. Even though the newly minted US faculty members desired an environment where they could engage in research and scholarly inquiry, the institutional leaders felt that the faculty's role was primarily to transmit what was known through their teaching duties.[2]

A series of well-publicized events caused faculty to agitate further for "freedom of inquiry." A liberal economist by the name of Richard Ely lost his job at the University of Wisconsin in 1894 due to his support for unions. John Mecklin, a professor of philosophy and psychology at Lafayette College, was compelled to resign in 1913 because he embraced philosophical relativism, pragmatism, and evolution in his teaching and research. Scott Nearing, another economist who was well known as a political and social activist, was dismissed by the University of Pennsylvania in 1915 when he voiced strong criticisms about the use of child labor in coal mines.

In 1915, professors from a variety of disciplines and universities joined together to create a national faculty organization led by John Dewey: the American Association of University Professors. During the first two years of its existence, the Association examined more than thirty cases that involved violations of academic freedom. In response, it developed a statement, still used by many colleges and universities today: "The purpose of this statement is to promote public understanding and support of academic freedom and tenure and agreement upon procedures to assure them in colleges and universities. Institutions of higher education are conducted for the common good and not to further the interest of either individual teacher or the institution as a whole. The common good depends upon the free speech for truth and its exposition. Academic freedom is essential to these purposes."[3] Perhaps the most well-known case concerning academic freedom in the late-nineteenth to early twentieth centuries involved Edward Ross, an economics professor at Stanford University. After speaking out against the employment of Chinese workers on privately held railroads, he was summarily fired in 1900 by Jane Stanford, the widow of Leland Stanford, who once was president of the Southern Pacific Railroad. Or, at least, that's how the common perception of the Ross case has been passed along over the years. In reality, Jane Stanford, as well as other influential people at the university, had long-standing issues with Ross that dated back to 1896, when Ross first worked for William Jennings Bryan to support the Free Silver Movement.

Ross made numerous speeches on behalf of Bryan that perplexed the president of Stanford University at the time, David Starr Jordan. And yet, he acknowledged Ross's right to freedom of expression: "No one has the right to speak for the University in any matter of opinion," wrote Jordan, "but each man as a private citizen is perfectly free to take any stand in politics he may choose."[4] Despite the fact that Ross appeared to be using his Stanford professorship as a tool for legitimacy (rather than speaking as a private citizen), he was never sanctioned for his activities with Bryan.

However, Ross's views on race were far more problematic than his support of free silver. In fact, Ross was a eugenicist who believed "the theory that races are virtually equal in capacity leads to such monumental follies as lining the valleys of the South with the bones of half a million picked whites in order to improve the condition of four million unpicked blacks."[5] Today, it is difficult to square Ross' beliefs about race with his socialist perspectives on labor. On May 7, 1900, he gave a racist speech that Jane Stanford read in the newspaper:

> The Oriental can elbow the American to one side in the common occupations because he has fewer wants. To let this go on, to let the American be driven by coolie competition, to check the American birthrate in order that the Japanese birthrate shall not be checked . . . is to reverse the current of progress, to commit race suicide. . . . We are resolutely determined that California, this latest and loveliest seat of the Aryan race, shall not become, if we can help it, the theater of such a stern, wolfish struggle for existence as prevails throughout the Orient.[6]

Immediately after seeing Ross's words, Jane Stanford composed the following to President Jordan: "I am grieved to the depths of my heart. . . . This movement . . . is but a repetition of the old prejudice against the Chinese, and a repetition of "Kearneyism" when a reign of terror pervaded our city. . . . The teaching of violence is inconsistent with the Founding Grant."[7] It is worth mentioning that Stanford was coeducational at a time when many similar colleges and universities were not. Stanford also admitted students from various racial and ethnic groups when other colleges remained steadfastly white. Edward Ross, on the other hand, responded to a student protest against Chinese and Japanese workers by remarking, "I argued against letting in the coolies." The Stanfords, conversely, rejected the students' complaints as ignorant and vulgar. Given this additional information and context, it is understandable why Jane Stanford might feel the need to fire Edward Ross.

The elaboration of this narrative is important for two reasons. First, it corrects a heroic, yet mistaken, portrait of a professor who purportedly needed the protection of academic freedom to stand up for marginalized individuals. Second, Ross's unfortunate words would be defined as hate speech on most campuses today. Despite their objectionable and racist tone, though, his words would still fall under the protections of tenure, which ensures that academic freedom endures.

In recent history, professors have been denied tenure for their public airing of unpopular views. Joel Samoff, for instance, was denied tenure in 1978 because he used a Marxist approach to teaching and researching political science that was deemed "unscientific" by his University of Michigan tenure-review board. Bruce Franklin opposed Stanford University's involvement with the Vietnam War and was fired as well for allegedly instigating a riot.

These examples are also clear violations of a professor's academic freedom. US academics have defined academic freedom as "the right of the professorate to a significant degree of autonomy in the manner in which they conduct their work in order to have the freedom of thought and expression that is seen as necessary to advance knowledge and learning."[8] According to Burton Clark, academic freedom is a "totem"— the sine qua non of academic life.[9] Academic freedom most often gets enacted within one of two places: the classroom or the campus. What does a professor get to profess in a classroom? What kind of speech and actions can a professor make on campus? With the rise of social media and the concomitant negative attention a video can bring to an institution, the academic freedom that a professor enjoys has only become a more contentious topic.

As a professor of education, I have the right to express opinions about education in my classroom. Obviously, I do not have the right to say, "President Trump is against educational reform; you must vote for the Democratic candidate for president, or I will fail you." Similarly, like any professor, I am able to talk informally about my gay husband, but I cannot require that students vote for a gay rights initiative that is on the ballot.

On campus and outside of the classroom, the scope of what I might say is broader. I might sponsor a rally for a political candidate or a particular initiative. I could speak on behalf of both at a campus meeting. Further, shared governance came about to enshrine the idea that the faculty had a say in how the university was governed. The result is that I also have the ability to speak about any number of issues that are germane to campus life. I can speak against what a president has done or said, and because of academic freedom, I will not be threatened with expulsion. Academic freedom is not merely a totem of the academy; it also has a structural protection—tenure—which I shall discuss in the next chapter.

Although many of the challenges have remained the same over the last century, the rise of social media also has brought new controversies. When am I speaking as Professor Bill and when am I simply Citizen Bill? Some of these issues are maddeningly difficult to parse. If I use the email server and the website of the university, then presumably I am speaking as a member of the faculty. At the same time, many of us might list on a website our participation in a gay rights march, so what happens when a faculty member posts a biblical admonition against homosexuality based on his own beliefs? What about a biology professor who spreads fake news? Who gets to define *fake news*? As with so many other issues facing the United States right now, my sense is that there has never been as great a threat to academic freedom in the past century as we are now experiencing.

To think through the parameters of academic freedom, we must be willing to give a great deal of consideration about what we think the academy should do, and what professors can and cannot do.

The Psychic Cost of Free Speech

As with many complex ideas, there is no clear definition of what constitutes academic freedom. Moreover, the concept of academic freedom has been made much more complicated with the recent discussions about microaggressions, hate speech, and trigger warnings. As I noted in the previous section, a fair question can be raised about why the person who faces a microaggression must have to suffer in order to support the abstract idea of academic freedom. Does academic freedom enable what some will interpret, but not everyone, as racist language? How we define academic freedom also will be a matter of considerable discussion. I am not sure how we get around an argument where two individuals hold fixed positions that are inherently contradictory.

A hypothetical example close to my own experience highlights the inherent tension. Assume a college of education has a core course entitled Education and Diversity that I have taught. The master-level course has units on African Americans, Latinx, women in science, disability, undocumented youth, homeless youth, religion focusing on Jews and Muslims, and a session on LGBTQ+ youth. The majority of students are studying to work in student affairs, many of them in residential education.

A new instructor inherits the course from a previous teacher, appreciates the work that has been done, and points out that she will change a few readings and discussions based on her own background. The department chair stops in from time to time and sees very little difference from previous units in the classes on African Americans, Latinx, women in science, disability, undocumented youth, and homeless youth.

The sessions on undocumented and homeless youth are particularly well done, and the students like the service-learning component of the class.

The discussion about religion and LGBTQ issues, however, goes off the rails. The instructor is Evangelical Christian, and she served in Iraq. She sees herself neither as bigoted nor racist. She also knows that when I taught the class, I let individuals know that I was gay, and I had them over for a luncheon where they met my husband. She has let people know about her religion and uses all the readings that I had included, but she also includes readings about Christianity and homosexuality; she includes other texts addressing Islam's oppression of women and beliefs about man's superiority. She welcomes robust discussion and has been clear from the first class that she does not mind if individuals disagree with her. When she teaches the sections on Islam and education and LGBTQ youth, she is respectful of the many gay students in the class who say they are uncomfortable with readings that say their lives are sinful; the lone woman who is Muslim and wears a headscarf sits quietly in class when they discuss the reading about Islam. At one point, the instructor asks, "Let me provoke a conversation since I know we have different viewpoints. If I'm teaching high school and a student comes to me and says he's struggling with the fact he's gay, and I think that's a sin, shouldn't I tell his parents?" At another time, the instructor smiles and looks to the young Islamic woman, and says, "Why don't you give us a different view of the article" they have been discussing. The student looks at the floor and shakes her head, saying quietly, "I have nothing to add." At the end of the semester, the instructor hosts a Christmas party at her house. Her husband is a minister, and they begin the meal with a brief prayer thanking "the Lord our Savior for bringing everyone together in fellowship."

By the end of the semester, many of the students have complained to me. The gay students and the Islamic woman feel unnerved. They want to complain to the dean; they plan a boycott for the last day of class. When I speak to the instructor, she is sympathetic, but unmoved. At one point she says: "To be honest, I don't really get it. You spoke about being gay in class, and all those readings were very pro-homosexual. Two of the readings slammed Christianity as homophobic and sexist. I even kept those readings in, and I know that students feel free to say the same things. Why is it not okay to show that Islamists stone adulterers and what they did to that little girl in Pakistan? Can't you say the same things about students of faith who took your class and had to hear things they disagreed with? I've tried to be respectful and exhort people to examine their ideas."

Assume the next year I teach the class and one of those very students takes the class. He is thoughtful and does not purposefully disrupt the class, but he is outspoken. He was on the debate team in high school and is adept at provoking the class to see his point of view, even if the other students vehemently disagree with it. In many respects, he is a prototype of a conservative Christian fundamentalist. He is against affirmative action and for a merit-based system of admission to college. He believes undocumented students should not be provided public monies to attend college. Although he supports the American with Disabilities Act, he feels there are too many accommodations for people "who don't really have a disability," like those who use emotional support animals (one of whom is in the college, but not in the class). He thinks homosexuals are OK, but he is against gay marriage. He points out that he even has a cousin who is gay; he regularly plays pickup games of basketball with him and has no problems showering after working out with him. His objections to Islam parallel those of the previous instructor. He is against abortion and believes that schools and universities should actively teach against it. He is Asian American and lets it be known that his girlfriend is African American and his best friend in high school was in a wheelchair. "I can't be biased; I've just thought about things, and I know what I know."

Although he speaks in an engaging manner and welcomes debate, many of the students grow weary of him. Students come to me and make a point that I have been thinking about all semester. His views, although shared by many citizens, actively work to place students who not only disagree with him but are different from him in a position where they feel attacked. His writing has been like his comments in class: well constructed, well argued, and consistently thoughtful, even though I disagree with virtually everything he has written. I give him an A for the course. My teaching assistant finds out what grade I have given him and is upset. "You shouldn't normalize that behavior," she says.

The issues I have raised here are not that far-fetched from what happens in classrooms on college campuses all over the United States. I purposefully have not tried to create caricatures because the issues that confront us are rarely the cartoonish portraits that make their way into the media. An absolutist on academic freedom would likely support my colleague's position, as well as mine, with regard to what gets taught and discussed in class. Insofar as the materials, discussions, and grading did not penalize individuals for having ideas different from the instructor, I cannot find much to criticize. Even the activities at their homes paralleled one another and were voluntary. No one was punished if they skipped the meals—or rewarded if they attended.

My teaching assistant may have been correct that I was normalizing the conservative student's idea, but from an absolutist stance on academic freedom, it is fair to ask: What was I normalizing? The student was respectful of the ideas of his classmates and never closed down conversation. Indeed, he welcomed it. He never shifted his opinions during the class, but I had never thought that my class was framed around the philosophy that my ideas were correct and that a successful student would be someone who thought like me.

At the other extreme are individuals who will point out the position in which individuals are placed, not because they intellectually disagree with the professor and student but because of their identity. The young Islamic woman, or the gay students, or the raft of individuals whom the articulate conservative student disagrees with, each feel attacked because of who they are, not what they believe. Indeed, from this line of logic, a fair argument can be made that my own critiques of Christian students confronted not simply their ideas but who they are. Whenever they enter the terrain that touches on a person's identity, discussions of topics on which we disagree become even more difficult. Even the social occasions might be cause for concern: while individuals may not be required to attend a social function, they may have the sense that they are missing an event that brings the class together. At the same time, for a Christian to feel compelled to attend an event in a gay home or a Muslim to be in attendance at a party that honors Jesus Christ may be problematic.

Although I acknowledge that these issues are fraught with tension, I ultimately come down on the side of academic freedom. I do not find the manner in which my hypothetical successor taught her class to be flawed. Indeed, I might have included some of the texts she used in a subsequent class. I also do not find the comments of my bright conservative student to be out of bounds. I entirely understand and honor the concerns of students and believe that the dynamic of the class is crucial in determining whether some action or reading should be criticized or sanctioned. I also appreciate, especially at this point in time, that a great deal of what gets discussed in class is laden with potential for controversy. To avoid the issues, however, seems mistaken. I certainly aim to honor those identities that I previously outlined, but honor ought not imply that we simply provide an environment where individuals are not able to respectfully question one another's positions and beliefs. Similarly, it seems mistaken to avoid voluntary casual activities, when we know that such events can be conducive to learning.

Fake News and Academic Freedom

The question of academic freedom becomes more complex when we move beyond the classroom to consider what we allow or forbid on our campus at large. I am not particularly concerned with flamboyant speakers who espouse values that run counter to my core beliefs. Rather, what troubles me greatly are those who engage in the extreme version of what has come to be called fake news.

Alex Jones and his Infowars website is perhaps the best known of the perpetrators of conspiracy theories that generate millions of listeners. Among others, Jones and his ilk have popularized the idea that Sandy Hook was a government conspiracy and no children were slaughtered that day. Although they tend to believe that there was a massacre at Stoneman Douglas High School in Florida, they have perpetuated the narrative that many of the students who have spoken out against gun violence, in particular David Hogg, are paid actors. Some other popular ideas are that Hillary Clinton ran a pedophile ring in the basement of a pizza parlor in Washington, DC; Barack Obama was the head of Al-Qaeda; the Boston Marathon bombing, like 9/11, was an inside job, and the government uses juice boxes to make kids gay.

Such ideas are laughable. Unfortunately, millions of people listen to Jones and read his broadsheets daily. Many conservatives make use of his information and do not verify the ideas; they simply spread them by saying, "Some are suggesting that in a pizzeria in Washington, DC . . ." To be fair, many conservatives disavow his ideas.

I do not believe these sorts of individuals and their ideas constitute much of an issue with regard to academic freedom. Although I believe that climate change is real and caused by human activity, support the rights of Palestinians, have benefited from gay marriage, and share any number of positions with progressive thinkers, I also believe we can have thoughtful discussions about the utility of having controversial speakers who fundamentally disagree with a position I hold and then invite those speakers to campus.

What I cannot countenance, however, are individuals who put forward crackpot ideas with no basis in fact that harm people. Although

I'm distressed to be labeled a deviant by those who believe homosexuality is a sin, I can at least understand how such mistaken notions may have been derived, and I am willing to air those views on campus. But I cannot stomach the idea that parents of children murdered at Sandy Hook should be subjected to the accusation that they are part of a government conspiracy, or that a kid who has the courage to speak up after his friends were murdered at a high school in Florida should be accused of being an actor, or that 9/11 was a government conspiracy.

Academic freedom, at its core, is about the search for truth. Conspiracies are in the search for an audience that generates income for the perpetrators, or they are the delusional thoughts of individuals in need of psychiatric help. They have nothing to do with academic freedom, and to claim that they do makes a mockery of the very real dilemmas that we face.

The Monetary Cost of Free Speech

Until recently, most of the arguments for and against free speech pertained to the idea of whether there were limits on free speech and whether individuals had an unfettered right to say whatever they wanted to say on campus. More recent discussions have revolved around codes and locations. *Speech codes*, university policies that attempt to define which forms of expression are both allowed and prohibited, have been attempted on multiple campuses, both public and private. The struggle is to balance the idea of academic freedom with attempts, largely by student affairs and the general counsel's offices, to restrict hateful speech. The assumption is that just as the designation *hate crime* is used as a legal weapon to prosecute crimes against individuals who are members of protected categories, so too should hate speech be limited on a college campus. Hate speech codes, however well intended, have mostly failed, since the courts tend to see such efforts as restrictions of free speech.

Some campus administrations also have tried to cordon off free speech. They might decide that students and others in the community have a right to exercise free speech but need to apply in advance for a permit to speak. This point has less to do with restricting free speech, they will say, and more to do with campus safety. Others have said that free speech exists on campus but can only take place in free speech zones, not unlike the arrangement in London at Hyde Park Corner or (with prior registration) Singapore's Speakers' Corner. Still others have defined the parameters of the event where free speech will take place. In the free speech zone, individuals might condemn the administration or protest against a particular action, but they could not do so outside of that zone. Without augmentation, the ability of a speaker or group to express their opinions to a large crowd is minimal. This geographic framing of academic freedom has been generally successful, unless there is a major uproar on campus where the campus convulses on an issue. Administrations prefer not to arrest students for failure to secure permits or for movement outside of a free speech zone. Who wants to have their campus flashed on television and the internet, with young kids being tackled and thrown into vans by helmeted police?

Over the last few years, however, the free speech issue has taken on a monetary toll. The events at the University of California (UC) in Berkeley are instructive. Milo Yiannopoulos was a writer at a conservative website and a provocative comedian. His various appearances on the UC campus brought out not only his supporters and detractors but also individuals and groups on the ideological extremes. Protestors caused $100,000 in damage the first time he appeared. Coincidentally, at the same time, the administration needed to lay off about 500 staff members because of budget shortfalls.[10]

In a subsequent event, the university was adamant that the scheduled event would take place, and they were willing to spend more than a million dollars to enable Yiannopolous's conference to be held. Carol Christ, chancellor of the university, again announced budget cuts of more than $20 million for the 2017–2018 academic year.[11]

A university the size of UC Berkeley, with a long tradition of supporting free speech, typically allocates about a quarter of a million dollars for security. But the university spent more than $2 million during the various performances of Mr. Yiannopolous and his friends. The president of the UC system, Janet Napolitano, offered another quarter of a million to the beleaguered campus, saying, "It's a cost that the university is bearing to protect the speakers but also to protect the value of free speech."[12]

These are admirable sentiments, but are they affordable? The UC system, not unlike other public and private institutions, is struggling to make ends meet. At one point, UC Berkeley had a budget deficit of $150 million and a governor who was not very sympathetic to providing extra funds from the state.[13] Should a university fall on its fiscal sword to defend academic freedom at any cost?

Those who support Mr. Yiannopoulos, or Nazi storm troopers such as Richard Spencer, point the finger and shout invectives at liberal snowflakes on campuses who simultaneously melt because of the speakers' offensive statements. According to Yiannopolous and Spencer supporters, the problem lies with the liberals and the anti-fascist left, Antifa, who will try to shut down speakers such as Nazis by any means necessary: if they just let speakers speak, there would be no problem.

Those who are most vociferous in protesting the likes of Yiannopoulos and Spencer claim that there need to be limits to free speech and blame these speakers for inciting violence. Similar to how I argued that those who support conspiracies (such as a secretary of state running a pedophile ring in the basement of a pizza parlor) have no relation to academic freedom, some will say that Richard Spencer spouting Nazi ideology or Yiannopoulos hurling epithets about lesbians or transgender people ought not be conflated with exercising academic freedom.

I have no problem with conflict where individuals disagree with one another in a manner that provokes thoughtful dialogue. I am concerned, however, with a learning environment where individuals feel threatened. On one level, I assume that virtually all of us will agree that physical violence is unacceptable. The purpose of academic freedom is in part to foster learning. The point of keeping postsecondary institutions safe is so that learning might occur. When physical violence occurs, the learning environment has evaporated.

The UC Berkeley experience seems to have perverted the ability to learn. The cost for security was real in the sense that it could have been spent on something else. And the redirected security detail had other effects. For example, a lecture by Anna Tsing, a well-respected anthropologist, was rescheduled because the campus did not think individuals could safely make their way across campus.[14] What is the fiscal and psychic cost of enabling someone to speak if it means that normal campus activities are replaced by those of a police state?

I appreciate the difficulty and complexity of deciding which campus speakers are able to speak and which are not. We cannot base our decisions on whether we agree or disagree with the speech, but rather whether their words contribute to a greater intellectual discourse on campus. Ann Coulter, Steve Bannon, David Horowitz, and Ben Shapiro are all extremely conservative ideologues with whom I agree on virtually nothing. I am dismayed that we are still debating climate change, and there are still those in the United States who look on homosexuality as morally repugnant. But their ideas are informed (or misinformed, in my opinion) by a particular line of intellectual thought.

Yiannopoulos has no informed opinion. Simply stringing words together, or shouting epithets, or perpetuating conspiracy theories is not the stuff of academic freedom. When we create an intellectual umbrella that encompasses everything, we debase the idea of academic freedom. We bankrupt the university not only fiscally but also morally.

On Censoring Others and Oneself

We all have moments when we censor ourselves. We generally do not blurt out "what a horrible-looking outfit" to a colleague. We teach our children when and when not to speak out of turn. Numerous times during every day, we think twice about what we are going to say for any number of reasons: we wish to be polite; we don't want to engage in an argument; we don't want to offend someone; we want to move the conversation along to another topic.

We have to recognize, however, that censorship on a college campus is not simply about being polite. Some countries prescribe the social and political mores that are enabled or disabled on college campuses. After the failed coup in Turkey, the universities were targeted. Numerous academics have detailed the extreme care they take in what they say to one another. In Malaysia, because of the pervasive influence of Islam, female academics, even those who are not Muslim, feel pressured to wear a headscarf to avoid harassment. In Saudi Arabia, no one would ever speak against the royal family on a university campus. In India, the screening of various movies and texts has been banned because they offend the religious beliefs of a certain conservative strain of Hinduism. Chinese universities do not allow Facebook on their campuses. An academic at Hong Kong University is under attack for suggesting the island might consider independence from China and become more like Singapore.

Self-censorship, and the censorship of others, also has occurred on US campuses throughout our history. When the American Association of University Professors began in the early twentieth century, it investigated infringements on academic freedom. Some years ago, I examined what those cases entailed; curiously, I never found a case where, in over the past half century, someone's academic freedom was hurt either because the person was gay or because the individual tried to present a pro-gay perspective. Clearly, there were gay people on campuses, and by the 1930s, there was a growing body of research that worked toward lessening the stigma around homosexuality. In spite of this, people censored themselves because they knew the consequences of coming out.

Anyone who has worked on a college campus is aware of how individuals will censor themselves and others for either well-intended or perverse reasons. We suggest to assistant professors that they may not want to argue a specific point because it may annoy someone and jeopardize their chances for tenure. Tenured faculty are often on the lookout for the next promotion, prize, or symbolic gift, which makes them hesitate to speak their minds. More pernicious are those moments when a campus or school initiative ought to be challenged, but individuals fail to speak because they fear some real or imagined retribution. In countries such as Turkey or Saudi Arabia, those penalties are genuine and could result in expulsion from the university and a prison term or worse.

For the record, I have generally spoken out on my own college campus and not suffered any particular penalties (that I know of). I have viewed tenure as the protection of academic freedom, which enables scholars to speak out on issues. During my own time in academe, however, I have seen that even if there are structural protections, a university's culture circumscribes what one says and does. To be sure, when I am on a campus in a foreign country, I adapt to the mores of that country. My words and behavior were distinctly different in Malaysia and India from that of my home campus in the United States.

The result is that academic freedom is a social construction that gets defined first by a nation and then on a campus. And we would be foolish to assume that academic freedom is precisely defined from campus to campus, regardless of nation. Indeed, even in the Unites States, there are significant differences with regard to how institutions define academic freedom.

One irony is that those on the right often are the most ardent critics of free speech limitations, on the basis that they infringe on conservative ideas. These critics point to legitimate cases where conservative intellectuals may have been banned or harassed from speaking on a campus, or less legitimate cases, such as Richard Spencer not being able to speak without protests erupting about his love for Nazism at the University of Florida.

However, the most severe cases of the infringement of academic freedom occur not because of liberals, but because of conservative beliefs. Shane Claiborne, for example, is a Christian pacifist. I disagree with many of his ideas, including his opposition to abortion. However, like me, he is also opposed to the death penalty, and he is a proponent for immigrant rights. Although he had tried to work and pray with Reverend Jerry Falwell at Liberty University, Claiborne was threatened with arrest and a $2,500 fine if he set foot on the Liberty campus.[15] A Liberty student who is an assistant news editor for the university paper, the *Liberty Champion*, asked Falwell for a statement about the incident, and he responded with the following: "Let's not run any articles about the event. That's all these folks are here for—publicity. Best to ignore them."[16]

Numerous Christian institutions would never allow a speaker on campus to offer a dispassionate analysis on any number of issues. At a Christian college, a sociology department that invited someone to speak about the challenges gay people face would never be countenanced. Some years ago, I did a case study of a Christian university in the northwest, and it was quite open about what it would and would not allow. The university conceded that someone might be allowed to speak about abortion, but only within a framework that it was evil. Cedarville University in Ohio fired two philosophy professors because they penned an editorial against the candidacy of Mitt Romney.[17] Faculty on other campuses are fired because they are deemed to be insufficiently pro-life, or antigay, or not strict enough in their adherence to Christian doctrine of the religion of that particular institution.

Larycia Hawkins, a professor at Wheaton College in Illinois, donned a hijab and claimed that Muslims and Christians were all brothers and sisters and worshipped the same God. She lost her job because her statement contravened Christian doctrine.[18] Gay rights groups have been arrested at Baylor University and Brigham Young University because of what they wanted to say, not because of their actions.[19]

Private universities have some discretion in how they frame their activities and free speech stances. However, the examples that get discussed frequently revolve around much more than the public–private distinction. Conservatives are just as concerned about Harvard and Stanford as they are about UC Los Angeles and UC Berkeley. Fair enough. But in that case, we also need to look at these abuses of academic freedom that occur at the thousand private Christian institutions in the United States.

The result of shutting speech down has cascading consequences. Universities are supposed to stand for free inquiry. Cardinal Newman's invocation of the university never mentioned academic freedom or free speech, but his conception of the university's purpose and role was clear. Academics debate and study controversies, and universities, at their best, are arenas where disagreement occurs. Individuals have different interpretations of particular phenomena and ideas; through discourse, we strive to understand an issue better tomorrow than we do today. When we do not have such conversations, then the university ought to be seen as a failure—not only to itself but to the larger society.

I am troubled that it seems we are moving in the exact wrong direction from where we should be with regard to this essential function of the academy. We discuss academic freedom when a crisis arises, such as the unfortunate occurrences at the University of Virginia with the Nazis or the circus at Berkeley when Milo Yiannopoulos came to speak. But we also exist in a polluted democratic environment soiled by Trumpism where disagreements mean we not only disagree with an individual but should not speak with one another. In essence, we work from the stance that the individual with whom I disagree is my enemy.

Those who disagree with Trumpism, or an agenda of right-wing extremism, curiously come to a similar conclusion with regard to academic freedom. The literature about microaggressions fosters a singular narrative about how to speak about an issue. Because most faculty are not trained in the dynamics of provoking and enabling dialogue, the result is one of avoidance. Rather than raise difficult topics, we avoid them—just as we are doing with regard to conservative speakers. We find ways to marginalize provocative dialogue because we worry about the consequences of enabling such conversations.

Three critical steps need to be taken. First, as participants in higher education, collectively we have to acknowledge that in this climate, academic freedom is at the lowest point it has been in our lifetimes, and we have to work assiduously to protect it. Faculty need to reclaim the radical center and foster dialogues where they disagree with one another and invite provocative thinkers with whom they disagree. A rigorous intellectual environment needs to embrace disagreement rather than shy away from it.

Second, collectively we need to be clearer about how we define academic freedom and free speech. This is an essential issue not only for those of us who work on college campuses but also for those of us who are educators. The rejection of the request (or demand) for someone to speak on campus does not automatically mean that academic freedom has been infringed but rather that some individuals have nothing to add to the serious exchange of ideas that characterizes an intellectual community. When we allow all speakers on a campus, we demean the idea of the search for truth.

On a national level, such civil discussion is even more difficult. If we dare to speak up, we tend to speak about issues on our campuses and ignore what happens elsewhere. That's a mistake. Private institutions obviously vary tremendously and have their own cultures and ideologies. But I do not believe that academics should simply look the other way when the academic freedom of our colleagues on other campuses is shortchanged because of a stifling intellectual culture. We also need to be clearer that intellectual rigidity is much greater on the right than on the left—and it is the faculty's obligation to fight it wherever we may find it.

This is also necessary at the international level. Faculty are inherently introspective; most of us go about our business and are more prone to look inward than outward. The violations that occur with regard to academic freedom, however, require us to speak out when academics are threatened on foreign campuses. We ought not collectively shrug our shoulders when a professor is jailed in Turkey and denied a lawyer or a professor is whipped in Saudi Arabia because of what he said in a blog. While I appreciate that cultures vary, I reject that academics throughout the world have nothing to say when a colleague's life is put at risk simply because the individual said or wrote something that angers the authorities. The obligation of the intellectual is not only to search for truth but also to support others in their search, regardless of geographic location.

Third, on an individual basis we need to take more responsibility not only for our own words but also for the conduct of all of us on our campuses. I mentioned earlier that the current climate in academe is the most fraught I have found in more than a quarter century. The temptation is to keep one's head low. To dodge controversy, however, is the exact opposite of what we should be doing. When we avoid speaking up because we fear what someone will say or we let intellectual blowhards claim the intellectual space in our school, department, or institution, we demean the purpose of academic life.

CHAPTER 9

Goodbye, Mr. Chips

Why Tenure Came into Existence

The concept of tenure can be traced to the traditions of academic free-dom and university life. Once academic freedom was recognized as a cornerstone of scholarly life, professors needed a corresponding structure to ensure neither internal nor external interference in their daily affairs. As a result, the American Association of University Professors (AAUP) published a *Declaration of Principles* in 1915 that contended the "dignity" of professors' work required the "security of tenure."[1] Although the con-cept was not well defined at the time, tenure eventually allowed faculty to interrogate important questions in their disciplines, write about new research developments, and critique their colleagues' work without fear of losing their jobs.

Throughout the twentieth century, both tenure and academic free-dom were frequently tried in the US court system. Courts have regularly affirmed the value of both concepts, with the Supreme Court writing that "our Nation is deeply committed to safeguarding academic freedom, which is of transcendent value to all of us and not merely to the teachers concerned."[2] The transcendent value of academic freedom is in its affir-mation of individual rights and its commitment to the search for truth in a nation where democratic principles are vital to the national discourse.

Before tenure was established in US higher education, professors were hired and fired as administrators saw fit. In the nineteenth century, most faculty did not have contracts, their salaries were low, and teach-ing constituted the bulk of their daily work. Those few faculty members who did have contracts were subject to terms dictated by the institution's president. Faculty senates, as well as promotion and tenure committees, did not yet exist.

Although hindsight is always twenty-twenty, one should not have been surprised to find that a crisis erupted in the early twentieth century over the nature of faculty work. Nationwide, the size of the faculty had more than doubled. Faculty from the United States returned from Europe with a desire for greater autonomy in their work. Professional associations began to take hold. The professorate became interested in research. At the same time, college presidents still ruled in a manner to which they had been accustomed, and authority remained vested at the top of the organization. Conflict was inevitable.

As I noted in the previous chapter, the violations of professors' academic freedom (from Ely to Ross) between 1890 to 1915 are legendary and well documented. One result of all these occurrences was the creation of the AAUP with John Dewey as its first president. Dewey initially approached the creation of a group of university professors "as an association representing the interests of US university teachers, comparable to the US Bar Exam or medical associations."[3] Professor Dewey did not envision the association as a labor union and, interestingly, did not consider the protection of academic freedom a top priority of the AAUP. He believed the role of the association was to promote scholarship to the US public.

In his inaugural address to the AAUP, Dewey rejected the notion that the need to investigate violations of academic freedom was of chief importance. Nevertheless, during its first two years, the AAUP dealt with more than thirty cases of infringements on academic freedom; Dewey subsequently acknowledged his initial misconception. He also recognized that an investigation was not simply intended to remedy a specific incident. Rather, Dewey understood that infringing on an individual's academic freedom was tantamount to an attack on the academy itself. The result was the invention of tenure, or lifetime employment.

By the end of the twentieth century, more than 95 percent of all traditional postsecondary institutions in the United States had some form of tenure.[4] Modifications had occurred to the tenure system, such as longer probationary periods, posttenure review, and family-friendly tenure-clock policies where an individual gets a set amount of time after the birth of a child, for example. Nevertheless, by the beginning of the twenty-first century, tenure as a structure looked pretty much like it had for a half century. Although individuals occasionally bemoaned tenure for its inefficiencies, more often than not, after consideration and research, tenure was reaffirmed as a bulwark for academic freedom.

Over time, individuals explicitly or implicitly agreed on six core assumptions about tenure. First, tenure was a structure of and for the institution. Tenure placed the onus on the institution to protect academic freedom.

Second, tenure provided academic freedom not only to those who held it but to those who did not as well. The assumption was that when individuals held tenure, they were able to speak out on behalf of others and thereby ensure the protection of academic freedom as an institutional belief. This assumption has been attacked by many individuals, especially early career faculty, who point out that tenured faculty can be an obstacle to academic freedom. There can be a sense, for example, that those who vote on one's tenure assume assistant professors will teach lower-level courses and not challenge senior faculty. The overwhelming rise of nontenure-track faculty points out the problem of the few protecting the many.

Third, tenure decisions are determined by tenured faculty. The assumption is that the quality of a scholar's work should be the only determining factor for earning tenure, not that individual's opinions or whether the person is liked or disliked.

Fourth, and relatedly, tenure enables faculty to assume some sort of role in governance and control over the institution, especially in aspects such as the curricula and admissions. If the raison d'etre of the institution is academic freedom, then those who are best able to ensure its survival are the tenured professors who can govern it.

Fifth, tenure is a contract for life. Once one has tenure, term limits do not apply. Although a great deal of discussion has recently turned on the idea of posttenure review, the vast majority of effort has considered how to help tenured faculty develop (rather than question whether tenure should have term limits or how to remove tenure from faculty).

The sixth assumption is that tenure means not only that an individual has a lifetime contract but also that the individual has a salary attached to that contract.

Permit me also to point out three details about what tenure is not. First, tenure is not a sinecure for intellectuals or guaranteed lifetime employment free of any responsibilities. Tenure is inevitably attached to the idea of academic freedom. A tenured professor's responsibility is to search for truth and to ensure that others can search as well.

Second, tenure does not give individuals carte blanche to express whatever they wish to say or write as a university professor. If my area of expertise is educational policy, I do not have the right to campaign for a presidential candidate in my classroom based on the candidate's position on global warming. If I write an op-ed and attach my institutional affiliation to my name, I cannot claim my academic expertise enables me to assert anything if the article does not fall within my domain of expertise.

Third, tenure does not give individuals the right to say that they want to teach only on Tuesdays, or that because they are tenured, they will not teach undergraduates, or that they have decided only to teach one course in a given year. Tenure is related to an individual's ability to seek truth and to speak about the life of the institution.

A generation ago, a contract with the university was a relatively casual affair. The general counsel's office on a campus was primarily a lawyer who served on staff or on contingency. An initial offer letter may have served as the only formal agreement a faculty member ever received. Every summer, the individual found out informally what the raise pool would be. Although merit raises always have existed, the norm was that either someone's salary went up by steps or what one individual received was the same for everyone else. The step scale was akin to being on a perpetual escalator that only went up, albeit slowly. The raise pool assumed that everyone deserved a raise. On rare occasions, an individual may have committed a transgression such that his or her salary was not increased, or an individual might win an important prize and find his or her salary increased significantly, but the general culture of higher education fostered a belief in measured annual raises.

If professors were to say that they had tenure, then the assumption was that they received a full salary from tenure. Individuals might earn additional income in the summer, or they might consult every now and then, but their base salary derived from the institution.

Over time, of course, conditions changed. Informal agreements became formalized. Offer letters also had contracts attached to them. Merit pay became more the norm than the exception. Stipulations about how much consulting an individual could do—or how much an individual could earn in the summer—became standardized. Significant discrepancies occurred across disciplines and departments. Business school professors earned more than their counterparts in philosophy or education. However, an individual's base salary was still tied to the institution because of the obligation of tenure. When individuals stated that they had tenure, the implicit fact was that they received a core salary from the institution. But increasingly, we are seeing a change in the overall percentage of faculty who hold tenure-track appointments.

Why Tenure Is Going Away

When I started at the University of Southern California a quarter of a century ago, 80 percent of the faculty in my school was tenure-track, and 20 percent was nontenure-track. Today, the situation has flipped. Now, not only is 80 percent of the faculty nontenure track but we have many part-time workers. Let's first consider why these changes have occurred and then whether the changes have made the academy stronger.

Conspiracy theorists often allege a plot is afoot, as if all administrators gather at American Council on Education meetings and decide to move away from hiring tenure-track faculty to increase their administrative power. I don't think that's it at all, even though the increase of administrative control has been one outcome. Instead, these decisions are made unit by unit, dean by dean across campuses and the country.

Why the shift? Ostensibly, we have fewer resources to meet the needs of running the institution. Public institutions, in general, are receiving fewer public dollars today than a generation ago. There is no precise date to point to declining academic dollars, but the Reagan era cemented a public philosophy that fewer public resources are a good thing, and tax cuts are even better.[5] The neoliberal agenda has put forward the idea that the less dollars for the public sector, the better. There is no honest research that suggests a decline in taxes increases public coffers, but that is the mantra that has been sold throughout my time in academe. The result is that we have fewer dollars to spend on all public investments—roads, schools, public safety—and our colleges and universities.

Insofar as most public dollars come from the state, rather than the federal government, we find academic institutions fighting over scraps with those who want prenatal care, health care, and better care for the homeless. It's a hard sell when the public's portrait of academe is of faculty who get to take the summer's off, even if that's no longer the case.

An additional issue for most public institutions pertains to pensions. Some pensions make sense; others do not. Frequently, the projections that administrators and unions inked out to develop a pension plan assumed absurdly high interest rates on an annual basis that enabled them to draw up absurdly high pension plans. One does not need to have a Nobel Prize in economics to know that, over the long haul, a system is not sustainable if people can earn more than 100 percent of their salary for a decade or more after retiring, and the revenue coming in does not match the revenue going out. Nonetheless, that has occurred in some instances, resulting in even fewer public dollars available for the university's operating expenses.

At the same time that public dollars have declined, administrations have grown dramatically, and senior administrative salaries have increased. Both changes are understandable, but lamentable. One of the first lessons anyone learns from reading Max Weber is that bureaucracy rationalizes itself.[6] I hire someone to oversee communications in the Pullias Center. The individual is energetic and hardworking and makes the case that we need to hire an assistant communications director. We hire an assistant communications director who also is ambitious; over time, they point out that we need someone to deal with social media, as well as print, plus a coordinator. And so it goes.

It is also true that we live in a litigious and regulatory environment, and a greater cost has to ensure that the institution and its members are neither sued nor out of compliance. The result is fewer resources for the institution to spend on other cost items, such as tenure-track faculty.

Coupled with the increases in bureaucracy and regulation are gigantic increases in administrative salaries. At no time in the past century has the discrepancy between the highest paid officials and the incoming assistant professor been greater. In many respects, the earnings differential between the wealthiest and poorest among us in an organization simply mirrors what is taking place within society. The top 1 percent of academe's earners are making more; the bottom 10 percent are earning less. Such a fact is lamentable in a democratic society, and it is even more lamentable in an environment ostensibly focused on the search for truth.

I'm not interested in arguing the finer points of university budgeting, but in acknowledging that we have less revenue to spend, we are increasingly focused on where we can make additional cuts to cost.

An analogy to the federal government is apt. First, they cut taxes. Then they recognize they do not have the revenue to pay for everything and say they need to cut the budget. They then say that the defense budget is off the table, and they may even increase it, making the budget deficit even more problematic. The result is cutting necessary services.

In academe, there are fewer resources, and they say they need to cut the budget. The articulation of bureaucracy cannot be trimmed. Those who are making the decisions are also the ones who decide their salaries cannot be cut. Where to cut? We outsource custodial jobs, resulting in miniscule cost savings and significant pay cuts to the poorest workers. We switch from an environment of tenure-track faculty to nontenure-track faculty.

This results in significant cultural changes for the organization. Many nontenure-track faculty actually want full-time permanent employment. Even though they have to teach a great deal more and do less research, they still want to be involved in the life of their schools and universities. Consequently, we see the augmentation of service-related activities over relatively meaningless tasks to give the appearance of faculty involvement in decision-making. Because individuals do not have tenure, they refrain from making their opinions clear on important issues, lest they face nonrenewal.

I am aware of no one who will argue that teaching is better today than when I entered academe. I am not blaming nontenure-track faculty for the decline in academic standards. Structures matter. The replacement of permanent with temporary faculty has achieved one goal: it has helped institutions balance their budgets. Balanced budgets have come at the expense of quality.

Much has been written about the decline in tenure-track faculty and the poorer quality of life that nontenure-track faculty have. Very little commentary, however, has been made about the impact nontenure-track faculty have had on academic freedom.

Three responses are possible. First, a structure always can be replaced with a better structure. It's entirely possible that in the interest of protecting academic freedom, a better arrangement than tenure could be put forward, and tenure would no longer be necessary. Unfortunately, no such structure has been suggested. The movement away from tenure has had nothing to do with improving the protections for academic freedom; instead, it has resulted in its weakening.

A second possibility is that the particular idea that has made the structure necessary is no longer needed, in which case the structure can be eliminated. Surely, academic freedom is still necessary insofar as we have numerous, seemingly daily, cases that lessen the ability of people to search for truth—the sine qua non of academic life. In an era where fake news bombards us on a daily basis, faculty work ought to be even more important than in the past with regard to explaining what is real and what is fake.

The third possibility is the likeliest culprit in the demise of the structure of academic freedom, and of academic life. Neither the faculty nor the administrators have made a good enough case about the import of academic values. As long as we argue over budgeting or our own individual benefit at the expense of the good of the academic community, we place our collective values at risk. Perhaps tenure has failed as a structure because we have not done a good job at protecting what it ostensibly safeguards. In this case, the failure is not in the structure but in those of us who are faculty who use the structure.

The Color of the Academy

Even before the rise of US higher education after World War II, the twentieth century professorate was more alike than dissimilar. Faculty may not have held tenure, but they were likely full-time professors. They were also usually white and male. They spent their lives teaching but came to accord research higher status. Although slight shifts have occurred, the professorate is still overwhelmingly white and male. During that time, the makeup of the students has changed considerably. We can bemoan that the student body is still too white or Asian American, that too many upper-class students attend elite institutions, and that low-income, first-generation students are overrepresented in community colleges. Even within the institutions, we know that white and Asian American students take majors with higher earning power than those majors where we find students of color and low-income.

As I noted, a college degree generally provides a better income than not having a college degree. A more elite institution generally enables students to earn higher incomes than open-access institutions. Sure, discrepancies exist. Whenever I speak with those individuals who wish to debate the finer points of college-going, however, I always ask them to speak about their own children. Are you saying that you won't send your son to college? Are you saying it's better for your daughter to start at community college rather than at Stanford? Why has your kid chosen to major in electrical engineering? Tell me about that summer camp you sent your teenagers to where they mixed camping with coursework? Inevitably, the answers are clear. If those who are middle and upper class, as well as college educated, want the best for their own children, then what do we need to do to ensure the best for all of the children of the United States?

Although we can't say that all students would succeed if we simply placed them with a teacher of the same race (or class, or sexual orientation, or gender), there is growing research to support the theory that the teacher's implicit biases can inform the learning of the student. As I mentioned in chapter 7, the research is not determinative, and we cannot make simplistic statements such that a student who is black and has a black teacher will succeed.[7] If such a fact were true, then teaching would be much easier—and much harder. We know that one's racial identity informs the learning environment. It is one factor that we need to take into account. If the fact was certain, then all students would succeed if we simply placed them with a same race (or class, or sexual orientation, or gender) teacher. We also know, however, that preparation and content matter factors into the learning environment.

If we harken back to my painful learning experience in that graduate seminar many years ago, it seems possible that the class may have been less painful if the professor had been gay. While we can't know how a gay professor might have handled my classmate's comment, one might hope that a homophobic comment would have elicited some commentary from the instructor.

To say that an instructor's background informs learning is not to insist that identity trumps everything else. We know that the environment is shifting with regard to who gets hired and on which contracts. Just as race matters with regard to learning, so does the stability of the workforce. A constantly shifting contingent workforce weakens the learning environment regardless of race, gender, or sexual orientation.

However, the background of the faculty cannot be discounted. As the student body becomes more diverse, so must the faculty. Biases, both real and implicit, are baked into our lives. We can and must try to overcome those biases, which requires first that we acknowledge they exist and, next, that we expand our communities to include individuals of different backgrounds and life experiences. Not only does teaching and learning in the classroom shift when students experience a diverse faculty but the sorts of conversations, curricula, and short- and long-range plans also change to become more dynamic and inclusive. Simple tests have taken place that highlight the problems again and again. A resume is sent to potential graduate professors asking if they would mentor a student; the student's name is Robert Smith; the same resume is sent, and the student's name is Roberto Gonzalez. Who do you think gets chosen more often? The same is true with potential employers. A resume is sent and the potential employee's name is either Robert Smith or Roberta Smith. Again, who do you think gets chosen more often?

Change does happen. When my mother went to Fordham University, she wanted to major in math and was told that girls could not, because they were not good in math. She persisted. The department chair finally relented, and she was the first woman to major in math; she graduated third in her class. It's comforting to know that we can look back and shake our heads and acknowledge that such limitations could never happen today.

Yet, these changes often feel glacial. I have consulted with numerous faculty who are predominantly or exclusively white. I have visited campuses where LGBTQ+ flags or notifications are nowhere to be found. I have spoken in schools or colleges of engineering where less than 10 percent of the faculty are women, and frequently those women are from Asia. Many of us are impatient for change, and we should be. The challenge is that our impatience can either depress us or enable us to make unforced errors.

The sense that change is never going to happen can lead to a crippling sense of defeatism that forces us into isolation, even nihilism. At the other end is the assumption that race trumps everything else. We will have a speaker series and only invite faculty of color, or we will state that we are only interested in hiring individuals of a particular race or gender. I appreciate the need and desire. I am hard-pressed to understand what happened when I look at a faculty's last half dozen hires and see that no person of color made the cut. Each time, I hear numerous rationalizations about why the isolated hire had to be a white male, but when I add up the hires to discover that the result is an all-white faculty, it's clear the organization has a cultural problem. One reflexive strategy is then to say that we will only hire African American faculty or only Latinx women, which, if not handled correctly, will end up being one of those unforced errors I just mentioned.

Alternatively, we see a climate of duck and cover. Faculty do not think a particular decision should be made, such as a hiring initiative aimed at a particular group, or a curricular change that tries to be more explicit about racism, but they do not want to be labeled racist or sexist or obstructionist, so they simply avoid getting involved. Such a climate, and the ensuing postures, presents roadblocks to the sort of organization that I'm trying to foster in the twenty-first century. To move forward, we need to hold discussions about difficult topics, including thorny issues pertaining to identity. We need to make space for open dialogue and disagreement and move away from a certain intellectual fascism where an individual might blurt out a statement that, rather than provoking thoughtful debate, shuts down discussion.

So, where are we? Let's jump forward a decade. If there are not significantly more tenured faculty, faculty of color, and women in the sciences than there are today, the academy will be weaker. If Black students still are underrepresented then the academy will have fallen short yet again.

As I stated earlier, tenure protects academic freedom. We have created no other structure that provides the protections that tenure afford faculty. If you believe, as I do, that academic freedom is essential for the health and well-being of the institution and of society, then having a substantial number of tenured faculty is essential. The continued slide toward contingent faculty may have a basis in budgeting, but that is a canard. Fewer tenure-track faculty make the institution less able to promote academic freedom.

Fewer tenure-track faculty also make the institution pedagogically weaker. As individuals, contingent faculty are not to blame. Their pay-for-performance is the culprit. We know that student engagement with the campus and with the faculty is more likely to produce better outcomes. Hence, paying an individual to teach courses like piecework belies the kind of creative engagement that campuses actually need. Contractual obligations defined principally by contact hours defeats the idea of an engaged campus with engaged intellectuals.

Similarly, a lack of progress with regard to diversifying the faculty would be a tragedy, regardless of the makeup of the student body. All students benefit by learning from instructors whose backgrounds are both similar and different from their own. Insofar as the student body is likely to grow increasingly diverse, it is imperative to ensure that more faculty come from diverse backgrounds. We need women scientists not only for women undergraduate and graduate students but also for their male counterparts.

CHAPTER 10

Paying for College

Understanding Costs

If I had taken a college knowledge quiz when I was applying to college, I would have failed. I could not have discerned the difference between a public and private institution, much less what a for-profit meant. I had no idea what the cost of college was, I did not worry about loans, and I could not have explained what a grant was. An income never went into my calculus about whether I should go to college or not.

My family never made it to the upper class, and by the end of my college years, we were sliding into the lower middle class, but money for college was never really an issue. My parents instilled in us a work ethic. During high school, my brothers and I worked in the summer. I cut lawns and gardened and made two dollars per hour. I'm not entirely sure what my parents would have said if I did not work, but we were not a family who *needed* their youngest kid to earn money. I never thought I was earning money to pay for college; I was saving it for some amorphous reason. When I went to college, I took a job for a few hours a week where I worked in the library, but even that money was simply to have some spare change for the weekend. During the summers of my college years, I worked most of the summer, then traveled for a little bit as well. While I worried about the academic side of college, my parents took care of the cost. I graduated from college debt free and never considered how much I might earn upon graduation. The Peace Corps advertised that volunteers earned ten cents an hour.

Pierre Bourdieu, a French sociologist who made famous the idea that individuals functioned in networks that created social and cultural capital, made the most common sense about issues of class in the 1960s and 1970s.[1] Some individuals in one class assumed they had the right to attend college; others in another class did not. Few middle- and upper-class students thought about the cost of college in the 1970s, because it was not prohibitive. And the poor and working-class people did not think about the cost of college either. Those who rent a one-bedroom apartment and have children hope to be able to move into a two-bedroom apartment. They try to save money to make it happen; they may even talk with a loan officer. They save to buy a car or a TV or a refrigerator, not to take a trip to Europe or have lavish dinners. Until about a generation ago, everyone implicitly understood the established order: college was for some and not others.

As I mentioned previously, education always has been seen as the great equalizer. We wanted children to attend grammar school and then high school. We wanted all of children to graduate from high school based on the assumption that, to make it into the middle class, individuals needed a high school degree. By the 1970s, we got it into our collective imagination that college should be available to all people, regardless of class or income—and not just community college, either. Economics didn't enter the discussion; rather, the assumption was that attending college was a cultural good: workers would be better trained, and citizens would be more civically engaged.

Unfortunately, the massification of higher education took hold as the country moved away from a collective embrace of college learning as a public good. Instead, we shifted toward the individualist assumption that if you wanted something, you should pay for it. Regardless of administration, the country has continued to narrow the definition of what we mean by a public good since the 1970s.

In 1977, John Travolta had his breakthrough role as Tony Manero in *Saturday Night Fever*. Tony is from a working-class area of Brooklyn and a good dancer. Throughout the movie, he has an on-again, off-again romance with his girlfriend. At one point, she asks Tony, "Why don't you think about bettering yourself? Have you ever thought of going to college?" Tony stops dead in the Brooklyn street and says, "No. I never thought about it." Tony's response is telling because it highlights the way the working class initially thought about a postsecondary education. His girlfriend's question reflects a cultural shift: by the 1970s, we had begun to think about all of us going to college. She assumes even Tony should have thought about it. He hasn't. If my friends at Horace Greeley High School in Chappaqua, New York, had been asked the same question, they would have answered, "Of course we've thought about it. We're going on college tours and discussing where to go with our friends." If the kids of the parents who bought their way into elite colleges in the 2019 admissions scandal were asked, they undoubtedly would say, "You bet I've thought about it. We talk about it every day."

Working-class kids live in a different world than the one that embraced massification. The cost of a bachelor's degree is a very real issue for individuals thinking about going to college. As more people consider a degree, we have more individuals who need revenue to make that happen. The costs also have risen, and, as with many complex issues, the reasons for that are multiple. There is no singular explanation for rising costs. If the problem was that simple, then we could fix it.

The pandemic has made the situation even more dire. Students have fewer resources to call on, and states have fewer resources to provide. Institutions also took a significant economic hit when they had to move students off campus in 2020, which made the ability for an institution to help students pay for college virtually impossible. Usually, in a recession or depression, more students go to a college or university because they cannot get a job. The reverse may happen over the long-term with regard to the pandemic, although it is possible that some community colleges may hold steady or experience an increase in student enrollment. Students still want a degree, but they cannot afford it.

Administration and administrative salaries have seen inordinate increases. I'll elaborate on that problem in the following chapter. And yet, even if we reduced the salaries of the handful of senior administrators who earn more than a million dollars a year, we would still have trouble balancing collegiate budgets. It's true that bureaucracy has dramatically increased and some staff positions are likely unnecessary, but bloat in administration is also not the central problem. Others will complain about the research infrastructure being too large and not paying for itself; while this point has merit, it alone cannot explain the rise in costs. Conservative critics love to pillory institutions for what they see as absurdly frivolous gewgaws--climbing walls, fancy recreational centers, eateries with sushi chefs, a potpourri of counselors--the reality is that today's consumer (i.e., student) at institutions that have those extravagances expects those goods and services. We once had to pay extra for air conditioning in a car; today, it is basic.

Some will point out the cost of red tape and regulations, and, as with the other points, there is truth in the observation. I have many more hoops to jump through today than when I began a quarter-century ago. We also no longer just arrive at the airport fifteen minutes before the plane takes off, walk up to the gate with our families, kiss them goodbye, and hop on a plane. They don't go back to their car they left at curbside and drive home. Why would we expect our postsecondary institutions to be different from what has happened everywhere else?

The cost to the consumer also has risen because states pay less than they once did. While we can try to parse out precisely which services states are paying for, to the college-goer, that information is irrelevant. That is, some might suggest that the state still pays for teaching services, but other costs have risen for an institution or system. However true that might be, the customer still has to pay for the entire bill. I don't get to say, "I'll pay for the main course, but I'm not paying for the appetizer, sides, dessert, and tip."

The result is that going to college today is not just a cultural decision; it's very much an economic decision as well. Although people have made broad statements about lowering the cost of college, I don't see that happening anytime soon. Sure, the overall cost of college can be reduced if we improve the efficiency of the system. Taking six years to graduate costs more than four. Students who need remedial education pay more for their education. When students drop out and return, or never return, the individual and the system both lose money. And yet, all these inefficiencies will not solve the overarching costs of a postsecondary institution.

At both nonprofit and for-profit institutions, distance learning and online courses have helped only in minimal ways around the edges. Those who proclaimed that the college world was about to undergo a digital revolution, up to now, have been false prophets. Higher education is still a labor-intensive undertaking. We are digitally savvy, but we have not been replaced in a manner that drives down cost.

How Much Is a Degree Really Worth?

Periodically, there are well-documented stories about individuals who either did not go to, or dropped out of, college and accumulated vast wealth. Even though Bill Gates dropped out of Harvard to become, for a time, the world's wealthiest man, he is circumspect and speaks about the importance of a college education. Peter Thiel is more of an iconoclast, arguing that because college wasn't useful for him, it's not useful for others. Bryan Caplan, a radical libertarian economics professor, has written an engaging book about how virtually all of education "is a waste of time and money." He suggests that degrees are "signals" of what one has learned but disputes that anyone really learns anything of value.[2]

Some, like Caplan, acknowledge that vocational training is important, and they have a broad conception of "vocation." Individuals don't go to a training school only to learn a trade like masonry; they can learn medicine as well. However, Caplan has a very narrow definition of what skills should be taught and assumes that values-based learning—old-fashioned citizenship skills—is best left to the family. One might think of his thesis as a human capital argument on steroids: education should train the citizenry, and if they are not going to learn a productive skill, we'd best not waste public funds or personal time on the activity. From this perspective, individuals and their families are responsible for education, and Horace Mann was wrong.

I agree with some of Caplan's ideas about signaling. As a professor, as I've already discussed, I am something of a proxy. When I give a student a good grade, I am attesting that the student is knowledgeable in a particular area. I have written a great many letters of reference over the years where my signature on the University of Southern California letterhead is probably the most important part of the letter. With the signature and the University's logo, I am giving the reference my conferral of authenticity. This is not evidence that the student is knowledgeable; it is merely evidence that I *think* he or she is.

We also know that some people fill positions for which they are overskilled. Certainly, a worker does not need a college degree for delivering pizzas. However, numerous white-collar positions state that candidates should have a bachelor's degree and that an advanced degree is preferred. Does that mean the guy with a master's degree is better qualified for the job? A host of qualities beyond skills also go into hiring. An individual with an advanced degree may be older and more willing to stay in the position than someone who sees the job as a stepping stone to something else. The advanced degree may not make the person more skilled in technique, but it could conceivably make the person more valuable to the company. At the same time, there are jobs that people have which could be held by someone less qualified, and the work could be done adequately. As with all complex issues, it's complicated. When we reduce such issues to an either/or scenario—either one needs to go to college to learn skills for a white-collar job or no one needs to go to college because what's learned is unnecessary—we are forcing people into making an intellectual Hobson's choice.

Learning agricultural techniques from your parents may not adequately equip farmers who face new farming methods. An individual who studies agriculture in school might learn useful new ideas about farming. Fields like agriculture also help individuals learn skills that are more than simply vocational. Farmers may need to adapt to fluctuating environmental conditions, weigh the advantages and disadvantages of various crop rotations and livestock migration patterns, and implement novel innovations in sustainable farming on a monthly, if not daily, basis.[3] A great deal of research continues to come in that points out the importance of not simply learning a specific skill but also developing cultural competencies and higher cognitive skills, such as creativity, complex information processing, and the capacity to adapt to changes in communication technologies.[4] In a democracy, we ought not dismiss the importance of individuals learning how to be civically engaged.

When I work with high school students in low-income schools, I have no problem encouraging them to go to college. I am certain that the vast majority of students will be better off with a college degree than without one. Such an assertion, however, does not come without contingencies. Not all students need to go to college; recall that estimates are about two-thirds of high school graduates need some form of postsecondary education to be viable in the labor market of the twenty-first century. Not all students need a four-year degree either; an associate's degree or a certificate will be sufficient for some forms of employment.

For a study, I've tracked two hundred and fifty students who graduated from a school populated by low-income, first-generation students. More than half of them had been enrolled in community college by their college advisor, but they had no information about what they were getting themselves into or why they should even attend college. Less than half of them remained in college one year after graduation. Those who were not in college were employed, generally in minimum wage jobs: cashiers, stock clerks, and various warehouse-type positions. After two years, they had not received additional training, and all were making less than $30,000 per year. Most lived at home.

There's no question if these students had gotten some type of college degree, they would most likely be better off. Unless, of course, they go into debt. Fear of debt is one key reason twenty-first century students dismiss the idea of going to college. We do not do a very good job of providing students with the financial literacy they need to understand the costs and benefits of debt, and unfortunately, the problems often get portrayed as a victimless crime. Let me offer some real-world examples.

Roberto, one young fellow I've mentored, recently graduated from an elite university with a degree in computer engineering. He will start, at the age of twenty-one years, a job in the Bay Area where he will make $105,000 per year. He earned a number of scholarships and has no debt. He's the rare example of a poor kid who has not had to worry about debt.

Another fellow I met is getting a doctoral degree in the social sciences; he already has a master's degree in education. At the age of twenty-eight years, his accumulated debt is $185,000; his likely earnings are to be slightly south of $100,000. Another individual I mentored has graduated from two elite universities with bachelor's and master's degrees, earns about $50,000 per year and is $25,000 in debt. She will pursue her PhD. Another student earned bachelor's and master's degrees, is very happy teaching middle school math, and has about $50,000 of debt. The final student is the saddest. He went to an elite university, accumulated about $60,000 worth of debt along the way, got his girlfriend pregnant in his junior year of college, had to drop out to help raise his autistic son, has accumulated another $60,000 of debt, and works two jobs to make ends meet. He also is raising his teenage brother since his parents are dysfunctional.

The nonmonetary lessons from these individual cases are instructive. Each of them, for different reasons, enjoyed college and learned a great deal. They were all low-income youth and typical of the students I mentor. They were first in their families to go to college and did not really know what to expect. They worked hard, enjoyed both in-class and out-of-class activities, and eventually figured out what they needed to do to succeed. The engineer graduated with a GPA above 3.5 and was able to concentrate on his studies because he accumulated no debt. All of the others had GPAs above 3.0—even the fellow who had to drop out. With slightly different luck, they all might have been in the same boat as the other students in their class of 2015. Or they all might have been working dead-end jobs and living at home. All but the hard-luck case earned a degree and have jobs that pay more than their colleagues who have not gone to college, though debt affects them in different ways.

What are the implications for these students? The saddest story is the young fellow who has debt totaling $120,000 and has nothing to show for it. Without remarkable good luck, he will not be able to go back to college to earn a degree; he will remain in debt, never own a home, and struggle to support his autistic son. Even now, he is accumulating more credit card debt as he struggles to pay off various loans. The fellow who is getting his PhD and is in debt to the tune of $200,000 is in slightly better shape, but not much. He is most likely not going to earn a sizable salary, and any catastrophe could put him in the same situation as the fellow who dropped out of college. If he has a productive career, then he will eventually pay off his loans. I do not imagine he will own a home. The woman pursuing her PhD with $25,000 in debt is likely to have a good life and has a chance of owning a home; the math teacher may eventually be able to own a home. Other than the young man who dropped out, I expect them to live middle-class lives, but they will likely be less financially secure than my colleagues and I have been. The only individual who seems set for success is the fellow who will be earning more than $100,000 with his bachelor's degree.

Individuals need to make informed choices, and in the twenty-first century, information about the costs and benefits of college is essential. It seems absurd, absent more pertinent data, to suggest that the students I follow who did not go to college are going to be well-off. They are all stuck in low-end, minimum-wage jobs with little hope for advancement. The students I have mentored largely made the choice to attend college, but the consequences of how they paid—and keep paying—for college loom large. To rack up debt and fail to earn a degree is a recipe for disaster. Without better college knowledge (and/or someone to watch over student's plans and the loans he or she accumulate), a student may get a useful degree but remain stuck economically. These students are all in an economically precarious position.

One might bemoan the economic situation that I have painted for these individuals. Although there is a fair amount of reporting pertaining to student debt, I do not think we recognize that the real culprit has less to do with higher education and more to do with the social safety net society has created—or dismembered—for the country's citizens. The neoliberal framework in which we function assumes that massive debt is OK. It is not. We also assume that predator companies can feed on students–consumers so that they rack up enormous debt, and it's the student–consumer's fault. It is not.

Recall that I never worried about what I was going to do upon graduation, and that lack of worry is not because I am a carefree fellow. It also has very little to do with the career counseling I received at Tufts, because I do not think there was any. Rather, I grew up at a time where the social safety net provided me with opportunity—and I did not even need to be aware of those opportunities to afford myself of them. I also grew up in a middle-class family that afforded me enormous benefits. In a democracy, we should look out for everyone.

It is essential for us to ensure that students make informed choices. I am not suggesting that eighteen-year-olds have to understand the intricacies of establishing a 401(k), but they do need more information about the implications of debt in a world where loans are going to be needed to graduate from college. I would prefer an environment where students do not need to take out loans to get a college degree, but if they do, then they need financial literacy. Most individuals who graduate from college eventually want to settle down with a family, own a home, and save for retirement. That is becoming increasingly harder. We need to equip students with the necessary financial literacy so that they can make informed decisions that will be beneficial not only while they are in college but also once they enter the workforce. The challenge, then, is not merely to graduate from college but to accumulate as little debt as possible.

How to Avoid (or at Least Minimize) Debt

I attended a Catholic grammar school. I was the first Tierney to attend a public high school. Although my parents had to pay the tuition to attend St. John and St. Mary's, the cost was a pittance. The place was staffed by nuns and affiliated with the next-door church. When labor costs are low or nonexistent, and the Monsignor shovels the Sunday collection plate and special requests into the educational budget, parents can afford to send their kids to Catholic school. We had to pay for dorky uniforms and a few extra costs, but the price was right for a family raised on saying the rosary during Lent. My mom did not have a paying job, so I stayed home during the summer when I was a little guy in grammar school, and I worked during the high school summers. We usually took a modest vacation for a week or two in July.

There were no costs in Chappaqua's public high school. The physical plant of Horace Greeley was a modernist setting of buildings; the teachers were among the top-paid instructors in New York, and we had a full complement of afterschool activities. I took driver's education, participated in track, wrote for the school newspaper (which had its own offices where the cool kids hung out), and got extra help when I needed it. Virtually everyone went on to a four-year college, and we were ready for it.

The contrast with how education works today sets the stage for a discussion of debt. We have neighbors who send their three kids to a private school because they feel the public schools in Los Angeles are not preparing their children for college. The cost of sending three kids to elementary and middle school is about $130,000 per year. Both parents work so they have to find additional activities for the children in the summer. Because all afterschool activities also cost money, they have to fork out additional dollars for their children to participate in sports, music, and math camp. The private high school where they will send the children has a high college-going rate, whereas the local high school does not—or at least it does not send their graduates to the type of institution they want for their kids.

When the children of these middle-class parents reach college, they almost certainly will have to take out loans. The total cost of attendance at a University of California institution, when all is said and done, is about $40,000 per year. Out-of-staters pay even more. If my neighbors' children go to a private college like the University of Southern California, the cost approaches $80,000. Admissions officers will hasten to point out that the real price is not the real price, and that's part of the problem; paying for tuition can be like buying a used car. There are always special deals where students can get a discount. I honed my bargaining skills as a Peace Corps volunteer in Morocco where we bargained for everything, from the milk at the local store to the rug at the market, but most US residents do not recognize how much one has to bargain his or her way into college. When we were in India, the landlady's son applied to college in the United States. He got his dream school, but they said he had to pay full tuition. I helped him pen one letter and then a second letter saying how much he wanted to attend the institution, but how difficult it would be to pay the tuition. In the first letter, the institution came down in price by about $5,000; in the second letter, they promised him work study, a low-interest loan, and a small grant. He accepted the offer.

Regardless, however much students may get this or that price cut, they are likely to be encumbered by loans unless they are standout students, or their parents are rich. My neighbors' friends' children will likely go into debt upon graduation from college. From 2000 to 2016, the United States had 28 percent more students entering the postsecondary system, which costs more.[5] It is estimated that between 40 to 60 percent of first-year college students are underprepared, which also drives up costs.[6] Most significantly, we have a government that is less willing to shoulder the burden of paying for public goods. In the 1960s, US public capital investment was around 3 percent of GDP; by 2007, the percentage of public capital investment had fallen to 1.7 percent, and by 2014, it was a mere 0.4 percent.[7] The trends are similar for higher education. After adjusting for inflation, researchers have shown that state funding for public higher education in 2017 was $9 billion less than it was in 2008. During that same period, annual tuition at four-year public institutions has risen by 35 percent; in eight states (Alabama, Arizona, California, Colorado, Florida, Georgia, Hawaii, and Louisiana), tuition has risen by more than 60 percent.[8] While not all tuition increases are directly attributable to divestments by state governments (remember the wasteful spending on university recreation centers), they are significantly accountable, and they force the burden of tuition onto the college-goer. Another recent study, in fact, indicates that students enrolling in college after 2000 can expect to pay $318 more in tuition for every $1,000 cut from public funds.[9] Moreover, reductions in state appropriations for higher education have negative effects on almost all of the expenditure functions of a college or university, as well as negative impacts on degree completion, especially at open-access institutions like community colleges.[10]

Many, but not all, of these issues are beyond the province of postsecondary institutions. Higher education cannot control wages in society, what families are able to save and earn, or what the government contributes to public goods. With suppressed wages and the rising cost of living, loans are going to be a fact of college life for the foreseeable future unless a progressive wave sweeps into power and makes free college for all a priority.

First-generation students will not have answers to many of the questions that they are supposed to ask to avoid debt. They do not know the difference between an interest-free loan and one that has high interest. Frequently, they do not even understand the difference between a grant and a loan. Today's students are not unlike I was; they do not really know what they want to do. Yet, because they now worry about salaries, a preponderance of students say they want to major in engineering or the sciences because they think it generates good salaries. When asked, most students cannot define what *good* is, and without knowing how much money they will earn, it's difficult to gauge how much of a loan they should take out.

We do know that indebtedness is rising among our college-age youth and that young black adults incur greater debt burdens than whites.[11] When we couple that with the awareness that salaries are not rising, and benefits are decreasing, it is incumbent on us to recognize the challenges that exist for today's college-going students and help resolve them. The students with whom I have worked largely have a low level of financial literacy. They generally do not know the difference between a grant and a loan, and they frequently see the large basket of revenue that comes their way—scholarships, need-based aid, Pell Grants—as free money. When it comes to loans, they tend not to understand interest or the different payment plans. Some students I have met have extraordinary interest on a credit card—upward of 20 percent. Others do not understand the difference between interest that starts accruing as soon as the loan is taken out as opposed to when the individual graduates from college. Credit card companies look at first-year college students as ripe for the taking. They will send complimentary notes encouraging the individual to take out a credit card because of their "extraordinary potential."

Similarly, the student loan industry has been able to charge interest and make enormous profits from those who take out loans. Similar to other forms of debt, such as mortgages, student loans can be grouped together into larger financial products called *securities*. These student loan asset-backed securities constitute a $200 billion market that attracts prominent financial institutions, such as Bank of America and Wells Fargo. The reason student loan securities are so popular is that student loan borrowers are not able to declare bankruptcy and have their debt forgiven; instead, their wages, unemployment benefits, and even Social Security payments can be garnished. And the federal government is on the hook as well, having insured approximately 80 percent of these student loan securities.[12]

What do we need to do, other than try to reinvigorate the notion of a public good where consumers do not need to go into debt to get the education they need to secure a good job and financial stability? While choosing a college involves a lot of factors—urban or rural, full-time or part-time, humanities or science—there are certain general guidelines that every prospective student should keep in mind.

If a student is intent on receiving a four-year degree and seems likely to complete the degree, then I would be hard-pressed to recommend that the individual start at a community college. Although transfer rates have generally increased and attending a two-year institution is much cheaper, the detours and missteps are too common to recommend a two-year degree with a serious intent to transfer.

There is also a significant difference in the cost of attending a private, rather than a public, institution. If a student is guaranteed graduation within four years, and the private institution has a great deal of available grants, then it's a worthwhile consideration. My biggest caution has to do with for-profit institutions; I would generally steer a student away from attending a for-profit college for the reasons I have outlined in a previous chapter, with the result being the student will accrue too much debt without necessarily earning a degree.

Debt is a gamble. When we incur debt, we do so assuming that whatever good we are buying is either necessary or useful for our lives. However, there is always the possibility that the good will not be useful, and the loan will therefore be a waste of money. My young friend who did not finish college bet that a loan would someday earn him a college degree, which, in turn, would earn him a big salary; it did neither. The fellow who became a math teacher incurred more debt than he should have, and he stumbled a few times, but he has a good job that he enjoys. The individual who is getting his doctorate with $200,000 of debt assumed a bad bet: he may well get a job that he likes, but he is unlikely to escape his debt.

If we assume that most students will complete college and earn somewhere between $50,000 and $200,000 and have relatively healthy and productive lives, fall in love, and raise a family, then that average poor or middle-class student should not assume more than about $5,000 per year of debt. If a student is headed in the right direction and, at the age of twenty-seven or twenty-eight years, has a master's degree and no more than $50,000 in debt, then my alarm signals do not go off. I'd pre-fer, obviously, that the individual had less debt. However, in addition to the cost of college, the student also is likely to buy a car and have other noneducational costs.

Let's take things step by step. The finer points of loans are critical. One might expect that the government should protect consumers from companies out to make a quick buck on unwitting college students, but when a free market ideology exists, we generally have no such luck. The result is that loan agencies and banks may charge exorbitant interest rates that, in the long run, will harm the student. That's yet another reason why colleges need to have a consumer protection agent who guides students through the loan process. Another way, of course, is to minimize or eliminate loans.

The Pluses and Minuses of Working in College

As I've pointed out, if a student does not have enough money to pay for college, then college life will be difficult. A student with parents who will pay for everything also faces a curious challenge. If the ability to avoid working in college enables the individual to participate in a full complement of activities on campus, that financial freedom may enable the student the time and resources for a great college career. Financial freedom, however, is not a guarantee that the student will succeed. The student could simply spend his or her time playing games on a cell phones and start partying on Thursday night for the long weekend ahead. Too often, economic freedom does nothing more than make college free-form when it cries out for structure, especially for adolescents.

Those students who come from working-class backgrounds arrive on campus with the knowledge that they need to earn some money not only to pay for college but also to send money home. First-generation students are likely to turn to jobs they are already familiar with: they will be a cashier at a fast-food joint, a stocker at a grocery store, or perhaps a barista at a coffee shop. These jobs are often off campus, which means the student will spend time commuting to the job and then putting in hours to meet their economic needs. Ten or twenty hours a week as a bagger at the local grocery store may help make ends meet, but what does it do for the student's college experience? Today, extracurricular experiences are essential. Employers no longer believe that simply getting a 4.0 GPA is sufficient for a job; they are now looking for additional criteria that would enhance a young adult's resume.[13]

The curious aspect of the individual who commutes back and forth to a coffee shop and dutifully opens the shop at 6:00 a.m. is that the tasks may not be resume worthy—"almond or soy milk with your latte?"—yet they require substantial fortitude and resilience. Nevertheless, we should discourage students from taking whatever job they can find off campus if it involves a significant amount of time in entry-level work.

How, then, can we ensure that students have enough income to survive and their experiences are more than simply perfunctory tasks? The first possibility is to provide students with enough grants and subsidies to cover the cost of college. It's entirely possible that they might also take out a reasonable amount in loans. Graduating without debt is preferable to having debt, but we live in the real world, and I'm not interested in putting forward ideas that are simply unworkable. Assuming that a mixture of loans and grants is still insufficient to meet the financial needs of the student, we should counsel students not to take the same job they did in high school.

Work-study and campus-based job may present better alternatives, though the nature of these jobs varies tremendously. We have had three or four students work in the Pullias Center every semester for a number of years. The experience is extremely positive for them. They have no commute, we let them work around their schedules, and when it's exam time, we cut them some slack.

More importantly, they are made aware of what I define in my academic texts as social capital and cultural capital (i.e., Bourdieu's terminology). Simply stated, social capital pertains to networks that enable an individual to prosper. Cultural capital concerns objects or ideas that acquaint individuals with information that will help them gain entry into, or maintain their status in, the middle and upper class. When they work in the Pullias Center, the student workers are surrounded by adults who take an active interest in not only the tasks the students are accomplishing but their lives as well. When we hold meetings, they attend, and they gain a sense of what professors and graduate students think is important. We treat them as adults and solicit their opinions. The result is that working for us not only pays the bills but also gives them experiences that will be useful on their resume and in future employment. Indeed, working for us helps these students frame the kind of work they want to pursue when they graduate, or if they want to go to graduate school. They also are likely to have found one or two individuals who will write letters of reference attesting to their skills.

Contrast those experiences with other types of campus work. A student can work in food services and help dish out food for hungry students. They can work in housing and deal with the numerous problems that arise in a dormitory. They can help deliver the mail or work in the library stacking books or delivering them around campus. These jobs enable the student workers to earn some cash but do not equip them with the skills and competencies necessary to assume a position of either civic or economic responsibility after college.

We need to do a better job of creating paid internships and activities that are more than mere drudgery. Our educational experiences have to mirror the culture, with out-of-class activities that are educationally rewarding and financially compensatory. If we are to develop such activities, we are not necessarily going to get stable funding from state and public coffers. Instead, we need to develop partnerships with an array of for-profit and nonprofit workplaces that will benefit from the experiences of college students. Community colleges have been particularly successful in this regard by identifying local and regional workforce development needs and tailoring curricula that will appeal to industry partners in sectors like culinary arts, marine engineering, and energy technology.[14] Such a scenario calls for much more engaged interactions with external audiences than most colleges and universities currently have. Institutions will need to cultivate relationships with boundary spanners who can build and preserve relationships among different industry and educational actors, and they have to have a long-term vision that is realistic in size and scope while identifying multiple funding sources.[15] To develop such outreach, we need to work with those ambassadors to the universities who are our main external agents—the boards of trustees.

CHAPTER 11

Noses In, Fingers Out

Rethinking Shared Governance

Shared Governance No More

Recall that the idea of shared governance came about to protect academic freedom in the early twentieth century. Although it has been employed, or at least been given lip service, in virtually all of our public and private nonprofit institutions, shared governance always has been a punching bag for flawed decision-making. Throughout the century of its existence, individuals have constantly bemoaned the glacial pace of academic decision-making. They have largely placed the onus on the faculty and pointed out that faculty decision-making is not nimble. The joke used to be that it was easier to move a graveyard than to get the faculty to change the curriculum.

The assumption used to be that senior tenured professors got together in the senate and debated arcane issues, adjourned for the summer, and then came back in the fall with a new cast of characters and started anew. But over the last twenty years, the makeup of the faculty has changed: there are fewer senior tenured professors and many more nontenure-track faculty. Rightly, the nontenure-track faculty want to participate in governance; unfortunately, they are extremely hesitant to challenge the administration on any number of issues because they do not want to jeopardize their employment. One need not be a political scientist to recognize that when there is a vacuum in authority, someone else will fill that vacuum. When we couple the change in faculty profiles with the continued criticism of faculty lethargy, the result is an increase in presidential power and authority.

There has been a great deal of literature written on presidential leadership. There also has been a smaller but substantial set of investigations pertaining to the various roles of the faculty, such as department chairs and senates. Frequently, both bodies of literature are more prescriptive or exhortative than theoretical or intellectual. All in all, the literature is not particularly helpful or enlightening.

Boards of trustees have a very thin body of work. Most of the literature derives from the Association of Governing Boards, based in Washington, DC. College presidents and their boards pay a fee to receive their various mailings and the magazine (*Trusteeship*) and attend various conferences and proceedings the Association holds throughout the year. For a new board member, the literature can be modestly useful. The problem is that frequently the descriptions of best practices rely on the guesswork and experiences of individuals rather than any empirical evidence.

Boards are not studied because they do not allow themselves to be studied. I know of no major, detailed empirical investigations of the inner workings and decision-making processes of boards of trustees. Occasionally, the Association of Governing Boards will publish a descriptive survey of a select number of board members. It's a curious fact that one of the most important components of US higher education is also one of the least understood.

We do know two points. First, most board members come from business and industry or elected office. Second, over the last generation, boards have delegated considerable authority to the institution's president. Both points are troubling.

Private and public board members differ. Public boards tend to be appointed by the legislature or governor, or they are elected. The appointments are frequently stipulated in the institution's or system's charter and take a Noah's Ark approach: one from this category and one from that category. Sometimes the categories are geographic areas of the state, for example, and at other times, they are representatives from specific organizations or community-based groups. Depending on the mood of the legislature or governor, the members can be extremely political or more thoughtful. Those who are elected also can have extreme opinions on one topic but care very little about everything else. Some years ago, I recall a board member of a university was adamantly opposed to professors who taught gay studies classes but had no opinion about virtually any other issue that came before the board. Single-issue board members are not helpful, given the broad array of issues that a board faces. Indeed, single-issue candidates can keep a board from accomplishing anything.

Private universities generally focus more on individuals who are able to make sizable donations to the institution. "Give or get" is the adage often employed where the president recruits an individual to the board. The expectation is that the person either will give a substantial donation or find individuals who will. Private boards can be just as ideological as public boards. Public boards frequently have stipulations that their meetings must be done in public; private institutions have no such requirement. The result is that the board of a private institution, on occasion, will take a position that is extremely conservative, but the decision will not be broadcast to the community; the president is left to handle the implementation.

Because boards do not meet very often, they receive information about the institution either by way of official documents sent by the president's office, by what they read in the general press, or by anecdote. In general, the assumption about good board governance is that they will have their noses in the academic tent, but their fingers out of everyday events. Board members should not think of themselves as uber-administrators who drop in and out of meetings on campus. They do not have jobs on campus. They are not gadflies who monitor teaching, learning, and research. At the same time, they should have their noses in if they are to properly guide the organization. But to guide the organization effectively, they must have reliable information about the campus.

Any president is going to provide particular information to the board about campus activities, and the president does not want to share information that portrays him or herself in a negative light. Even information that is difficult, but necessary to share—such as a drop in enrollment—is usually presented in a light that does not make the president look weak or incompetent. The community at large is also discouraged from communicating with the board. In most cases, communication with the board goes through the president's office, which vets what a board member can or cannot see. Some universities have more fulsome representation from the larger academic community, such as a faculty and student member or two, and perhaps even a staff or community representative, as well as an alum. These positions, however, are largely honorific and carry very little real power. The individuals rarely are able to raise issues, much less set an agenda. The result is that the board generally discusses only what the president deems appropriate and useful.

Insofar as board members largely derive from the business community, an odd dualism exists. On the one hand, board members who come from business and industry know a great deal about the business world but not a lot about the purpose and function of a college or university. On the other hand, they tend to operate in a manner akin to what they do in the business world; they often do not, for example, question a president's expense accounts. What might seem exorbitant to the faculty seems consistent with the business world. One might logically assume that a board member for a Fortune 500 company will know a tremendous amount more about the institution's investments than the individual who is placed on a university board because he or she is an alumnus. That same board member, however, may know little about student life, the curriculum, or what kind of computing center should be built. The result is the board usually pays deference to the institution's president, and that deference has only increased over time.

Another humorous aphorism is that the board should have a vote at the start of every meeting that resolves "to fire the president." If the motion fails, then the board should adjourn. This idea, of course, is at the extreme end of the idea that board members should not be involved in the life of the organization. And yet, how do board members acquire the necessary information to offer guidance to the college or university?

Over the last generation, we have seen all governance at our postsecondary institutions move in the same direction. The rise of nontenure-track faculty has lessened what we think of as traditional faculty governance. Although unions have played a significant role in trying to protect the working conditions of faculty, they have not played a part in the multitude of other actions that take place in academe. The result is that today the faculty are the weakest part of the "shared" governance model. Faculty have much less of a say in presidential searches than they did a generation ago. Indeed, they have less voice and less authority in virtually every aspect of academic life. Student voice waxes and wanes based on the personality of a particular student activist. And staff have never really had any significant involvement in university governance, other than when a union represents its working interests.

Consequently, postsecondary institutions revolve around presidential prerogative. An interesting dichotomy is that while university presidents are stronger today than they have been in a century, their tenure is shorter today than it has been since we began tracking presidential terms. What gives?

Presidents at the Trough: Perks and More Perks

In 1925, Willa Cather wrote *The Professor's House.*[1] The book is primarily about the titular professor, but it contains a noteworthy portrayal of the president. He is viewed as an administrator, not an intellectual, and he is running after money, trying to do whatever he can to get a grant from a prospective donor. We may look at current college presidents and think their scurrying after money is a new ambition, but Cather shows that this aim has been part of the job for a century. We are just seeing it intensified. Public universities used to receive the vast majority of their funding from the state government. Today, we have universities that receive less than a quarter of their fiscal needs from the government. The remainder is made up by tuition dollars and capital campaigns. Most presidents will acknowledge that three-quarters of their time is now spent fundraising, and at many institutions, lower-level administrators such as deans will have the same job requirements.

What has changed is not only the power of the presidency, which I alluded to earlier, but also the way we now think of the individuals who take the job. Woodrow Wilson was president of Princeton before he became president of the United States. Robert Hutchins of the University of Chicago was thought of as an intellectual colossus and advised US presidents. Father Hesburgh of the University of Notre Dame was one of the most admired men in the United States in the 1960s and chaired the Civil Rights Commission from 1969 to 1972.[2] To be sure, not all presidents were intellectuals, or social and political giants, but they were generally regarded as pillars of the community. They were not typically wealthy: they earned more than the professors at the institution, but they had very few trappings of grandeur. Yet, I do not wish to romanticize all presidents of yesteryear. Some were petty. Some were racist. Some were ideologues.

Today, many more women and people of color are presidents, although the numbers certainly remain overwhelmingly tilted toward white men. It is also possible in some, but not all, institutions to have a gay man or lesbian, who has a spouse, as president. Such a possibility would have been unheard of only a generation ago. In the past, most presidents rose to their positions through the academic ranks: an assistant professor achieved tenure and promotion, then perhaps went on to serve as a department chair, then dean, provost, and finally president. Although that is still the norm, today we also have many more individuals who come from different walks of life. Candidates come from business and industry; they are entrepreneurs or politicians; they are executives at nonprofits or think tanks.

Because faculty have largely been cut out of the decision-making process for hiring presidents, there is usually a great deal of angst when an individual with a nonacademic profile is chosen as president. Although the trepidation is to be expected, and sometimes is warranted, an outsider can provide a useful perspective. The faculty at Texas A&M University, for example, were extremely hesitant to embrace Robert Gates when he was chosen as president. He came from the CIA, and the faculty were not sure what to expect. Yet, when he left his position to become secretary of defense for President Bush, there was general sadness by most of the faculty at the institution. Gates was celebrated for raising substantial funds for the construction of new facilities, raising the research and teaching profile of the institution, and perhaps most importantly, significantly increasing racial and ethnic diversity among students on campus.[3] His was a successful presidency. Similarly, when Mitch Daniels, the former governor of Indiana, became president of Purdue University, the faculty had doubts. Although he is not the typical college president, he also has not forged an assault on the institution. He has also demonstrated a command of the major issues confronting higher education, from academic freedom to student retention and completion, and a disposition to engage both qualitative and quantitative data in rigorous pursuit of greater understanding about the trajectory of his own institution.[4] By contrast, some presidents with more typical trajectories have been myopic in their institutional purview, eschewed data in making decisions, and had careers that ended in disaster.

I have pointed out how academe mimics the larger society. The college presidency is perhaps the best example. Throughout the twenty-first century, we have seen the erosion of the working class's standard of living and the astronomical rise in the earnings of what has come to be known as "the one percent." When we look within a business, we also find that managerial salaries and compensation have skyrocketed, while the salaries of those who fill lower-level service positions have stalled or been eroded. A Walmart employee earning roughly the median salary for the company pulls in about $20,000 per year, while the company's CEO makes over $20 million a year.[5] The employee would need to work a thousand years to earn the CEO's annual salary. As the power of unions has been curtailed, so too have the salaries and compensations of those individuals whom the unions serve. Tax cuts have largely served to aid the upper class. The premise that they will reinvigorate the economy by creating more jobs with their additional revenue has not come to pass.

We have seen the same pattern in academe. At our most elite institutions, the salaries of presidents approach, and at times exceed, one million dollars. When this is seen as a marker of prestige, boards at other institutions try to achieve the same for their own presidents. Board members, coming from business and industry, do not believe that a college president earning one million dollars is excessive. The CEO of their company could be earning ten times that amount.

The perks that come with the job may appear de rigueur to business executives, but they are excessive to those of us on the faculty. One's spouse may get a salary. The president will have an entertainment budget and perhaps a clothing allowance. Travel is first class, and lodging will be on the executive level of a hotel. Often unreported, memberships on boards can effectively double an individual's salary. Retirement packages can be exorbitant—the same salary one has been earning, coupled with a research budget. All of these presidential perks can be explained away with logical rationales. We want presidents to arrive where they are going fresh and ready to raise money, so first-class travel makes sense. They need to entertain donors, and how would it look if they stayed at a Motel 6 or split the bill at dinner? A spouse's job is full-time entertaining.

The problem with presidential compensation is that postsecondary institutions are nonprofit entities. There has never been as great a discrepancy between the president's salary and the lowest paid, full-time faculty member as there is today. Higher education has mirrored the business world; the difference is that higher education is a nonprofit, while business and industry are profit-generating entities. Should we countenance the same sort of income distribution at public and private nonprofit colleges and universities? We have presidents flying first class, while the faculty do not receive enough travel support to attend a conference. We have presidents with an unlimited amount of revenue to entertain individuals, while the faculty pay out of their own pockets. The president makes a salary of a million dollars, and a full-time, nontenure-track professor brings in $65,000. The annual raise for presidents is usually quite hefty. In 2015, the board at the University of Southern California (USC) gave my own university president a bonus of $1.5 million to match his annual salary; I received the standard 2 percent raise.[6] While a retiring president has all expenses covered, plus a salary and research budget, retiring faculty must bargain for basic health benefits. In 2018, my own president was forced to step down because of irregularities, but the board gave him a 7.5 million dollar buyout.

Presidents and boards are largely tone deaf when it comes to the people they ostensibly serve: the students and faculty. Students are told that tuition needs to increase because the institution needs to balance its budget, then they see the president's limo. Faculty do not get a pay raise because enrollment is down, then they pass the president in first class as they head to steerage. All of these cost-cutting and budget-balancing arguments ring hollow in a nonprofit institution.

Presidential tenures are also down. The presidency has become a stepping stone to a better presidency, so it is not uncommon to see an individual start at a small institution or a state university, then move on to a better institution and then possibly a state system. There certainly is nothing wrong with upward mobility, but the challenge of leadership turnover is that the members of the organization get mixed signals about institutional priorities when there is a new president every few years. As a result, board members tend to ignore presidential missives because they have grown cynical, assuming the president is less concerned with the institution than with the next big raise and perks.

I do not wish to imply that we once had an academic utopia. What we have lost, however, is the intellectual leadership that helps define not merely what a curriculum might be but also what kind of institution we want to have for one another. Because of the reduction in faculty ranks and the move toward paying faculty as piecemeal workers who get paid to teach a class or two, rather than being gainfully employed in a full-time job, the faculty participate much less effectively in governance. Initially, the board and administration may have privately rejoiced at the commodification of the faculty. The lethargic decision-making pace could be picked up with the implementation of a more business-like line of thinking and acting. Unfortunately, such decisions have not turned out for the betterment of academe; instead, these changes only underscore the fact that the board, in general, has been asleep at the wheel.

Boards Asleep at the Wheel

In the recent past, we have seen three celebrated universities find themselves on the first page of major newspapers throughout the country because of scandals. Pennsylvania State University had a football coach, Jerry Sandusky, who abused young boys for a number of years. Senior administrators, including the president, knew about the coach's actions and did nothing about it.[7] Michigan State University had a trainer, Larry Nasser, who abused young women gymnasts over decades. Senior administrators sat on the sidelines and did nothing.[8] My own institution, USC, had numerous scandals: one involving a rogue dean, Carmen Puliafito, who took drugs and partied with young people and prostitutes, and a second involving a staff gynecologist, George Tyndall, who was accused of sexually assaulting hundreds of students in the exam room for two decades. The dean's actions had been reported to the provost and president, and the gynecologist's actions were known within the unit, but the information was ignored.[9] The dean of social work allegedly participated in a pay-to-play scandal with an elected official to get his son into a master's degree program; the university had to pay UC San Diego $50 million for corrupt practices related to poaching its faculty, and we were a centerpiece of the admissions scandal.

The result in each case was the removal of the university's president. Other actions were taken: President Spanier and two of his associates at Penn State were charged with criminal behavior, as was President Simon at Michigan State. Many associates of each president were dismissed or simply resigned. At Penn State, the iconic coach Joe Paterno, Sandusky's boss, was fired after a storied career. The reputations of each university were severely damaged.

What is remarkable about each case from an organizational perspective is that these three presidents were previously considered exemplars of good leadership. Each of them had garnered accolades and respect for their leadership. They played major roles in the elite Association of American Universities. They received honorary doctorates. They commonly consulted with presidents, governors, and legislators. President Spanier had been on the short list for a cabinet position if John Kerry had won the presidency. He was credited with expanding the university's research capacity and improving student quality, and the Association of Governing Boards cited Penn State for its good governance. President Simon made Michigan State a leader in the Big Ten. She had been a primary force in attracting federal contracts to the university. As a public university, Michigan State's global reach was unrivaled. It once did not have name recognition beyond the borders of the state; under President Simon, it came to plant the flag in far-off locations such as Uzbekistan. President

Nikias was a remarkable fundraiser who, in a little over half a decade, raised enough revenue to build a $700 million new campus adjacent to the main campus.[10] USC rose in the global rankings, and many world-class faculty who regularly went to other universities now came to USC because of its prestige and ability to compensate them. New presidents commonly made their way to USC to understand the secret that led to such a rapid rise in the rankings.

Presidents Spanier and Simon had been in office for approximately fifteen years; President Nikias for slightly less than a decade. Prior to his tenure as president, Nikias had been provost at USC for a half decade. Their downfalls were swift and unexpected. What happened? How did three institutions and three presidents fall from grace when they had seemed untouchable?

One could look to the character of the individuals. Spanier was detached and buried difficult issues under the administrative rug. Simon had been at the institution since graduate school and risen through the ranks, so she did not question the established patterns for making decisions. Nikias was imperious and ignored or banished those who opposed him.

But to my mind, the real failures of the institutions were the manner in which the boards of trustees functioned and provided (or failed to provide) oversight. Earlier, I noted the old adage that a board might convene, hold a vote of no confidence in the president, then adjourn the meeting upon the vote's failure. Unfortunately, in each of the instances above, this is essentially the way the boards functioned. Penn State's board, as a public university, had a makeup determined by its charter in which different constituencies, such as representatives from the agricultural, business, and industry communities, had seats. The board was large, whereas Michigan State's board was small and composed largely of ex-football players. USC's board had fifty-nine members, and virtually all of them gave significant sums of money to the university. The board chair at the time of Nikias's resignation, for example, had donated more than $100 million for scholarships for low-income youth.

Board meetings were sporadic and largely inconsequential. I was an expert witness for a victim of Sandusky; the individual sued Penn State, and I read hundreds of pages of transcripts pertaining to the board. I also was president of the Academic Senate at USC and subsequently attended board meetings as president when the administration asked me to make a presentation. The president's office always took extreme care to arrange and orchestrate the meetings, from seating arrangements to the sort of food that is served, yet the meetings are largely inconsequential insofar as the most important decisions were made by the president, his senior staff, and a small group of the board.

Until the eleventh hour (and sometimes not even then), none of these boards had a firm grasp of the issues confronting their respective universities, nor what role the president had in enabling the problems. Only a short time before the crises brought the downfall of their presidents, the boards appeared extremely content with their president. Those individuals who raised red flags were marginalized or ignored.

Board members tend not to take their roles seriously because the roles are ambiguous. They also recognize that their participation in committees—student affairs, academic affairs, athletics, and the like—is not a great burden. It may require little more than a meeting or two a year over lunch at the university. They see their participation as useful and important because the president often shows up for committee and subcommittee meetings.

At the same time, everyone recognizes that the only subcommittee that really matters is the one that oversees financial affairs, often called the executive committee. These committee members are essential to the running of the organization, and the president meets with them on a regular basis. This can create a tendentious dynamic, as individuals may be miffed when they are left out of the in-group.

Boards members are not irrelevant. Board members often have extensive connections with state and federal governments, as well as with other wealthy individuals. They can play critical roles in forging relationships that are financially beneficial to the university. Rich in social capital, members of the board can extend and enrich their own connections while also benefiting the university. Moreover, membership on the board of trustees guarantees invitations to all of the home football games, great seats on the fifty-yard line, and invitations to the president's tailgate parties (which tend to be elegant lunches or dinners). Many board members see fall football games as the highlight of their membership.

Some years ago, I did a study of governance and interviewed several former and current governors.[11] They all had a common lament. Each governor had a state with an extensive postsecondary system that needed good guidance. Unfortunately, when they contacted individuals about serving on the board, the potential board members all wanted to serve on the most prestigious university that had a football team. They were less interested in serving on public institutions further down the academic food chain, which offered entre to fewer social capital networks than those with football powerhouses.

Faculty frequently forget that presidents do not report to them. Presidents report to the board and, therefore, spend a great deal more time on the care and nurture of the board. The challenge for presidents is to keep faculty busy doing menial administrative work to make them feel that they are engaged in shared governance and cultivate the board such that it willingly takes a bystander role while granting enormous power to the president.

The president of a university should never have the absolute power and authority that the leaders of Penn State, Michigan State, and USC accumulated. The faculty enabled the accumulation of power in large part because nontenure-track faculty have grown enormously and, with it, their representation in decision-making bodies. Although all faculty should have a rightful voice in the governance of the university, individuals who lack job security are likely to fear speaking out on issues that will place them at odds with the president.

Since the faculty voice has been muted, with messages curated by the president's office, the board heard very few complaints about the campus and therefore neglected its oversight responsibilities. This results in a system that does not reflect the ideal of shared governance whatsoever. I have concentrated on these three elite institutions because how they have conducted themselves has ripple effects across all of academe.

When a crisis erupts the board goes into overdrive. "Do something" seems to be the mantra—even though what they should do is entirely unclear. Increasingly, we see boards unable to grapple with complex issues because they are unprepared. An enrollment crisis occurs, and they blame the president and assume stronger leadership is the answer. Boards tend to spring into action at the eleventh hour when actually they should be actively engaged at all times. How to define that engagement is the challenge.

Monkey See, Monkey Don't

Most developed countries have a pretty clear postsecondary system. There is an elaborated public structure akin to our premier public systems, perhaps a few regional institutions, no community colleges, and then a handful of private colleges or universities. Only a few countries have any form of for-profit higher education. The governing boards of institutions are largely irrelevant, as state ministries run public institutions like public entities.

US higher education is quite different. We have thousands of universities and colleges and an elaborated private system. Virtually every institution has some form of a board. Even though I have pointed out how the power of US boards is relatively weak, they do ultimately have the trust of the institution in their collective hands and statutory authority. Relative to other countries, US boards have much more power and authority. Many scholars of postsecondary education in the United States have commented on the elaborated structure and marveled that such a complex system not only can function but also has become the envy of the world.

Observers also have noted that the decision-making triumvirate—the board, faculty, and senior administration—are often at odds with one another. I actually think the overall goals have been more in sync than not. Throughout the twentieth century, an institutional isomorphism was at work. Those lower on the food chain sought ways to move up; rather than an ecological approach where different organizational species thrived, institutions sought similarity. By and large, the faculty, administration, and boards all bought into the idea. Most institutions throughout the twentieth century tried to improve—everyone wanted to move up the hierarchy. The teacher's college became a state college, then a state university, then one that offered graduate degrees. The community college might first offer four-year degrees and then become a four-year college. The small regional public or private college needs to expand beyond its current geographical environment.

Faculty work also changed over the past forty years. Recent graduates armed with PhDs from research universities wanted to do what they had been trained to do: research. The problem is that the vast panoply of institutions supposedly gave more importance to teaching than research. When a majority of a department's faculty wanted to do research, then the institutions would try to find ways to reward research—through higher salaries, improved job protections, sabbaticals, and graduate student assistants—more than teaching. In a study conducted some years ago, we found that in all types of institutions, faculty received greater rewards and recognition for their research than teaching.[12] More and more, teaching loads were decreased so that faculty might do more research. As state appropriations began to shrink, administrators began to think that faculty members who could generate external funds through research grants were a more valuable asset than faculty members who excelled at teaching.

Faculty sought work lives akin to those of their graduate school mentors. Presidents wanted a track record they could show for the next job. Success was being able to demonstrate that there had been an increase in research funding, or they had grown from a regional to a national institution, or they had become more selective, or they had risen in research-biased rankings, or they had introduced or expanded graduate offerings.

These changes were catnip for too many boards. Recall that governors have lamented that recruiting members to low-status institutions was difficult. How might one make board service more prestigious? Make the institution more like the prestigious institutions! Multiple small-tier colleges and universities organized sports teams and formed leagues to mimic major universities. Attending football games on a Saturday afternoon was important for not only the boards at Baylor and Berkeley but also Boston College and Bucknell. The implicit strength of social capital also rose for board members as they rose in prestige.

Correspondingly, the trustees raised presidential salaries, sought newer accoutrements, tried to raise the prestige of the faculty by hiring "star" faculty, and began to see themselves as fundraisers or conduits to funding. Granted, all of these actions were mostly done on scale. Bucknell did not join the Big Ten. California State University's faculty did not rival the University of California in research productivity. The University of Cincinnati's incoming first-year class did not have the SAT scores of Northwestern. Yet, each institution would say it had improved by the standard criteria of prestige and productivity as defined by elite institutions like Stanford and Harvard.

The way forward in the twenty-first century will be a distinct departure from the last century. Rather than mimesis, we will look toward differentiated best practices. We need to return to the core values of the institution and then consider how these values get articulated based on the fundamental mission of each college or university. Rather than let the institution drift toward isomorphism (or actively embrace it), the board must step back and try to invent an institution that best meets the needs of the board's constituency and environment. If US higher education is going to reinvent itself, then boards need to break away from the crippling assumption that the accumulation of social capital is desirable, which, in turn, suggests the institution needs to move in the rankings so that board members can enjoy pleasurable fall afternoons on the fifty-yard line.

Leadership for the Twenty-First Century

Clearly, we need an engaged form of governance that maintains the ideals that framed shared governance in the twentieth century but also responds to the structural and demographic changes that have taken place in the twenty-first century.[13] Shared governance suggests we cannot do an end run around the faculty, and the board of trustees has to be fully engaged with its role. Many of us have been quick to highlight the flaws in the lethargic pace of shared governance. I fully appreciate the model's shortcomings. We ought to recognize, however, that US higher education rose to worldwide prominence at the same time this model took hold: our stature came about, in part, not in spite of but because of shared governance.

No form of governance is going to be perfect. Academic decision-making must be informed by faculty input. The lack of participation not only leads to autocratic rule but also ignores that faculty have a special place in the organization. Faculty are not workers who have no voice in the decision-making of the organization. Rather, they have a key role in fomenting reasoned intellectual dialogue. Those who think that professorial passivity is a good thing are misinterpreting academic life. When faculty are disengaged, then the sorts of disasters that I previously discussed take place. Administrators always can trick the faculty into being involved in menial decision-making, but history suggests that we are served best when the professoriate is actively engaged in those matters that are essential to determining and then implementing academic quality.

Just as the US system of shared governance helped us vaunt into primacy in the world, I would also argue that true structural democracy holds institutions and systems back. Latin American higher education, generally, has a system where presidents (or vice rectors) are elected by the faculty. I've spent a year in Central America and returned numerous times to lecture and do research; what I have seen is not a structure I would want to replicate. When the leaders of the institution are constantly aware of the term limit of their presidency, the university is always politicized. The individual has to have opinions on topics within the university but also be allied to a particular party in the country. The result is a system that is riven by one side arguing with another, decision-making is stymied, and the ability to create a consistent message about the worth of the university and why someone might want to support the institution gets muted.

I do not want board members acting like administrators telling people what to do. Their ability to give or get is also essential on private and public boards. What needs to change, however, is the makeup of the boards and the manner in which they approach oversight. The underrepresentation of people of color on our Boards and as college and university presidents is unacceptable in organizations that value diversity as a core principle.

I mentioned how many captains of industry populate our boards. That is shorthand, as well, for white men. This concern does not have to do with being politically correct. There is zero research to suggest that a Noah's Ark approach to board composition is effective—two from this and two from that. Nevertheless, groupthink is dangerous to shared governance. Far too often, trustees go on autopilot because they all come from the same walks of life and therefore tend to interpret situations in the same manner. If we are more careful about board composition, we can improve board effectiveness.

Further, anyone whose primary interest in serving on the board is access to football games is not someone we need in the twenty-first century. We have to have individuals who are committed to the educational legacy of the organization, rather than the perceived advantages they might accrue by being on the board. We need to continually remind ourselves about the meaning and purpose of the academic organization, rather than simply try to fill open slots.

Finally, we need a new brand of leader, or perhaps, an old brand. I appreciate the manifold responsibilities of any president today, whether it's fundraising or lobbying for funds with the legislature or trying to put forward new ideas to the various communities we serve: local, regional, national, and international. At the same time, we are urgently in need of intellectual and cultural leaders more willing to serve the organization than themselves. I'm not suggesting that college leaders should take a vow of poverty, but the gross inequity between those who are the highest paid and those who are struggling in the gig economy requires a new form of leadership. Rather than trying to manipulate the board and silence the faculty, we need leaders who can enable, foment, and encourage creative conflict. Our challenge is to reclaim the idea of building communities of difference.

CHAPTER 12

Lessons Learned

Inconvenient Truths

I have approached writing this book with a mixture of concern and calm. The concern should be obvious based on the preceding chapters. The context in which I have penned this book also cannot be overlooked; we dealt with a recession only a decade ago, and we have confronted a pandemic that presumably is a "game-changer." In the midst of the pandemic we also have had to deal with the murder of George Floyd, the recognition of criminal behavior on the part of some of the police, and the acknowledgement on a societal level that racism is baked into the structure of American society. We have an enormous array of problems, new and old, and we must face up to them. A writing instructor in graduate school once cautioned me that I ought not use *must* in academic work because academics never *must* do anything. Perhaps that's where the calm enters. Yes, we need to change, but we ought not lose sight of our central focus. Understanding the idea of a university is not a call for maintaining the status quo or returning to a golden age that I do not think for many of us was all that golden. I believe we face eight compelling problems.

1. The erosion of academic freedom and tenure. When faculty and administrations agree, or a professor has a research area without political ramifications, or when faculty have no issues with how the institution is governed, then we don't worry much about academic freedom. Not all controversies fall solely within the domain of academic freedom, though we need to defend academic freedom when controversy arises. All institutions should have procedures in place to provide support to individuals when their academic freedom is under attack.

There is a more insidious problem, however. The erosion of tenure and the increase in nontenure-track faculty has created a climate where people are less likely to speak out, lest they risk their employment. The culture of the organization is shifting in a manner that tamps down controversy at the expense of moving the institution forward, putting academic freedom in ever greater peril.

2. The assault of fake news. One new problem that has arisen is the issue of conspiracy theories and unfounded rumors being passed off as news. We always have had conspiracy theorists and individuals who rejected fact. There are those, for example, who believe the moon landing was staged. Because of the ubiquitous nature of social media and talk radio, many more people are able to have conspiracies spoon-fed to them. Conspiracies also are big business; the right wing has a goldmine on its hands—just ask Alex Jones. We ought to be clear that these purveyors of dangerous falsehoods are not part of the parameters of academic freedom that we aim to foster. I acknowledge that how we determine what is fake news is a complicated question, and I am more willing to allow dialogue than to restrict it.

To that end, I have no problems debating issues about climate change, even though the facts are clear. Every umbrella has some limits, and the recent rise of fake news tests those limits. To be sure, gatekeeping is always going to be controversial, but rather than sidestep the responsibility, I am encouraging faculty to embrace it. Even a thoughtful discussion, for example, about why we might allow a conversation about climate change but not one about a president's birthplace, would be helpful to all in the community, but especially students, about how to assess facts and information.

3. The cost of higher education. We have two interrelated problems: cost and paying for the costs. The costs of higher education have risen, and at the same time, the support for students to attend college has dropped. The result is that the students are left with the bill.

Some of the rising cost of higher education is entirely unnecessary. Presidential salaries and perks are absurd. The expansion of administration is understandable but can be curtailed. Institutions take on too many tasks, and if they were more focused on a finite number of goals, they would be able to trim costs. Part of the problem is that institutions frequently try to mimic the actions of the most expensive institutions. Institutions with more constrained missions will save revenue. I do not think that many of these problems will go away, and even if we were able to curtail spending in these areas, I do not believe we will be able to save enough money to stop student tuition from continuing to rise. Declining public support, coupled with the increase in costs, suggests students have to pay more.

The second problem to be faced, then, is that students are facing a wall of debt. There are some important ways to stem the tide of debt, including working with students to improve their financial literacy before they take on loans they will be unable to support. However, for students not to walk away from college with a mountain of debt requires much more government oversight and assistance than we currently have. The Obama administration was on the right track: increase grants to those who need them; force institutions to spend more on need-based aid than merit scholarships; regulate for-profits; force greater accreditation oversight; have the government cover loans; and ensure that the banks do not charge an absurd interest rate. These sorts of commonsense solutions will go a long way toward overcoming the challenges students and their families face, but the country does not yet seem able to force Congress to function in such a fashion.

All of these issues have been exacerbated by the pandemic. Fewer students can afford the cost of a four-year degree—but jobs are hard to find. States have less revenue to replace the dollars that have been lost. Philanthropy has taken a hit. Summer revenue took a nosedive since no one could come to campus. The challenges are perhaps more daunting than at any time since the Great Depression.

4. Students are not (only) customers. Due to an increasingly consumerist society and inexorably rising costs, institutions have responded by thinking of students as customers. This idea is not entirely wrong. We do need to meet the needs of the market. We do need to be more accommodating to what students need and want. Indeed, as I mentioned, a large part of the initial success—both in attracting students and enabling them to get the credentials they wanted—of the University of Phoenix was simply that it was willing to offer classes at times and locations that its customers wanted. The University of Phoenix was among the first institutions to embrace online learning (in 1989), and by 1994, it was successful enough to have a public stock offering. By the turn of the century, the influx of public capital allowed the University of Phoenix to boast that it had more than one hundred thousand students.[1]

The problem is that when we think of students only as customers, then we lose the essence of higher education. Faculty are more than baristas trying to deliver an expresso. We are not simply a business, and we need to go back to a framework that delineates the essential ingredients that define learning and helps prepare students to be active participants in democracy. Clearly, students need a more thorough understanding of the country's past, and its troubled relationship with race. They need intellectual spaces that enable them to think through their own and one another's identities, and how to create a more responsive community. When we forget that, we lose our brand—to use a business term—and although we may think we have solved one problem, we have created a bigger one.

5. The increase of globalization and the decline of jobs. Colleges and universities are not businesses, but they also are not immune to the larger environment. Who could question such a statement given the immediate and long-term implications of COVID-19? Perhaps the day will come again when students enter college without worrying about the sort of job they will get upon graduation, but I do not see that happening any time soon. Therefore, higher education needs to do a better job at preparing students for the workforce. This point is not just about having a more elaborate career-training center, although that is useful. I am not arguing that all learning should be strictly vocational.

Rather, I am suggesting that we have to have a more coordinated effort about what students need, and what they need to know, from the moment they start to apply to college. The disconnect between high school and college is unacceptable, as is the lack of readiness both when students arrive to college and when they graduate from college. Of all the problems that I have outlined here, this one is the easiest to resolve, but it requires a change in culture in terms of how faculty work with others, what we want students to know in a class, and what takes place outside of class. Higher education professionals, for example, need to be more involved with students at the high school level, as I have suggested, and work more closely with high school educators and administrators.

6. The unwillingness to talk through differences. Fundamentally, a university is a conversation. We talk with students. We do research and, through discourse, discover the errors in our work and how to improve them. Recall that the first article I ever published was entitled "Governance by Conversation." Yet, we bemoan how much conversation consumes us. Our work cannot be done by fiat; because so much conversation occurs on a campus, it is a conundrum how little occurs today. We tend to avoid difficult dialogues when they are precisely what we need to enable.

At our best, we model for society how to think about particular phenomena and provide information about how to live a better life.

Whether such puzzles pertain to cures for cancer or how to improve the flow of traffic, universities exist in large part to improve the discourse of human life. Despite the old adage about ivory-covered walls, we are not hermetically sealed off from the world: we come from the world, and unfortunately, we reflect back the insecurities at work in that world. The intolerance for contradicting perspectives in society, in part, creates a climate on campus that wants to wall off disagreeable arguments and ideas. If we are unwilling to speak across differences and sit in communion with those with whom we disagree, have we not then lost the raison d'etre of academic life?

7. **The challenge of governing today.** Governance is always going to be messy and imperfect. Two current challenges make governance that much more problematic. The rise in nontenure-track hires means that faculty are less comfortable confronting the administration when they disagree. At the same time, boards are more likely to grant senior administrators significant executive power. The result is a sort of imperial presidency. The good news about strong central administration is that decisions are more likely to occur in rapid fashion, and external actions, such as fundraising, are likely to increase. The downside is that the culture of the organization is likely to be rendered ineffective. When individuals' voices are not important, they are less likely to be involved and less likely to care about the future of the organization. As individuals' voices are muted, we lose nuance and the richness of diverse perspectives when it comes to strategic planning. We also lose people's sense of involvement, as well as care and concern for the institution. The result is an organization that has moved far afield from one focused on the search for truth.

8. **The lessening of individual and public commitment to higher education.** Surveys continue to show that individuals believe attending college is useful, but a recent Gallup Poll indicates that, from 2015 to 2018, our confidence in higher education has slipped. In 2015, 57 percent of US adults had "a great deal" or "quite a lot" of confidence in higher education, yet in 2018, only 48 percent were willing to make the same endorsements.[2] The slippage is not terrifying, but it is cause for concern. There is a curious dualism that the citizenries seem to like higher education and, for the most part, want their children to attend college. At the same time, they vote conservative politicians into office who tend to advocate cutting public support for higher education. Republicans hold a majority of state houses, and they have controlled at least one branch of Congress for much of the last two decades. We have had to deal with the election

of one of the country's most conservative presidents. Consequently, the public's commitment to higher education is weaker today than it has been in a century. A narrow definition of the public good that relies on a neoliberal framework implies not only that higher education will be less well supported but that related public entities such as primary and secondary education will also suffer. The result is that academe faces a quiet crisis that we have been unable to stem.

Building a Community of Difference

Sometimes in baseball, a very good team seems to lose it all at once. As a Los Angeles Dodgers fan, I know of what I speak. The team goes from World Series caliber to assorted errors and mental lapses that are more similar to a minor league team than an elite club. No magic potion exists that enables a club to return to top form. If the best pitcher in baseball hurts his arm, then the team faces a challenge. A rookie might face the "sophomore slump." A great team, however, does not succeed or fail because of one individual—it's a group effort. Over the years, I have seen a collective fail to a baseball team—everything and everyone seem to be flailing, as if there is an infection surging through the clubhouse. The correct response in such a situation is not simply to remain calm but to go back to basics and think through what has been working, what might need to change, and how to move forward.

US higher education is in that position now. Different institutions and systems face different problems. Some face enrollment declines and budget shortfalls. Others face campus unrest because of imperial leaders. Many face problems around student diversity and increasing part-time faculty. Others tiptoe around issues where bold action is required; still others make broad proclamations where discretion might be advised. All of us must deal in some fashion from the ramifications of the COVID-19 pandemic and the resulting economic hardship. The result is that higher education's fan base—US families—starts to waver. To staunch the bleeding and avoid a death spiral, boards look to saviors who can save them with whatever tonic the leader proposes to be the cure.

To solve our myriad problems, we cannot act as though we are on the *Titanic*, either looking away or making cursory changes as if rearranging the chairs to get a better view of the iceberg. As a faculty member, I know that when I say we should go back to basics, I run the risk of watching readers' eyes roll, as if I am suggesting nothing more than more talk.

I get it. Problems are real, and as someone who likes to solve problems, simply saying we should talk only leads to indecision. And we have
to do something! Now!

No we don't. Take a breath.

Let's review five quick principles of the idea of the university that
I've outlined. First, we have a dedication to the search for truth. Second,
based on our desire for understanding truth, we have an abiding concern
for free speech, as we have defined it here. Third, we are focused on
enabling opportunity for students and society in all its many manifestations.
Fourth, we not only want educated citizens who are able to be gainfully
employed but we also want individuals who will be active participants in
democracy. And fifth, we see the intellectual and sociocultural diversity
of the country as a strength that needs to be mirrored in, and led by,
postsecondary organizations.

When people are confused, we need relentless conversation. The
point is not to bloviate about the same topics again and again, focusing
on instrumental actions that frequently do not work because they fail to
take into account the larger framework in which we find ourselves. We
have a budget shortfall, so we hire part-time faculty. The interrelatedness
of academic life defies easy solutions, but such complexity ought not to
suggest that action is impossible.

We frequently fool ourselves into thinking that similarity is essential.
We've heard adages such as, "We all have to be on the same team," and
assume that those who offer alternative opinions are naysayers or "not
team players." Higher education, however, is not a team sport. What has
made higher education in the United States great is not our similarity, but
our difference. We have fallen down when we've overlooked diversity and
tried for similarity. We still have a long way to go with regard to gender
diversity in the sciences and racial and economic diversity throughout all
of higher education, especially in our most elite institutions. But we have
at least acknowledged these problems rather than brushed them aside. We
have been forced to acknowledge our shortcomings because students or
faculty have raised uncomfortable issues. The progress we've made over
the last century has been because of, rather than in spite of, our commitment to issues such as diversity and the principles that underscore them,
such as free speech.

Don't get me wrong. Instrumental actions are important, and simply
practicing our breathing exercises will not overcome the slump in which we
have found ourselves. And yet, if we are to get our groove back, we need
to first understand the fundamentals, then articulate them for our many

constituencies, and then set to work on plans that enable us to reach our goals. Too often, we have platitudes but not commitment. What's curious is the vast majority of individuals I work with in academe—regardless of whether they are faculty, administrators, staff, or students—believes in the idea of higher education, but we often do not articulate our beliefs lest we be thought of as sanctimonious or silly.

Similarly, we disdain conflict, or at least overt conflict. We all too often eschew differences that require us to disagree with one another face-to-face. I understand. Who likes disagreeing with people, or being told we're wrong? A learning environment, however, has to embrace disagreement because differences of opinion are inevitable and integral to an intellectual community.

The most successful classes I have taught are the ones where students felt free to disagree with one another and me. At the end of class, we have grown closer rather than farther apart. Indeed, any intellectual undertaking has to be framed in a manner that enables individuals to follow Baldwin's dictate "to ask questions of the universe."[3] This ought not suggest that the answers that come back will all be the same. The unique and various responses of individuals and institutions will offer a fuller understanding of the problem at hand.

Our focus, then, is not simply on an amorphous meaning of excellence or on writing strategic plans that no one will read. We need to concentrate on building a community of difference for the twenty-first century.[4] We will work from our historical sense of what a university is about, confront the challenges I have outlined here, and develop unique responses to the challenges at hand.

The Way Forward

I admit there is cause for pessimism, especially since the recovery from the pandemic is so difficult, and to many the goal of racial equity seems further off today than yesterday. Our postsecondary institutions are decaying because of budget shortfalls. Students and their families are incurring costs for college that are exorbitant and likely to increase. Vitriolic attacks on the professoriate are now common. Tenure, once the coin of the academic realm, is now a rarity. Students arrive to college unprepared and depart for the workforce in the same manner. Faculty are working harder and getting paid less. Panaceas like online learning have turned into pipe dreams. No one is happy with how institutions deal with diversity. Simply removing a sculpture or renaming a building is easy work, and yet it has taken decades. Either the well-used bromide of political correctness gets tossed around by the right, or the left argues that campuses support the racist status quo. The belief in education as a public good that aids the development of the individual, the community, and society seems to have been lost, in an age when resources are finite.

The Austrian psychiatrist Viktor Frankl once quoted Nietzsche as saying, "He who has a why to live for can bear almost any how."[5] I have argued here that the central challenge that currently confronts us is neither fiscal nor structural, but moral—the why. Once we are clear about the why, we will figure out the how. We have arrived at a point where many of our most pressing concerns turn on how we define larger issues. Yes, the cost of a college degree is too great for many families, but to solve this problem, we first need to come to terms with what we expect of society and one another and how we define an academic institution.

If we assume that all students deserve the opportunity to go to college, then a closer relationship between high school and college needs to be created, and a seamless transition from one organization to another needs to be facilitated. One ought not assume that graduating from high school college ready is a remarkable feat. It should be the norm. All students should have the opportunity to graduate ready for college or for gainful employment.

Similarly, higher education does not need merely to reflect society, with its huge discrepancies in faculty and administrative pay. We can try to reassert that our colleges and universities are fountainheads for change that reflect the best of our democratic tradition. Rather than continue to see tenure erode, we will work assiduously to reverse the pattern, as well as ensure that those without tenure have the protections to speak their mind in service to the common good.

We will embrace the need for vigorous argument over ideas and ensure that students are exposed to a wide range of topics that may provoke passionate commentary. Because we are known as an arena for thoughtful disagreement, however, we should not entertain elaborate lies that parade as fact. The worth of the academic community can be judged by the embrace of a cultural citizenship aimed at understanding difference, but not by enabling those who seek to distort reality, grounds, and individuals by lies. To be sure, how we reach agreement on these issues is going to be difficult terrain to navigate, but ultimately, it is precisely the landscape we should traverse.

Academic life should be messy, but it should not be unequal. If we continue to accept a degraded form of academic life, then all the progress we have made in terms of gender and racial equity, for example, over the last century will have been for naught. When the country waxes poetic about the shining city on the hill, I am certain that a postsecondary institution exists on that hill in that city. Its role is to raise uncomfortable questions, empower people to lift themselves out of poverty, create a climate that stimulates innovation and creativity, and ultimately help enable a better world. I am sure we still have that ability. The question is if we have the will.

Notes

Chapter 1

1. Mann, H. (1845). *Lectures on education* (p. 216). Boston, MA: Fowle and Capen. Retrieved from https://archive.org/details/lecturesoneducat00mannuoft/page/216

2. Mann, *Lectures*, p. 216.

3. See https://www.census.gov/population/censusdata/table-4.pdf

4. See https://www.census.gov/population/censusdata/table-4.pdf

5. Goldin, C., & Katz, L. F. (2011). Mass secondary schooling and the state: The role of state compulsion in the high school movement. In D. L. Costa & N. R. Lamoreaux (Eds.), *Understanding long-run economic growth: Geography, institutions, and the knowledge economy* (pp. 275–310). Chicago: University of Chicago Press; also see Goldin, C. (1998). American's graduation from high school: The evolution and spread of secondary schooling in the twentieth century. *Journal of Economic History, 58*(2), 345–74.

6. Harris, G. G., & Cohen, H. S. (2012). *Women trailblazers of California: Pioneers to the present*. Charleston, SC: History Press.

7. Douglass, J. A. (2000). *The California idea and American higher education: 1850 to the 1960 master plan*. Stanford, CA: Stanford University Press.

8. See, for example, Labaree, D. F. (2006). Mutual subversion: A short history of the liberal and the professional in American higher education. *History of Education Quarterly, 46*(1), 1–15; Lanford, M., & Tierney, W. G. (2015). *From "vocational education" to "linked learning": The ongoing transformation of career-oriented education in the United States*. Los Angeles, CA: Pullias Center for Higher Education, University of Southern California; Oakes, J., & Saunders, M. (2008). *Beyond tracking: Multiple pathways to college, career, and civic participation*. Cambridge, MA: Harvard Education Press.

9. Johnson, H., Bohn, S., & Mejia, M. C. (2017). *Addressing California's skills gap*. San Francisco, CA: Public Policy Institute of California.

10. Organisation for Economic Co-operation and Development. (2018). *Education at a glance 2018: OECD indicators.* Paris: OECD Publishing; also see https://data.oecd.org/eduatt/population-with-tertiary-education.htm

11. Lumina Foundation. (2016). *A stronger nation: Postsecondary learning builds the talent that helps us rise.* Indianapolis, IN: Lumina Foundation; Bill and Melinda Gates Foundation. (2016). Postsecondary success advocacy priorities. Retrieved from http://postsecondary.gatesfoundation.org/wp-content/uploads/2015/03/PS-ADV-Priorities-V1.pdf

12. Clynes, T. (2016, June 4). Peter Theil's dropout army. *New York Times.* Retrieved from https://www.nytimes.com/2016/06/05/opinion/sunday/peter-thiels-dropout-army.html

13. Vedder, R. (2012). *Twelve inconvenient truths about American higher education.* Washington, DC: Center for College Affordability and Productivity.

14. Wadhwa, V. (2013, September 11). Peter Thiel promised flying cars; we got caffeine spray instead. *Venture Beat.* Retrieved from https://venturebeat.com/2013/09/11/peter-thiel-promised-flying-cars-instead-we-got-caffeine-spray/

15. Johnson, H., Mejia, M. C., & Bohn, S. (2015). *Will California run out of college graduates?* San Francisco, CA: Public Policy Institute of California.

16. Abel, J. R., & Deitz, R. (2014). Do the benefits of college still outweigh the costs? *Current Issues in Economics and Finance, 20*(3), 1–12.

17. Trostel, P. (2015). *It's not just the money.* Indianapolis, IN: Lumina Foundation.

18. Johnson, Bohn, & Mejia, *Addressing California.*

19. Baldwin, J. (1985). A talk to teachers. In *The price of the ticket: Collected nonfiction 1948–1985* (pp. 325–32). New York: St. Martin's Press. Excerpt from p. 326. (Reprinted from *Saturday Review* by Baldwin, J., December 21, 1963.)

20. Center on Budget and Policy Priorities. (2020). *States grappling with hit to tax collections.* Retrieved from https://www.cbpp.org/research/state-budget-and-tax/states-grappling-with-hit-to-tax-collections

21. National Center for Education Statistics. (2018). *Degree-granting postsecondary institutions, by control and classification of institution and state or jurisdiction: 2016–17.* Retrieved from https://nces.ed.gov/programs/digest/d17/tables/dt17_317.20.asp?current=yes

22. Clauset, A., Arbesman, S., & Larremore, D. B. (2015). Systematic inequality and hierarchy in faculty hiring networks. *Science Advances, 1*(1), e1400005.

23. Howe, J. (2013). Clayton Christensen wants to transform capitalism. *Wired.* Retrieved from https://afflictor.com/2013/02/20/i-think-higher-education-is-just-on-the-edge-of-the-crevasse/

24. West, C. (2020). Coronavirus fears may lead to big gap year for college students. *PBS News Hour.* Retrieved from https://www.pbs.org/newshour/education/coronavirus-fears-may-lead-to-big-gap-year-for-college-students

25. National Center for Education Statistics. (1993). *120 years of American education: A statistical portrait.* Washington, DC: Author.

26. Carnevale, A. P., Smith, N., Melton, M., & Price, E. W. (2015). *Learning while earning: The new normal.* Washington, DC: Center on Education and the Workforce, Georgetown University.

27. National Center for Education Statistics. (2018). *Digest of education statistics, 2016.* Retrieved from https://nces.ed.gov/fastfacts/display.asp?id=76

28. College Board. (2017). *Trends in college pricing 2017.* Retrieved from https://trends.collegeboard.org/college-pricing/figures-tables/published-prices-national#Published%20Charges%20over%20Time

29. Baum, S. (2015). The evolution of student debt in the United States. In B. Hershbein & K. M. Hollenbeck (Eds.), *Student loans and the dynamics of debt* (pp. 11–35). Kalamazoo, MI: Upjohn Institute for Employment Research; also see Fry, R. (2014). *The growth in student debt.* Washington, DC: Pew Research Center. Retrieved from http://www.pewsocialtrends.org/2014/10/07/the-growth-in-student-debt/

30. See https://www.ny.gov/programs/tuition-free-degree-program-excelsior-scholarship

31. See *Fast Facts* at the National Center for Education Statistics, https://nces.ed.gov/fastfacts/display.asp?id=40

32. Shapiro, D., Dundar, A., Wakhungu, P. K., Yuan, X., Nathan, A., & Hwang, Y. (2016). *Time to degree: A national view of the time enrolled and elapsed for associate and bachelor's degree earners* (Signature Report No. 11). Herndon, VA: National Student Clearinghouse Research Center.

33. Shapiro et al., *Time to degree.*

34. See, for example, https://registrar.fsu.edu/registration_guide/summer/registration_information/

35. Arum, R., & Roksa, J. (2011). *Academically adrift: Limited learning on college campuses.* Chicago, IL: University of Chicago Press.

36. Meacham, J. (2010, March 18). Bill Clinton discusses his war against obesity. *Newsweek.* Retrieved from https://www.newsweek.com/bill-clinton-discusses-his-war-against-obesity-69331

37. Trow, M. (1999). Lifelong learning through the new information technologies. *Higher Education Policy, 12*(2), 201–17.

38. Carlson, S. (2013). Competency-based education goes mainstream in Wisconsin. *Chronicle of Higher Education.* Retrieved from https://www.chronicle.com/article/Competency-Based-Education/141871

Chapter 2

1. Newman, J. H. (1852/1982). *The idea of a university.* Notre Dame, IN: University of Notre Dame Press.

2. Hauser, C. (2017, June 21). A Yale dean lost her job after calling people "white trash" in Yelp reviews. *The New York Times.* Retrieved from https://www.nytimes.com/2017/06/21/us/yale-dean-yelp-white-trash.html

3. Jaschik, S. (2018, February 22). Evergreen calls off "day of absence." *Inside Higher Ed*. Retrieved from https://www.insidehighered.com/news/2018/02/22/evergreen-state-cancels-day-absence-set-series-protests-and-controversies

4. Nichols, J. (2017, May 11). Black students matter: Black university sides with establishment. *The Hill*. Retrieved from http://thehill.com/blogs/pundits-blog/education/332926-black-students-matter-why-bethune-cookman-picked-white-power

5. Redden, E. (2019). Number of enrolled international students drops. *Inside Higher Ed*. Retrieved from https://www.insidehighered.com/admissions/article/2019/11/18/international-enrollments-declined-undergraduate-graduate-and

6. Medina, J., Benner, K., & Taylor, K. (2019, March 12). Actresses, business leaders, and other wealthy parents charged in U.S. college entry fraud. *The New York Times*. Retrieved from https://www.nytimes.com/2019/03/12/us/college-admissions-cheating-scandal.html; also see Jaschik, S. (2019, March 18). The week that shook college admissions. *Inside Higher Ed*. Retrieved from https://www.insidehighered.com/admissions/article/2019/03/18/look-how-indictments-shook-college-admissions

7. Rubin, J., & Ormseth, M. (2019, June 21). Rick Singer, the mastermind behind the college admissions scandal, know whom to target: The wealthy. *Los Angeles Times*. Retrieved from https://www.latimes.com/local/lanow/la-me-college-admissions-scandal-rick-singer-wealth-advisor-stanford-20190621-story.html

8. Mayhew, L. B. (1979). *Surviving the eighties: Strategies and procedures for solving fiscal and enrollment problems*. San Francisco, CA: Jossey-Bass.

9. Bauman, D., & Brown, S. (2019, September 26). The U. of Montana has lost more students this decade than any other flagship. What's going on? *Chronicle of Higher Education*. Retrieved from https://www.chronicle.com/article/The-U-of-Montana-Has-Lost/247227

10. Bauman & Brown, The U. of Montana.

11. Iloh, C., & Tierney, W. G. (2013). A comparison of for-profit college and community colleges' admissions practices. *College and University, 88*(4), 2–12; also see Iloh, C., & Tierney, W. G. (2014). Understanding for-profit college and community college choice through rational choice. *Teachers College Record, 116*(8), 1–34.

12. Iloh & Tierney, A comparison of for-profit; Iloh & Tierney, Understanding for-profit college and community college.

13. Wong, A. (2019, September 6). Colleges face growing international student-visa issues. *The Atlantic*. Retrieved from https://www.theatlantic.com/education/archive/2019/09/how-harvard-and-other-colleges-grapple-student-visa-problems/597409/

14. Grawe, N. D. (2018). *Demographics and the demand for higher education*. Baltimore, MD: Johns Hopkins University Press.

15. Christensen, C. M., & Eyring, H. J. (2011). *The innovative university: Changing the DNA of higher education from the inside out*. San Francisco, CA: Jossey-Bass.

16. Education Dive Staff. (2019, November 1). A look at trends in college and university consolidation since 2016. *Education Dive*. Retrieved from https://www.educationdive.com/news/how-many-colleges-and-universities-have-closed-since-2016/539379/

17. Education Dive Staff, A look at trends.

18. Newton, D. (2018, September 11). No, half of all colleges will not go bankrupt. *Forbes*. Retrieved from https://www.forbes.com/sites/dereknewton/2018/09/11/no-there-wont-be-massive-college-bankruptcies/#42b511cbd75b

19. Lederman, D. (2017, April 28). Clay Christensen, doubling down. *Inside Higher Ed*. Retrieved from https://www.insidehighered.com/digital-learning/article/2017/04/28/clay-christensen-sticks-predictions-massive-college-closures

20. Jaschik, S. (2019, March 4). Will Clay Christensen put his money where his mouth is? *Inside Higher Ed*. Retrieved from https://www.insidehighered.com/news/2019/03/04/university-president-challenges-clay-christensen-1-million-bet-future-private

21. National Center for Education Statistics. (2018). Degree-granting postsecondary institutions, by control and level of institution: Selected years, 1949–50 through 2017–18. *Digest of Education Statistics: 2017*. Washington, DC: NCES. Retrieved from https://nces.ed.gov/programs/digest/d18/tables/dt18_317.10.asp

22. See Bauman, D., & O'Leary, B. (2019, April 4). College closures, 2014–18. *Chronicle of Higher Education*. Retrieved from https://www.chronicle.com/interactives/college-closures#id=all_2_all

23. Buman & O'Leary, College closures.

24. Angulo, A. J. (2016). *Diploma mills: How for-profit colleges stiffed students, taxpayers, and the American dream* (p. 3). Baltimore, MD: Johns Hopkins University Press.

25. Angulo, *Diploma mills*, p. 9.

26. Rosenthal, C. (2012). The controversial history of for-profit colleges. *Minneapolis Star Tribune*. Retrieved from http://www.startribune.com/the-controversial-history-of-for-profit-colleges/175991601/

27. Angulo, *Diploma mills* p. 3.

28. Angulo, *Diploma mills*, p. 114.

29. Tierney, W. G. (2012). Too big to fail: The role of for-profit colleges and universities in American higher education. *Change: The Magazine of Higher Learning*, 43(6), 27–32.

30. Kelchen, R. (2017). *How much do for-profit colleges rely on federal funds?* Brookings Institution. Retrieved from https://www.brookings.edu/blog/brown-center-chalkboard/2017/01/11/how-much-do-for-profit-colleges-rely-on-federal-funds/

31. Cottom, T. M. (2017). *Lower ed: The troubling rise of for-profit colleges in the new economy*. New York: The New Press.

32. See, for example, the following scholarly papers: Armona, L., Chakrabarti, R., & Lovenheim, M. (2018). How does for-profit college attendance affect student

loans, defaults, and labor market outcomes? (FRB of NY Staff Report No. 811). New York: Federal Reserve Bank of New York; Belfield, C. R. (2013). Student loans and repayment rates: The role of for-profit colleges. *Research in Higher Education*, 54(1), 1–29; Cellini, S. R., & Koedel, C. (2017). The case for limiting federal student aid to for-profit colleges. *Journal of Policy Analysis and Management*, 36(4), 934–42; Cellini, S. R., & Turner, N. (2018). Gainfully employed? Assessing the employment and earnings of for-profit college students using administrative data (NBER Working Paper No. 22287). Cambridge, MA: National Bureau of Economic Research; also see the following publications: Fain, P. (2018, March 26). High default rates at New York for-profit colleges. *Inside Higher Ed.* Retrieved from https://www.insidehighered.com/quicktakes/2018/03/26/high-default-rates-new-york-profit-colleges; Smith, P., & Parrish, L. (2014). *Do students of color profit from for-profit college? Poor outcomes and high debt hamper attendees' futures.* Center for Responsible Lending; White, G. B. (2015, September 15). The empty promises of for-profit colleges. *The Atlantic.* Retrieved from https://www.theatlantic.com/business/archive/2015/09/the-failure-of-for-profit-colleges/405301/

33. Westervelt, E. (2016, January 29). For-profit colleges seeking veterans' GI bill dollars aren't always the best fit. *NPR.* Retrieved from https://www.npr.org/sections/ed/2016/01/29/464579497/veterans-to-higher-ed-big-room-for-improvement; also see Wong, A. (2015, June 24). "Dollar signs in uniform": Why for-profit colleges target veterans. *The Atlantic.* Retrieved from https://www.theatlantic.com/education/archive/2015/06/for-profit-college-veterans-loophole/396731/

34. Cassidy, J. (2016, June 2). Trump University: It's worse than you think. *The New Yorker.* Retrieved from https://www.newyorker.com/news/john-cassidy/trump-university-its-worse-than-you-think

35. Hansberry, L. (1994). *A raisin in the sun.* New York: Random House. (Original work published in 1958.)

36. Hillman, N. (2016). *Why performance-based college funding doesn't work.* The Century Foundation. Retrieved from https://tcf.org/content/report/why-performance-based-college-funding-doesnt-work/?agreed=1l; also see Hillman, N., Tandberg, D. A., & Fryar, A. H. (2015). Evaluating the impacts of "new" performance funding in higher education. *Educational Evaluation and Policy Analysis*, 37(4), 501–19.

37. For a comprehensive, and recent, discussion of the public good and higher education, see Marginson, S. (2018). Public/private in higher education: A synthesis of economic and political approaches. *Studies in Higher Education*, 43(2), 322–37; for the classic view of the public good as nonrivalrous and nonexcludable, see Samuelson, P. (1954). The pure theory of public expenditure. *Review of Economics and Statistics*, 36(4), 387–89.

38. Shaw, J. S. (2010). Education—A bad public good? *The Independent Review*, 15, 241–56.

39. Marginson, S. (2016). *The dream is over: The crisis of Clark Kerr's California idea of higher education.* Oakland, CA: University of California Press.

40. Smith, B. (2003, December 6). State colleges could privatize, Sanford says. *Spartanburg Herald-Journal*.

41. Johnson, J. (2013, September 11). U-Va. should break some ties with state, panel says in preliminary report. *Washington Post*.

42. Protopsaltis, S. (2006). The Colorado voucher system: Implications for higher education. *College and University, 81*(2), 45–48.

Chapter 3

1. See, for example, Seltzer, R. (2017, September 14). Disparaging interpretive dance (and more)? *Inside Higher Ed*. Retrieved from https://www.insidehighered.com/news/2017/09/14/kentuckys-governor-says-universities-should-think-about-cutting-programs-poor-job; Jaschik, S. (2016, February 1). Kentucky's governor vs. French literature. *Inside Higher Ed*. Retrieved from https://www.inside highered.com/quicktakes/2016/02/01/kentuckys-governor-vs-french-literature; Logue, J. (2016, January 20). Psych! *Inside Higher Ed*. Retrieved from https://www.insidehighered.com/news/2016/01/20/florida-governor-wants-know-why-all-psychology-majors-arent-employed

2. See, for example, Bruno-Jofré, R., & Schriewer, J. (Eds.). (2012). *The global reception of John Dewey's thought: Multiple refractions through time and space*. New York: Routledge; Rogacheva, Y. (2016). The reception of John Dewey's democratic concept of school in different countries of the world. *Espacio, Tiempo y Educación, 3*(2), 65–87; Turan, S. (2000). John Dewey's report of 1924 and his recommendations on the Turkish educational system revisited. *History of Education, 29*(6), 543–55.

3. A photo of the stamp is hosted by Southern Illinois University's Center for Dewey Studies at https://deweycenter.siu.edu/about-dewey/dewey-stamp.php

4. Baldwin, J. (1985). A talk to teachers. In *The price of the ticket: Collected nonfiction 1948–1985* (pp. 325–332). New York: St. Martin's Press. Excerpt from p. 326. (Reprinted from *The Saturday Review*, by J. Baldwin, December 21, 1963.)

5. Calcagno, J. C., Crosta, P., Bailey, T., & Jenkins, D. (2007). Stepping stones to a degree: The impact of enrollment pathways and milestones on community college student outcomes. *Research in Higher Education, 48*(7), 775–801.

6. Goldrick-Rab, S. (2010). Challenges and opportunities for improving community college student success. *Review of Educational Research, 80*(3), 437–69; Goldrick-Rab, S. (2016). *Paying the price: College costs, financial aid, and the betrayal of the American dream*. Chicago, IL: University of Chicago Press; Kiyama, J. M. (2010). College aspirations and limitations: The role of educational ideologies and funds of knowledge in Mexican American families. *American Educational Research Journal, 47*(2), 330–56; Roderick, M., Nagaoka, J., & Coca, V. (2009). College readiness for all: The challenge for urban high schools. *The Future of Children, 19*(1), 185–210.

7. Castleman, B. L., & Page, L. C. (2014). *Summer melt: Supporting low-income students through the transition to college.* Cambridge, MA: Harvard Education Press.

8. Kuh, G. D., Cruce, T. M., Shoup, R., Kinzie, J., & Gonyea, R. M. (2008). Unmasking the effects of student engagement on first-year college grades and persistence. *Journal of Higher Education, 79*(5), 540–63; also see Kronholz, J. (2012). Academic value of non-academics: The case for keeping extracurriculars. *Education Digest, 77*(8), 4–10; for a discussion of students transferring from community to four-year universities, see Townsend, B. K., & Wilson, K. B. (2009). The academic and social integration of persisting community college transfer students. *Journal of College Student Retention: Research, Theory, & Practice, 10*(4), 405–23.

9. Stripling, J. (2017). The lure of the lazy river. *Chronicle of Higher Education.* Retrieved from https://www.chronicle.com/article/The-Lure-of-the-Lazy-River/241434

10. Kelchen, R. (2016). An analysis of student fees: The roles of states and institutions. *Review of Higher Education, 39*(4), 597–619.

11. Paynter, B. (2017). *One trick for keeping kids in college: Forgive tiny debts that force them to leave.* Fast Company. Retrieved from https://www.fastcompany.com/40454950/one-trick-for-keeping-kids-in-college-forgive-tiny-debts-that-force-them-to-leave

12. Relles, S. R., & Tierney, W. G. (2014). *The summer before: Improving college writing before freshman year.* Los Angeles, CA: Pullias Center for Higher Education, University of Southern California.

13. See https://ies.ed.gov/ncee/wwc/Intervention/1043

14. Cassidy, L., Keating, K., & Young, V. (2010). *Dual enrollment: Lessons learned on school-level implementation.* Herndon, VA: SRI International.

15. See http://ecs.force.com/mbdata/MBQuestNB2?Rep=DE1512

16. See https://ies.ed.gov/ncee/wwc/Intervention/814

17. Arum, R., & Roksa, J. (2011). *Academically adrift: Limited learning on college campuses.* Chicago, IL: University of Chicago Press.

18. Jaschik, S. (2016, March 29). Grade inflation, higher and higher. *Inside Higher Ed.* Retrieved from https://www.insidehighered.com/news/2016/03/29/survey-finds-grade-inflation-continues-rise-four-year-colleges-not-community-college

19. Duncheon, J. C., & Tierney, W. G. (2013). Changing conceptions of time: Implications for educational research and practice. *Review of Educational Research, 83*(2), 236–72.

Chapter 4

1. Jost, J. T., Rudman, L. A., Blair, I. V., Carney, D. R., Dasgupta, N., Glaser, J., & Hardin, C. D. (2009). The existence of implicit bias is beyond reasonable

doubt. *Research in Organizational Behavior, 29,* 39–69; Purkiss, S. L. S., Perrewé, P. L., Gillespie, T. L., Mayes, B. T., & Ferris, G. R. (2006). Implicit sources of bias in employment interview judgments and decisions. *Organizational Behavior and Human Decision Processes, 101*(2), 152–67.

2. Karabel, J. (2005). *The chosen: The hidden history of admission and exclusion at Harvard, Yale, and Princeton.* Boston, MA: Houghton Mifflin.

3. Rasmussen, C. (1996, December 23). A pioneer of black Los Angeles. *Los Angeles Times.* Retrieved from http://articles.latimes.com/1996-12-23/local/me-12005_1_los-angeles-chapter

4. Liptak, A. (2016, June 23). Supreme court upholds affirmative action program at University of Texas. *The New York Times.* Retrieved from https://www.nytimes.com/2016/06/24/us/politics/supreme-court-affirmative-action-university-of-texas.html

5. Hsu, H. (2018, October 8). The rise and fall of affirmative action. *The New Yorker.* Retrieved from https://www.newyorker.com/magazine/2018/10/15/the-rise-and-fall-of-affirmative-action

6. Sue, D. W., Capodilupo, C. M., Torino, G. C., Bucceri, J. M., Holder, A. M. B., Nadal, K. L., & Esquilin, M. (2007). Racial microaggressions in everyday life: Implications for clinical practice. *American Psychologist, 62*(4), 271–86. Excerpt from p. 271.

7. See Merriam-Webster. (n.d.). No, "snowflake" as a slang term did not begin with *Fight Club.* Retrieved from https://www.merriam-webster.com/words-at-play/the-less-lovely-side-of-snowflake

8. Merriam-Webster. No, "snowflake."

9. Sue, et al. Racial microaggressions. Excerpt from p. 271.

10. Bellet, B. W., Jones, P. J., McNally, R. J. (2018). Trigger warning: Empirical evidence ahead. *Journal of Behavior Therapy and Experimental Psychiatry, 61,* 134–41. Excerpt from p. 134.

11. Lilienfeld, S. O. (2017). Microaggressions: Strong claims, inadequate evidence. *Perspectives on Psychological Science, 12*(1), 138–69.

12. See, for example, the following articles: Huber, L. P., & Solorzano, D. G. (2015). Racial microaggressions as a tool for critical race research. *Race, Ethnicity, and Education, 18*(3), 297–320; Solorzano, D., Ceja, M., & Yosso, T. (2000). Critical race theory, racial microaggressions, and campus racial climate: The experiences of African American college students. *Journal of Negro Education, 69*(1/2), 60–73; Sue, et al. Racial microaggressions.

13. Tierney, W. G. (1983). Governance by conversation: An essay on the structure, function, and communicative codes of a faculty senate. *Human Organization, 42*(2), 172–78.

14. Robert's Rules of Order is a frequently cited book that outlines parliamentary procedures for meetings held by a variety of organizations. See Robert III, H. M., Honemann, D. H., & Balch, T. J. (2011). *Robert's rules of order: Newly revised* (11th ed.). Philadelphia, PA: Da Capo Press. (Original work published 1876.)

Chapter 5

1. Chaffee, E. E. (1998). Listening to the people we serve. In W. G. Tierney (Ed.), *The responsive university: Restructuring for high performance* (pp. 13–37). Baltimore, MD: Johns Hopkins University Press.

2. Kezar, A., & Gehrke, S. (2014). Why are we hiring so many non-tenure-track faculty? *Liberal Education, 100*(1), 44–51. Retrieved from https://www.aacu.org/publications-research/periodicals/why-are-we-hiring-so-many-non-tenure-track-faculty; Kezar, A., & Sam, C. (2010). *Understanding the new majority of non-tenure-track faculty in higher education: Demographics, experiences, and plans of action.* (ASHE Higher Education Report, Vol. 36, Issue 4). San Francisco, CA: Jossey-Bass.

3. For a thorough and engaging summary of higher education as a business, see Kirp, D. L. (2004). *Shakespeare, Einstein, and the bottom line.* Cambridge, MA: Harvard University Press.

4. See https://www.ewa.org/profit-universities; also see https://capseecenter.org/research/by-the-numbers/for-profit-college-infographic/

5. Kelchen, R. (2017). *How much do for-profit colleges rely on federal funds?* Brookings Institution. Retrieved from https://www.brookings.edu/blog/brown-center-chalkboard/2017/01/11/how-much-do-for-profit-colleges-rely-on-federalfunds/

6. Pusser, B. (2008). For-profit universities in the political economy of higher education. *International Higher Education, 52,* 21–22; also see Harris, A. (2018, July 27). Emails from Trump educational official reveal ties to for-profit colleges. *The Atlantic.* Retrieved from https://www.theatlantic.com/education/archive/2018/07/early-emails-from-trump-education-officials-reveal-ties-to-for-profit-college/566273/

7. Pusser, For-profit universities. The 85-15 and 90-10 rules refer to the proportion of financial aid that could be derived from federal aid programs versus other sources.

8. Bailey, T., Jeong, D. W., & Cho, S. W. (2010). Referral, enrollment, and completion in developmental education sequences in community colleges. *Economics of Education Review, 29*(2), 255–70.

9. Kezar, A. (2004). Obtaining integrity? Reviewing and examining the charter between higher education and society. *Review of Higher Education, 27*(4), 429–59.

10. See, for instance, Mitchell, M., Leachman, M., & Masterson, K. (2017). *A lost decade in higher education funding.* Washington, DC: Center on Budget and Policy Priorities.

11. Green, E. L. (2018, August 10). DeVos ends Obama-era safeguards aimed at abuses by for-profit colleges. *The New York Times.* Retrieved from https://www.nytimes.com/2018/08/10/us/politics/betsy-devos-for-profit-colleges.html

12. Eder, S., & Medina, J. (2017, March 31). Trump University suit settlement approved by judge. *The New York Times*. Retrieved from https://www.nytimes.com/2017/03/31/us/trump-university-settlement.html

Chapter 6

1. Beck, J. (2016, January 22). The decline of the driver's license. *The Atlantic*. Retrieved from https://www.theatlantic.com/technology/archive/2016/01/the-decline-of-the-drivers-license/425169/

2. Etehad, M., & Nikolewski, R. (2016, December 23). Millennials and car ownership? It's complicated. *Los Angeles Times*. Retrieved from https://www.latimes.com/business/autos/la-fi-hy-millennials-cars-20161223-story.html

3. Marginson, S. (2016). *The dream is over: The crisis of Clark Kerr's California idea of higher education*. Oakland, CA: University of California Press.

4. Callan, P. (2012). The perils of success: Clark Kerr and the Californian master plan for higher education. In S. Rothblatt (Ed.), *Clark Kerr's world of higher education reaches the 21st century: Chapters in a special history* (pp. 61–84). Dordrecht: Springer.

5. Marginson, *The dream is over*.

6. Johnson, H., Bohn, S., & Mejia, M. C. (2017). *Addressing California's skills gap*. San Francisco, CA: Public Policy Institute of California.

7. Newman, J. H. (1852/1982). *The idea of a university*. Notre Dame, IN: University of Notre Dame Press.

8. Piketty, T. (2014). *Capital in the twenty-first century* (A. Goldhammer, Trans.). Cambridge, MA: Harvard University Press; Saez, E. (2018). Striking it richer: The evolution of top incomes in the United States. In D. B. Grusky & J. Hill (Eds.), *Inequality in the 21st century: A reader* (pp. 39–42). New York: Routledge.

9. Spellings, M. (2018, February 22). The perils of trashing the value of college. *Chronicle of Higher Education*. Retrieved from https://www.chronicle.com/article/The-Perils-of-Trashing-the/242614

10. Statistics from the Russel Sage Foundation, see http://www.russellsage.org/sites/all/files/chartbook/Educational%20Attainment%20and%20Achievement.pdf

11. Knobel, M., & Verhine, R. (2017). Brazil's for-profit higher education dilemma. *International Higher Education, 89*, 23–24.

12. Lanford, M., Maruco, T., & Tierney, W. G. (2015). *Prospects for vocational education in the United States: Lessons from Germany*. Los Angeles: Pullias Center for Higher Education, University of Southern California.

13. Tierney, W. G., & Duncheon, J. C. (Eds.). (2015). *The problem of college readiness*. Albany, NY: State University of New York Press.

14. Baldwin, J. (1985). A talk to teachers. In *The price of the ticket: Collected nonfiction 1948–1985* (pp. 325–332). New York: St. Martin's Press. (Reprinted from *The Saturday Review*, by J. Baldwin, December 21, 1963.)

Chapter 7

1. Tierney, W. G., Corwin, Z. B., & Ochsner, A. (Eds.). (2018). *Diversifying digital learning: Online literacy and educational opportunity.* Baltimore, MD: Johns Hopkins University Press.

2. Berry, T., Cook, L., Hill, N., & Stevens, K. (2011). An exploratory analysis of textbook usage and study habits: Misperceptions and barriers to success. *College Teaching, 59*(1), 31–39.

3. Killion, J. (2011). *Teachers agree that supporting diverse learners with high needs is a priority.* Learning Forward. Retrieved from https://learningforward. org/press-release/metlife-survey-american-teacher-explores-needs-diverse-learners/

4. Hart Research. (2015). *Rising to the challenge: Views on high school graduates' preparedness for college and careers.* Achieve. Retrieved from https:// www.achieve.org/rising-challenge-survey-2-powerpoint

5. Gilliam, W. S., Maupin, A. N., Reyes, C. R., Accavitti, M., & Shic, F. (2016). *Do early educations' implicit biases regarding sex and race relate to behavior expectations and recommendations of preschool expulsions and suspensions?* New Haven, CT: Yale Child Study Center. Retrieved from https://medicine.yale.edu/ childstudy/zigler/publications/Preschool%20Implicit%20Bias%20Policy%20Brief_ final_9_26_276766_5379_v1.pdf; also see Gregory, A., Skiba, R. J., & Noguera, P. A. (2010). The achievement gap and the discipline gap: Two sides of the same coin? *Educational Researcher, 39*(1), 59–68.

6. Gershenon, S., Holt, S. B., & Papageorge, N. W. (2016). Who believes in me? The effect of student-teacher demographic match on teacher expectations. *Economics of Education Review, 52,* 209–24.

7. Cheryan, S., Ziegler, S. A., Montoya, A. K., & Jiang, L. (2017). Why are some STEM fields more gender balanced than others? *Psychological Bulletin, 143*(1), 1–35; for a historical overview, see Tolley, K. (2003). *The science education of American girls: A historical perspective.* New York: Routledge; for a perspective on women of color in STEM fields, see Ong, M., Wright, C., Espinosa, L. L., & Orfield, G. (2011). Inside the double bind: A synthesis of empirical research on undergraduate and graduate women of color in science, technology, engineering, and mathematics. *Harvard Educational Review, 81*(2), 172–208, 389–90.

8. For a useful review of signaling theory, see Connelly, B. L., Certo, S. T., Ireland, R. D., & Reutzel, C. R. (2011). Signaling theory: A review and assessment. *Journal of Management, 37*(1), 39–67; the classic text on signaling is Spence, M. (1973). Job market signaling. *Quarterly Journal of Economics, 87*(3), 355–74.

9. Torpey, E. (2018). *Measuring the value of education.* Washington, DC: Bureau of Labor Statistics. Retrieved from https://www.bls.gov/careeroutlook/2018/data-on-display/education-pays.htm

Chapter 8

1. Rudolph, F. (1962). *The American college and university: A history* (p. 412). New York: Vintage Books.

2. Tierney, W. G., & Lanford, M. (2014). The question of academic freedom: Universal right or relative term. *Frontiers of Education in China, 9*(1), 4–23.

3. American Association of University Professors. (1940). *1940 statement of principles on academic freedom and tenure with 1970 interpretive comments.* Retrieved from https://www.aaup.org/report/1940-statement-principles-academic-freedom-and-tenure

4. Elliott, O. (1937). *Stanford University: The first twenty-five years* (p. 336). Stanford, CA: Stanford University Press.

5. Menand, L. (2001). *The metaphysical club* (p. 383). New York: Farrar, Straus, and Giroux.

6. Ross, E. (1900, November 15). Indignation at the dismissal. *San Francisco Chronicle.*

7. Bromberg, H. (1996). Revising history. *Stanford Lawyer, 30*(2), 116.

8. Tierney, W. G. (2001). Academic freedom and organizational identity. *Australian Universities' Review, 44*(1–2), 7–14.

9. Clark, B. R. (1971). Belief and loyalty in college organization. *Journal of Higher Education, 42*(6), 499–515.

10. Bodley, M. (2017, February 2). At Berkeley Yiannopoulos protest, $100,000 in damage, 1 arrest. *San Francisco Chronicle.* Retrieved from https://www.sfgate.com/crime/article/At-Berkeley-Yiannopoulos-protest-100-000-in-10905217.php

11. Hutson, S. (2017, August 11). UC Berkeley budget cuts campus deficit by nearly half. *KQED.* Retrieved from https://www.kqed.org/news/11611440/uc-berkeley-budget-cuts-campus-deficit-by-nearly-half

12. Gray, R. (2017, September 22). How Milo Yiannopoulos's Berkeley "free speech week" fell apart. *The Atlantic.* Retrieved from https://www.theatlantic.com/politics/archive/2017/09/how-milo-yiannopoulos-berkeley-free-speech-week-fell-apart/540867/

13. Watanabe, T. (2016, April 20). As UC Berkeley tries to close its deficit, administrators feel the ire of traditional faculty allies. *Los Angeles Times.* Retrieved from http://www.latimes.com/local/education/la-me-berkeley-deficit-20160421-story.html

14. Nwanevu, O. (2017, September 15). Berkeley's bind. *Slate*. Retrieved from http://www.slate.com/articles/news_and_politics/politics/2017/09/ben_shapiro_milo_yiannopolous_and_berkeley_s_tough_spot.html

15. Goodstein, L. (2018, May 23). "This is not of God": When anti-Trump evangelicals confront their brethren. *The New York Times*. Retrieved from https://www.nytimes.com/2018/05/23/us/anti-trump-evangelicals-lynchburg.html

16. Burton, T. I. (2018). For many, Christianity and Trumpism are synonymous. These evangelicals are pushing back. *Vox*. Retrieved from https://www.vox.com/identities/2018/4/12/17216258/lynchburg-rally-red-letter-revival-shane-claiborne-jerry-falwell-jr-liberty-university

17. Withrow, B. G. (2014). The outrageous idea of Christian academic freedom. In B. G. Withrow & M. Wecker (Eds.), *Consider no evil: Two faith traditions and the problem of academic freedom in religious higher education* (pp. 85–103). Eugene, OR: Cascade Books.

18. Graham, R. (2016, October 13). The professor wore a hijab in solidarity—then lost her job. *New York Times Magazine*. Retrieved from https://www.nytimes.com/2016/10/16/magazine/the-professor-wore-a-hijab-in-solidarity-then-lost-her-job.html

19. St. Amant, C., & Limmer, M. (2007, March 21). Soulforce members arrested on campus. *Baylor Lariat*. Retrieved from https://www.baylor.edu/lariat archives/news.php?action=story&story=44715; Walch, T. (2006, April 12). 24 arrested at BYU. *Deseret News*. Retrieved from https://www.deseretnews.com/article/635199006/24-arrested-at-BYU.html; also see Eckholm, E. (2011, April 18). Even on religious campuses, students fight for gay identity. *The New York Times*. Retrieved from https://www.nytimes.com/2011/04/19/us/19gays.html

Chapter 9

1. Rosenthal, C. (2011). Fundamental freedom or fringe benefit? Rice University and the administrative history of tenure. *AAUP Journal of Academic Freedom*, 2. Retrieved from https://www.aaup.org/sites/default/files/files/JAF/2011%20 JAF/Rosenthal.pdf

2. *Keyishian et al. v. Board of Regents of the University of the State of New York et al*, 385, U.S. 589 (1967).

3. Menand, L. (2001). *The metaphysical club* (p. 413). New York: Farrar, Straus, and Giroux.

4. Tierney & Lanford (2014). Conceptualizing innovation in higher education. *Higher Education: Handbook of Theory and Research*, *31*, 1–40.

5. For a critical view of this phenomenon, and its effect on higher education, see Giroux, H. (2002). Neoliberalism, corporate culture, and the promise

of higher education: The university as a democratic public sphere. *Harvard Educational Review, 72*(4), 425–64.

6. Waters, T., & Waters, D. (Eds.). (2015). *Weber's rationalism and modern society: New translations on politics, bureaucracy, and social stratification.* New York: Palgrave Macmillan.

7. Jost, J. T., Rudman, L. A., Blair, I. V., Carney, D. R., Dasgupta, N., Glaser, J., & Hardin, C. D. (2009). The existence of implicit bias is beyond reasonable doubt. *Research in Organizational Behavior, 29*, 39–69; and Purkiss, S. L. S., Perrewé, P. L., Gillespie, T. L., Mayes, B. T., & Ferris, G. R. (2006). Implicit sources of bias in employment interview judgments and decisions. *Organizational Behavior and Human Decision Processes, 101*(2), 152–67.

Chapter 10

1. See Bourdieu, P. (1973). Cultural reproduction and social reproduction. In R. Brown (Ed.), *Knowledge, education, and cultural change: Papers in the sociology of education* (pp. 71–112). London: Tavistock Publications; and Bourdieu, P. (1986). The forms of capital. In J. G. Richardson (Ed.), *Handbook of theory and research for the sociology of education* (pp. 241–58). New York: Greenwood Press.

2. Caplan, B. (2018). *The case against education: Why the education system is a waste of time and money.* Princeton, NJ: Princeton University Press.

3. See, for example, Pollan, M. (2006). *The omnivore's dilemma.* New York: Bloomsbury.

4. Bughin, J., Hazan, E., Lund, S., Dahlstrom, P., Wiesinger, A., & Subramaniam, A. (2018). *Skill shift: Automation and the future of the workforce.* McKinsey Global Institute. Retrieved from https://www.mckinsey.com/featured-insights/future-of-work/skill-shift-automation-and-the-future-of-the-workforce; also see Manyika, J. (2017). *Technology, jobs, and the future of work.* McKinsey Global Institute. Retrieved from https://www.mckinsey.com/featured-insights/employment-and-growth/technology-jobs-and-the-future-of-work; and Frey, C. B., & Osborne, M. A. (2017). The future of employment: How susceptible are jobs to computerisation? *Technological Forecasting and Social Change, 114*, 254–80.

5. National Center for Education Statistics. (2018). *Undergraduate enrollment.* Retrieved from https://nces.ed.gov/programs/coe/indicator_cha.asp

6. Jimenez, L., Sargrad, S., Morales, J., & Thompson, M. (2016). *Remedial education: The cost of catching up.* Washington, DC: Center for American Progress. Retrieved from https://www.americanprogress.org/issues/education-k-12/reports/2016/09/28/144000/remedial-education/

7. Manyika, J., Pinkus, G., Ramaswamy, S., Woetzel, J., Nyquist, S., & Sohoni, A. (2016). *The US economy: An agenda for inclusive growth.* McKinsey

Global Institute. Retrieved from https://www.mckinsey.com/featured-insights/employment-and-growth/can-the-us-economy-return-to-dynamic-and-inclusive-growth

8. Mitchell, M., Leachman, M., & Masterson, K. (2017). *A lost decade in higher education funding.* Washington, DC: Center on Budget and Policy Priorities.

9. Webber, D. A. (2017). State divestment and tuition at public institutions. *Economics of Education Review, 60,* 1–4.

10. Zhao, B. (2018). *Disinvesting in the future? A comprehensive examination of the effects of state appropriations for public higher education.* Boston, MA: Federal Reserve Bank of Boston. Retrieved from https://www.bostonfed.org/publications/research-department-working-paper/2018/a-comprehensive-examination-of-the-effects-of-state-appropriations-for-public-higher-education.aspx

11. Addo, F. R., Houle, J. N., & Simon, D. (2016). Young, black, and (still) in the red: Parental wealth, race, and student loan debt. *Race and Social Problems, 8*(1), 64–76; and Houle, J. N., & Warner, C. (2017). Into the red and back to the nest? Student debt, college completion, and returning to the parental home among young adults. *Sociology of Education, 90*(1), 89–108.

12. Carrillo, R. (2016, April 14). How Wall Street profits from student debt. *Rolling Stone.* Retrieved from https://www.rollingstone.com/politics/politics-news/how-wall-street-profits-from-student-debt-225700/

13. Thompson, D. (2014, August 19). The thing employers look for when hiring recent graduates. *The Atlantic.* Retrieved from https://www.theatlantic.com/business/archive/2014/08/the-thing-employers-look-for-when-hiring-recent-graduates/378693/

14. Soares, L. (2010). *Community college and industry partnerships.* Washington, DC: Center for American Progress; also see Kisker, C. B., & Carducci, R. (2003). UCLA community college review: Community college partnerships with the private sector—Organizational contexts and models for successful collaboration. *Community College Review, 31*(3), 55–74.

15. Lanford, M., & Maruco, T. (2019). Six conditions for successful career academies. *Phi Delta Kappan, 100*(5), 50–52; also see Lanford, M., & Maruco, T. (2018). When job training is not enough: The cultivation of social capital in career academies. *American Educational Research Journal, 55*(3), 617–48.

Chapter 11

1. Cather, W. (1925). *The professor's house.* New York: Knopf.

2. Jaschik, S. (2015, February 27). Father Hesburgh dies at 97. *Inside Higher Ed.* Retrieved from https://www.insidehighered.com/news/2015/02/27/father-hesburgh-leader-notre-dame-and-american-higher-education-dies-97

3. Tresaugue, M. (2006, November 8). Gates' departure stuns Texas A&M community. *Houston Chronicle*. Retrieved from https://www.chron.com/news/houston-texas/article/Gates-departure-stuns-Texas-A-M-community-1492985.php; also see Watkins, M., & Satija, N. (2016). At A&M, diversity increases without affirmative action. *Texas Tribune*. Retrieved from https://www.texastribune.org/2016/06/19/m-student-diversity-increasing-without-affirmative/

4. See, for example, *Annual open letter to the people of Purdue from Mitch Daniels*. Purdue University. Retrieved from https://www.purdue.edu/president/messages/annual-open-letters/1901-med-openletter-full.php

5. Nassauer, S. (2018, April 20). At Walmart, the CEO makes 1,188 times as much as the median worker. *Wall Street Journal*. Retrieved from https://www.wsj.com/articles/at-walmart-the-ceo-makes-1-188-times-as-much-as-the-median-worker-1524261608

6. Kamenetz, A. (2017, December 13). USC president is third-highest paid in higher education. *NPR*. Retrieved from https://www.scpr.org/news/2017/12/13/78835/usc-president-is-third-highest-paid-in-higher-educ/

7. For the full text of the Freeh Report into the Penn State University scandal, see the *Chicago Tribune* website: http://www.chicagotribune.com/sports/chi-freeh-report-sandusky-penn-state-20120712-pdf-htmlstory.html; also see Sander, L., & Stripling, J. (2011, November 10). An insular Penn State stayed silent. *Chronicle of Higher Education*. Retrieved from https://www.chronicle.com/article/An-Insular-Penn-State-Stayed/129713

8. Kozlowski, K. (2018, January 18). What MSU knew: 14 were warned of Nassar abuse. *Detroit News*. Retrieved from https://www.detroitnews.com/story/tech/2018/01/18/msu-president-told-nassar-complaint-2014/1042071001/

9. Pringle, P., Ryan, H., Elmahrek, A., Hamilton, M., & Parvini, S. (2017, July 17). An overdose, a young companion, drug-fueled parties: The secret life of a USC med school dean. *Los Angeles Times*. Retrieved from http://www.latimes.com/local/california/la-me-usc-doctor-20170717-htmlstory.html

Ryan, H., Hamilton, M, & Pringle, P. (2018, May 16). A USC doctor was accused of bad behavior with young women for years. The university let him continue treating students. *Los Angeles Times*. Retrieved from http://www.latimes.com/local/california/la-me-usc-doctor-misconduct-complaints-20180515-story.html

10. Fine, H. (2018, May 25). USC president Nikias to step down amid scandals. *Los Angeles Business Journal*. Retrieved from http://labusinessjournal.com/news/2018/may/25/usc-president-nikias-step-down-amid-scandals/

11. Tierney, W. G. (Ed.). (2004). *Competing conceptions of academic governance: Negotiating the perfect storm*. Baltimore, MD: Johns Hopkins University Press.

12. Tierney, W. G., & Bensimon, E. M. (1996). *Promotion and tenure: Community and socialization in academe*. Albany, NY: State University of New York Press.

13. Tierney, W. G. (2006). A cultural analysis of shared governance: The challenges ahead. In J. C. Smart (Ed.), *Higher education: Handbook of theory and research, vol. 19* (pp. 85–132). Alphen aan den Rijn: Kluwer.

Chapter 12

1. Hanford, E. (n.d.). *The story of the University of Phoenix*. American Public Media. Retrieved from http://americanradioworks.publicradio.org/features/tomorrows-college/phoenix/story-of-university-of-phoenix.html

2. Jaschik, S. (2018, October 9). Falling confidence in higher ed. *Inside Higher Ed*. Retrieved from https://www.insidehighered.com/news/2018/10/09/gallup-survey-finds-falling-confidence-higher-education

3. Baldwin, J. (1985). A talk to teachers. In *The price of the ticket: Collected nonfiction 1948–1985* (pp. 325–332). New York: St. Martin's Press. Excerpt from p. 326. (Reprinted from The *Saturday Review*, by J. Baldwin, December 21, 1963.)

4. Tierney, W. G. (1993). *Building communities of difference: Higher education in the twenty-first century*. Westport, CT: Bergin and Garvey.

5. Frankl, V. (2006). *Man's search for meaning* (I. Lasch, Trans.). Boston, MA: Beacon Press, p. 104. (Original work published 1946.)

Further Reading

Chapter 1

Baldwin, J. (1985). A talk to teachers. In *The price of the ticket: Collected nonfiction 1948–1985* (pp. 325–32). New York: St. Martin's Press. (Reprinted from *The Saturday Review*, by J. Baldwin, December 21, 1963.)

Johnson, H., Bohn, S., & Mejia, M. C. (2017). *Addressing California's skills gap.* San Francisco, CA: Public Policy Institute of California.

Johnson, H., Mejia, M. C., & Bohn, S. (2015). *Will California run out of college graduates?* San Francisco, CA: Public Policy Institute of California.

Mann, H. (2009). Lectures of education. *Schools, 6*(2), 226–40. (Reprinted from *Lectures on education*, by H. Mann, 1855, Boston, MA: Ide and Dutton.)

Tierney, W. G., & Rodriguez, B. A. (2014). *The future of higher education in California: Problems and solutions for getting in and getting through.* Los Angeles, CA: Pullias Center for Higher Education, University of Southern California.

Vedder, R. (2012). *Twelve inconvenient truths about American higher education.* Washington, DC: Center for College Affordability and Productivity.

Chapter 2

Angulo, A. J. (2016). *Diploma mills: How for-profit colleges stiffed students, taxpayers, and the American dream.* Baltimore, MD: Johns Hopkins University Press.

Hansberry, L. (1994). *A raisin in the sun.* New York: Random House. (Original work published in 1958.)

Hillman, N. (2016). *Why performance-based college funding doesn't work.* Washington, DC: The Century Foundation.

Kezar, A. (2004). Obtaining integrity? Reviewing and examining the charter between higher education and society. *The Review of Higher Education, 27*(4), 429–59.

Newman, J. H. (1982). *The idea of a university.* Notre Dame, IN: University of Notre Dame Press. (Original work published in 1852.)

Shireman, R. (2016). Public and nonprofit higher education as the optimal second-best. *Public Administration Review*, 76(5), 758–59.

Shireman, R. (2017, April 30). There's a reason the Purdue–Kaplan deal sounds too good to be true. *Chronicle of Higher Education*. Retrieved from https://www.chronicle.com/article/There-s-a-Reason-the/239954

Shaw, J. S. (2010). Education—A bad public good? *The Independent Review*, 15(2), 241–56.

Tierney, W. G., & Hentschke, G. C. (2007). *New players, different game: Understanding the rise of for-profit colleges and universities*. Baltimore, MD: Johns Hopkins University Press.

Tierney, W. G., & Lechuga, V. M. (2005). Academic freedom in the twenty-first century. *Thought and Action, 21*, 7–22.

Chapter 3

Arum, R., & Roksa, J. (2011). *Academically adrift: Limited learning on college campuses*. Chicago, IL: University of Chicago Press.

Castleman, B. L., & Page, L. C. (2014). *Summer melt: Supporting low-income students through the transition to college*. Cambridge, MA: Harvard Education Press.

Dewey, J. (1997). *Democracy and education: An introduction to the philosophy of education*. New York: Free Press. (Original work published 1916.)

Goldrick-Rab, S. (2016). *Paying the price: College costs, financial aid, and the betrayal of the American dream*. Chicago, IL: University of Chicago Press.

Pellegrino, J. W., & Hilton, M. L. (Eds.). (2012). *Education for life and work: Developing transferable knowledge and skills in the twenty-first century*. Washington, DC: National Academies Press.

Chapter 4

Huber, L. P., & Solorzano, D. G. (2015). Racial microaggressions as a tool for critical race research. *Race, Ethnicity, and Education, 18*(3), 297–320.

Karabel, J. (2005). *The chosen: The hidden history of admission and exclusion at Harvard, Yale, and Princeton*. Boston, MA: Houghton Mifflin.

Lilienfeld, S. O. (2017). Microaggressions: Strong claims, inadequate evidence. *Perspectives on Psychological Science, 12*(1), 138–69.

Solorzano, D., Ceja, M., & Yosso, T. (2000). Critical race theory, racial microaggressions, and campus racial climate: The experiences of African American college students. *Journal of Negro Education, 69*(1–2), 60–73.

Sue, D. W., Capodilupo, C. M., Torino, G. C., Bucceri, J. M., Holder, A. M. B., Nadal, K. L., & Esquilin, M. (2007). Racial microaggressions in everyday life: Implications for clinical practice. *American Psychologist, 62*(4), 271–86.

Tierney, W. G. (1983). Governance by conversation: An essay on the structure, function, and communicative codes of a faculty senate. *Human Organization, 42*(2), 172–78.

Chapter 5

Chaffee, E. E. (1998). Listening to the people we serve. In W. G. Tierney (Ed.), *The responsive university: Restructuring for high performance* (pp. 13–37). Baltimore, MD: Johns Hopkins University Press.

Kezar, A. (2004). Obtaining integrity? Reviewing and examining the charter between higher education and society. *The Review of Higher Education, 27*(4), 429–59.

Kezar, A., & Sam, C. (2010). *Understanding the new majority of non-tenure-track faculty in higher education: Demographics, experiences, and plans of action* (ASHE Higher Education Report, Vol. 36, Issue 4). San Francisco, CA: Jossey–Bass.

Kirp, D. L. (2003). *Shakespeare, Einstein, and the bottom line.* Cambridge, MA: Harvard University Press.

Tierney, W. G. (Ed.). (1998). *The responsive university: Restructuring for high performance.* Baltimore, MD: Johns Hopkins University Press.

Chapter 6

Duncan, G. J., & Murnane, R. J. (2011). (Eds.). *Whither opportunity? Rising inequality, schools, and children's life chances.* New York: Russell Sage Foundation.

Long, B. T., & Boatman, A. (2013). The role of remedial and developmental courses in access and persistence. In A. Jones & L. Perna (Eds.), *The state of college access and completion: Improving college success for students from underrepresented groups* (pp. 77–95). New York: Routledge.

Marginson, S. (2016). *The dream is over: The crisis of Clark Kerr's California idea of higher education.* Oakland, CA: University of California Press.

Tierney, W. G. (Ed.). (2015). *Rethinking education and poverty.* Baltimore, MD: Johns Hopkins University Press.

Tierney, W. G., & Colyar, J. E. (Eds.). (2009). *Urban high school students and the challenge of access: Many routes, difficult paths* (2nd ed.). New York: Peter Lang.

Tierney, W. G., Corwin, Z. B., & Colyar, J. E. (Eds.). (2005). *Preparing for college: Nine elements of effective outreach.* Albany, NY: State University of New York Press.

Tierney, W. G., & Duncheon, J. C. (Eds.). (2015). *The problem of college readiness.* Albany, NY: State University of New York Press.

Chapter 7

Carnevale, A. P., Jayasundera, T., & Cheah, B. (2012). *The college advantage: Weathering the economic storm.* Washington, DC: Center on Education and the Workforce, Georgetown Public Policy Institute.

Connelly, B. L., Certo, S. T., Ireland, R. D., & Reutzel, C. R. (2011). Signaling theory: A review and assessment. *Journal of Management, 37*(1), 39–67.

Moretti, E. (2012). *The new geography of jobs.* New York: Houghton Mifflin Harcourt.

Rosenbaum, J. E., Stephan, J. L., & Rosenbaum, J. E. (2010). Beyond one-size-fits-all college dreams. *American Educator, 34*(3), 2–13.

Spence, M. (1973). Job market signaling. *Quarterly Journal of Economics, 87*(3), 355–74.

Tierney, W. G., Corwin, Z. B., & Ochsner, A. (Eds.). (2018). *Diversifying digital learning: Online literacy and educational opportunity.* Baltimore, MD: Johns Hopkins University Press.

Chapter 8

American Association of University Professors. (2018). *Campus free-speech legislation: History, progress, and problems.* Washington, DC: American Association of University Professors.

Dewey, J. (1902). Academic freedom. *Educational Review, 23,* 1–14.

Fish, S. (2008). *Save the world on your own time.* New York: Oxford University Press.

Lawrence III, C. R. (1993). If he hollers let him go: Regulating racist speech on campus. In M. J. Matsuda, C. R. Lawrence III, R. Delgado, & K. W. Crenshaw (Eds.), *Words that wound: Critical race theory, assaultive speech, and the first amendment* (pp. 53–87). Boulder, CO: Westview Press.

O'Neill, R. M. (2005). Academic freedom: Past, present, and future beyond September 11. In P. Altbach (Ed.), *American higher education in the twenty–first century: Social, political, and economic challenges* (pp. 91–114). Baltimore, MD: Johns Hopkins University Press.

Schrecker, E. (2010). *The lost soul of higher education: Corporatization, the assault on academic freedom, and the end of the American university.* New York: The New Press.

Tierney, W. G. (1997). *Academic outlaws: Queer theory and cultural studies in the academy.* Thousand Oaks, CA: Sage Publications.

Tierney, W. G. (2004). The roots/routes of academic freedom and the role of the intellectual. *Cultural Studies/Critical Methodologies, 4*(2), 250–56.

Chapter 9

Caplan, B. (2018). *The case against education: Why the education system is a waste of time and money.* Princeton, NJ: Princeton University Press.

Giroux, H. (2002). Neoliberalism, corporate culture, and the promise of higher education: The university as a democratic public sphere. *Harvard Educational Review, 72*(4), 425–64.

Menand, L. (2001). *The metaphysical club.* New York: Farrar, Straus, and Giroux.

Tierney, W. G., & Bensimon, E. M. (1996). *Promotion and tenure: Community and socialization in academe.* Albany, NY: State University of New York Press.

Tierney, W. G. (Ed.). (1999). *Faculty productivity: Facts, fictions, and issues.* New York: Falmer Press.

Waters, T., & Waters, D. (Eds.). (2015). *Weber's rationalism and modern society: New translations on politics, bureaucracy, and social stratification.* New York: Palgrave Macmillan.

Chapter 10

Berliner, D. C. (2013). Effects of inequality and poverty vs. teachers and schooling on America's youth. *Teachers College Record, 115*(12), 1–25.

Bourdieu, P. (1973). Cultural reproduction and social reproduction. In R. Brown (Ed.), *Knowledge, education, and cultural change: Papers in the sociology of education* (pp. 71–112). London: Tavistock Publications.

Bourdieu, P. (1986). The forms of capital. In J. G. Richardson (Ed.), *Handbook of theory and research for the sociology of education* (pp. 241–58). New York: Greenwood Press.

Bowles, S., & Gintis, H. (2002). Schooling in capitalist America revisited. *Sociology of Education, 75*(1), 1–18.

Coleman, J. S. (1988). Social capital in the creation of human capital. *American Journal of Sociology, 94*, S95–120.

Dika, S. L., & Singh, K. (2002). Applications of social capital in educational literature: A critical synthesis. *Review of Educational Research, 72*(1), 31–60.

Portes, A. (1998). Social capital: Its origins and applications in modern sociology. *Annual Review of Sociology, 24*, 1–24.

Reardon, S. F. (2011). The widening academic achievement gap between the rich and the poor: New evidence and possible explanations. In G. J. Duncan & R. J. Murnane (Eds.), *Wither opportunity? Rising inequality, schools, and children's life chances* (pp. 91–116). New York: Russell Sage.

Chapter 11

Cather, W. (1925). *The professor's house.* New York: Knopf.

Chaffee, E. E., & Tierney, W. G. (1988). *Collegiate culture and leadership strategies.* New York: MacMillan.

Tierney, W. G. (Ed.). (2004). *Competing conceptions of academic governance: Negotiating the perfect storm.* Baltimore, MD: Johns Hopkins University Press.

Tierney, W. G. (2008). *The impact of culture on organizational decision making: Theory and practice in higher education.* Sterling, VA: Stylus.

Tierney, W. G., & Bensimon, E. M. (1996). *Promotion and tenure: Community and socialization in academe.* Albany, NY: State University of New York Press.

Chapter 12

Tierney, W. G. (1993). *Building communities of difference: Higher education in the twenty-first century.* Westport, CT: Bergin and Garvey.

Tierney, W. G. (2006). *Trust and the public good: Examining the cultural conditions of academic work.* New York: Peter Lang.

About the Author

William G. Tierney is university professor and Wilbur-Kieffer professor of higher education and founding director of the Pullias Center for Higher Education at the University of Southern California. He is a past president of the Association for the Study of Higher Education and the American Educational Research Association. He was awarded the Howard R. Bowen Distinguished Career Award from the Association for the Study of Higher Education and the Distinguished Research Award from Division J of the American Educational Research Association. Tierney is an elected member of the National Academy of Education, a disciplinary society of two hundred individuals recognized for their outstanding scholarship and contributions to education, and a fellow of the American Educational Research Association. At the University of Southern California Rossier School of Education, Tierney served as the associate dean for research and faculty affairs and as a department chair. He has served as academic dean at a Native American community college, a Peace Corps volunteer in Morocco, a scholar-in-residence in Malaysia, and a Fulbright Scholar in Central America, Australia, and India. He has been a fellow at the Rockefeller Foundation's Center in Bellagio, Italy, and a Fernand Braudel Fellow at the European University Institute in Florence, Italy. His recent books include *Rethinking Education and Poverty*; *The Impact of Culture on Organizational Decision-making, Trust and the Public Good: Examining the Cultural Conditions of Academic Work*; and *New Players, Different Game: Understanding the Rise of For-profit Colleges and Universities*. He earned a master's degree from Harvard University and a PhD from Stanford University.

Index

Made in the USA
Las Vegas, NV
17 November 2021